THE

PARISH REGISTER

OF

Saint Peter's, New Kent County, Va.

FROM

1680 to 1787,

PUBLISHED BY

THE NATIONAL SOCIETY OF THE COLONIAL DAMES OF AMERICA IN THE STATE OF VIRGINIA.

Parish Record Series, No. 2.

Southern Historical Press, Inc.
Greenville, South Carolina

This volume was reproduced from
an 1904 edition located in the
publisher's private library,
Greenville, South Carolina

Please Direct all Correspondence & Orders to:

Southern Historical Press, Inc.
P.O. Box 1267
375 West Broad Street
Greenville, S.C. 29602-1267

Originally published: Richmond, VA., 1904
Reprinted: Southern Historical Press, Inc.
Greenville, S.C., 2004
ISBN # 0-89308-770-X
Printed in the United States of America

INTRODUCTION.

New Kent county, which was formed from York in 1654, included not only the present county of the name, but also the section of country now embraced in King William, King and Queen, Hanover, and all upwards to the heads of the Pamunkey and Mattapony rivers. Bishop Meade states (*Old Churches and Families of Virginia*, I, 383), that there were originally in the county two parishes, St. John's, north of York and Pamunkey, and St. Peter's, south of those streams. It appears, however, that in 1655, the district, beginning at Poropotank creek, on the north side of York river and extending up the Mattapony, was organized into a parish called Stratton Major.

There appears to be no record to show when St. Peter's was formed, but the vestry book begins in 1682.

In 1704, St. Paul's parish, afterwards in Hanover county, was formed from St. Peter's. All persons, therefore, who trace their ancestry to Hanover, as well as those of New Kent descent, may find information of interest in the St. Peter's Register.

As the Virginia Society of Colonial Dames will follow the Register with the publication of the Vestry Book of St. Peter's, a more detailed history of the parish is deferred.

The copy from which this volume is printed was made, by permission of the trustees of the Virginia Theological Seminary, Alexandria county, Va., from the original register now in the library of the Seminary.

Register of St. Peter's Parish,

NEW KENT COUNTY, VA.

BIRTHS AND BAPTISMS.

—— daughter of James Blackwell and Lydia his wife baptized
—— 16—.

Edward the son of Edward Bell & Mary his wife baptized
—— 16—.

Mary daughter of Thomas Buttler & Mary his wife baptized
7 day of ——, 16—.

—— the son of Will Bingham & Jane his wife baptized ye
28th day of ——, 16—.

William the son of Will Bigger was born 28th January and
baptized 24th of March, 16—.

Thomas son to Thomas Browne baptz. ye 27th day of November. 168–.

Edward son to John Bayly baptiz. ye 30 day of May, 16—.

May daugh' to Charles Bostick baptiz⁴ fn. 24th day of June,
——.

—— son to Robert Bomps baptiz⁴ 16th day of August, ——.

—— son to John Bayly baptiz⁴ ye 8th of June, ——.

—— daughter to James Blackwell baptiz⁴ ye 27th of Sept.,
——.

—— son to Richard Brock baptiz⁴ ye 11th of Oct., ——.

Joe son to Abraham Benn baptiz⁴ ye 18th of Oct., ——.

John son of Charles Barker by Rebeck his wife baptiz' —, ——.

Jnº son of Jnⁿ Brown and Eliz. his wife baptiz⁴ ye 16th of June,
——.

Anne daughter of Jnº Baughan and Mary his wife born —,
——, and baptized the 10th day of July, ——.

An— daughter of Joseph Baughan bapt. ——.

Elizabeth daughter of John Barnes baptiz. —, ——.
Judith daughter of John Bumpus bapt. —, ——.
Jane daughter of John Burnley bapt. —, ——.
Katherine daughter of Richard Bullock bapt. —, ——.
John son of Thomas Bassett bapt. the 8th of Feby., ——.
John son of Henry Borne by Sarah his wife bapt. 19th Mar.,
        ——.
Ellener daughter Robert Brooks bapt. July —, ——.
Nathan son of John Barnett bapt. —, ——.
Dorothy daughter of Edwrd Bullock bapt. —, ——.
John son of James Blackwell bapt. —, ——.
Sarah daughter of Robert Brooks bapt. —, ——.
Margery daughter of Benj. Bulkley bapt. —, ——.
Sarah daughter of Henry Brown bapt. —, ——.
John son of Thomas Brook —— bapt. —, ——.
Mary daughter of James Blackwell bapt. 24th De——, ——.
Elizabeth daughter of Jn° Baughan Junr bapt. May —, ——.
Thomas son of Thomas Briggman bapt. the 3 Nov. —, ——.
Mary daughter of Richard Brooker bapt. —, ——.
John son of John Barnes bapt. the 29 ——, ——.
Elizabeth daughter of John Brown bapt. —, ——.
Amadiah daughter of Christopher Binns bapt. 23 ——, ——.
—— daughter of Henry Bone born 1st of March, ——. ——.
—— daughter of David Bell born 2 Jany., ——, ——.
—— daughter of John Burley bapt. ye 20 July, ——, ——.
—— daughter of Robert Brooks bapt. 6 July, ——, ——.
—— daughter of Robert Bumpus born 19 ——, ——.
—— daughter of Wm Bugg bapt. ——.
Baughan —— Jn° Baughan July bapt. ——.
—— belonging to Mrs. Sarah Bray.
Sarah born May ——, 1697.
Pegg born —— October, 1697.
Hannah born July ——, 1697.
Rebecca daughter of Henry Brown bapt. the 28th Mar. 170⅔.
Jane daughter of Henry Bon baptized the 4 of April, 1703.
Anne daughter of Tho. Bassett bapt. the 20th of June, 1703.
Joshua son of Geo. Brock baptized the 3rd of July, 1703.
—— son of Richard Brooker born 4 Feb'y, 1702–3.
—— of Jn° Burnley bapt. ye 21 Nov., 1703.

—— child belonging to Mrs. Alice Butts, ——, 1703.

—— John Boules Junr bapt. 13th Feb'y, 1703¾.

—— Barker bapt. 5 March 1703¾.

—— of David Bell bapt. ye 21 May, 1704.

—— of Edwd Bullock baptized ye 4 of June, 1704.

Thos. Brogman bapt. ye 25 of Feb'y, 1704-5.

—— of Thos. Bassett baptized ye 1 of July, 1705.

—— M. A. B. child born ye 17 day of August, 17—.

·—— of —— Baughan born ye 5 of May 1706.

—— Joseph Baughan born ye 17 day of Feb'y, 1702.

—— belonging to Mr. Wm Beek —— day of August, 1704.

—— of Thomas Bassett born ye 10th of Xbr, 1696.

—— son of Thomas Bassest born ye 18th Feb'y, 1701.

—— daughter of Wm Bayzy bapt. ye 5 Feb'y, 1705.

Negro girl belonging to Mr. Butts born ——, 1705.

—— of James Bullock baptized Jan'y, 1706-7.

—— Jn° Bibey bapt. ye 5 of Jan'y, 1706-7.

—— of Thomas Barnes bapt. April 2d, 1708.

Negro girl of Mad^m Sarah Bray born ye 4th day of July, 1707.

—— daughter of Rich. Brooker bapt. July ye 25, 1708.

—— a bastard child born March ye 27th.

—— of Nathaniel Brothers and Mary his wife ——· 4, 1706 and baptized Aug. ye 9th, 1708.

—— Henry Bardrick bapt. Sept. 5, 1708.

—— of Jn° Bacon born Aug. ye 14th, 1708.

—— of Jn° Bacon born 8^{ber} ye 30th, 1709.

—— belonging to Jn° Bacon born April ——, 1708.

—topher Binns bapt. —— b--- No—— 3^d ye 21st, 1708.

Thomas Cottorill son of Richard and Mary his wife bapt. ye 11th day of April, 169–.

Timothy ye son of Robert Chandler and Elizth his wife, bapt. ye 17th day of Oct., 168–.

John ye sone of Nicholas Cox and Mary his wife bapt. ye 31st day of Oct. not ye 11th of Oct. 168–.

Susanah daughter to Stephen Crump bapt. ye 4th of September 168–.

Robt sone of Robert Chandler bapt. ye 30th of May 168–.

Elizabeth daughter to Richd Cambo bapt. ye 15th of February, 168–.

Sara daug^t to Richd Chaslin bapt. ye 13th day of May, 168–.

Angelina daughter to John Chaford bapt. ye 21 of Nov., 1689.

Elizabeth daughter to William Crump bapt. ye 24 day of Aprill, 1960.

Rachell daughter to George Cox bapt. ye 1st of June, 1690.

Peter negro belonging to David Craford borne ye 10th of Oct., 1688.

Thomas sone of Thomas Cranshaw bapt. ye 25 of Decem., 169–.

John son to Robert Chandler bapt. ye 11 of Jan'y, 16—.

Barbara daugh. of Thomas Case and Mary his wife borne Dec. 9, 169– and baptized the 10 July 1698.

James son of Edwd Chambers and Eliz. his wife bapt. 7 Aug., 169–.

Hen^l son of Hen^l childs baptized the 13th of Nov^e 169–.

Elizabeth daughter of Hen^l Crumpton bapt. 2 October, 169–.

Margarett daughter of Robt Cade bapt. Nov. ye 27, 169–.

Hannah dau^t of Benj. Clark by Eliz. wife bapt. the 12 March, 169–.

Richard son of Edwd Bullock by Sarah bapt. the 16 Aprill, ——.

William son of Benj. Clarke by Mary bapt. the 25 June, 169–.

William son of Robert Chandler bapt. the 26 June, 169–.

Abraham son of Abra. Cox bapt. the 13 Dec., 169–.

Mary daugh. of William Crump bapt. the 9 of June, 1——.

Thomas son of Thos Case —— the 16 Nov., 169–.

Samuel son of Burnell Chapell bapt. the 4 ——, 16—.

Mathew, son of Abraham Cook born the 27 June ——.

Mary daug. of Thos Case baptized the 18 ——, ——.

Joseph son of Robt Chandler bapt. the 11 Aug^t ——.

Benjamin, son of Benjamin Clark bapt. the 29 Sept. ——.

Stephen son of William Crump bapt. the 3 November, ——.

Francis son of Thomas Cheney bapt. the 15 December, ——.

Walter son of Hen^l Childes bapt. the 5 of January, ——.

Susana daug^t of Robt Crump baptis. the 23 March, ——.

Hannah daugh^t of Abraham Cook baptized 21 Dec., ——.

Jane dauter of Hen^l Crumpston bapt. the 15 Mar., ——.

William son of Hugh Case bapt. the 24 ——, ——.

James son of Hen^l Childes Gent bapt. the 4 ——, ——.

Bryan son of Wm Cooker, bapt. the 10 Oct., ——.

Anne, daughter of Hen^l Crompton, bapt. 25 Dec., ——.

Francis a negro boy belonging to Wm Clopton ——, born the 5 of August, 1703.

Nanc negro belonging to Wm Clopton —— the 29 of Aprill, 1704.

Bart ye son of Wm Crump bapt. ye 12 May ——.

Joseph son of Robt Crump bapt. 17 July, 1706.

Negros belonging to David Clarkson Peg born in 1 ——ber, 1706 and Doll born June 28, 1706.

Mary daughter of Wm Crump born April ye 30th and bapt. May ye 8, 1709.

Gutrick son of Stephen Crump by Anne his wife born May ye 22, 1709.

Phillis a negro girl belonging to Rich. Cottorel Junr born Feb'y ye 10, 1708–9.

Charles son of Richard Crump born Feb'y 2 bapt. Feb'y ye 26, 1709.

Susana daugh^t of Thomas Cotterell bapt. April ye 1st, 1710.

Jno a negro belonging to Mr Wm Clopton bapt. June ye 25th, 1710.

Richard Cotterell son of Rich. Cotterell bapt. Dec. ye 17th, 1710.

John son of David Clarkson baptized February ye ——, 1710.

Lucy daughter of Robt Crump bapt. Mar. the 25th, 1711.

Thomas son of Thomas Cotterell baptized April ye 22nd, 1711.

Mary daughter of James Crump baptized May ye 13th, 1711.

Judith daughter of James Christian baptized May ye 21st, 1711.

Richard son of Richd Crump born 8ber ye 12th bapt. Nov. ye 11th, 1711.

Agnes daughter of Stephen Crump bapt. 9ber ye 25, 1711.

Anne daughter of Wm Crump born 7ber ye 8th & bapt. 8br. ye 4th, 1713.

Sarah daughter of Arthur Crue born April ye 21st, 1712.

Anne Daughter of Walter Clopton born July ye 3rd bapt. Aug. 3rd, 1712.

Bathyah (Birtha) Daughter of Robt Clopton born Aug. ye 19th bapt. 7br. ye 28, 1712.

Gideon son of Mr Wm Carr born January ye 1st & bapt. Feb'y
ye 8th, 1712.

Gilbert son of Tho. Cotterell Baptized March ye 1st, 1712.

Agnes Daughter of James Crump Baptized May ye 10th, 1713.

Charles son of Richd Cotterell Jr. baptized December ye 27th,
1713.

Thomas & Sarah son & daughter of Steph. Crump born Feb'y
ye 14th, 1713.

Negros belonging to Major John Custis (viz):

John a mulatto Born March ye 18th, 1709.

Patty a negro Born March ye 18th, 1709.

———— a negro Born 7ber, 1713.

———— a negro born May ——— 1712.

———— Daughter of Robt Case Born March ye 24th bapt. April
ye 25th, 1714.

———— a negro belonging to Major Custis Born April ye 18th,
1714.

———— a negro belonging to Mr Wm Clopton Born June ye 6,
1706.

———— a negro belonging to ye s^d Clopton Born May ye 8th,
1707.

———— a negro belonging to ye s^d Clopton Born May ye 30th,
1713.

———— negro belonging to Richd Cotterell Junr Born 7ber ye
15th, 1714.

———— Daughter of Robt Clopton and Sarah his wife Born July
Baptised August ye 29th, 1714.

———— negro child belonging to ye s^d Robt Clopton Born 7ber
ye 20th, 1714.

———— of Walter Clopton Born ye 19th of 9ber & Baptised Dec.
ye 19th, 1714.

———— Cotterell Born December ye 31st, 1714.

———— Daughter of Richd Crump by Fran. his wife Born Dec.
1714.

———— Daughter of David Clarkson Jnr. Baptised April ye 24th,
1715.

———— Stephen Crump Born ——— Baptised July ye 10th,
1715.

—— negro belonging to Major John Custis Born 8ber ye 16th,
   1715.

—— Girl belonging to Robert Clopton, 1715.

Richard the sone of Francis Day and his wife baptised ye 9 day
   of May, 168–.

Nitt the son of Henry Dillan & Elinor his wife baptised ye 1st
   day of August, 168–.

Geo. sone to Robert Douglas bap. ye 9 day of Aprill, 168–.

Robert son to Robert Douglas bap. ye 15th of February, 168–.

William sone to Rob᷈ Depress bap. ye 24th of October, 168–.

Mary daug. to Rob᷈ Depress bapt, ye 9 of November, 169–.

Margaret daugh. to Henry Dillan bapt. ye 15th of March,
   1690–1.

Rachel daugh. to Alice Doe bap. ye 15 of March, 1690–1.

David son of David and Bethea Bell bap. the 10 July, 1698.

Eliz. daugh. of John Denott & Eliz. his wife bap. 14 August,
   1698.

Sarah daugh. to Rob᷈ Depress & Mary his wife bap. 4 Sept.,
   1698.

Eliz. daugh. of Geo. Dabney bapt. ye 11th of Nov., 1698.

Nelthan daugh. of James Dabney bapt. the 8 Jan᷈, 1698–9.

Susanah daugh. of James Darrum by Eliz. his wife bap. 19
   March, 1698–9.

William son of Nitt᷈ Dowe baptized the 2 July, 1699.

Eliz. Daugh. of Francis Day baptized the 20 Jan᷈, 1699.

Elizabeth Daugh. of Rob᷈ Deprest baptized the 19 July, 1702.

Perthenia Daugh. of John Dennett borne ye 27 Nov., 1690.

Eliza Daugh. of John Dennett borne ye 13 June, 1698.

Thomas sone of John Dennett borne ye 11 of Feb'y, 1699.

John son of John Dennett born ye 21 of October, 1702.

James son of James Darrum baptized ye 23 May, 1703.

Mathen daugh. of Jeremiah Dumas bap. ye 10 October, 1703.

William son of William Dollard bap. ye 19 March, 1703.

Elizabeth Daugh. of James Doller bap. ——, 170–.

Mary Daughter of Henry Dicks Born the 5th November, 170–.

Edward son of Francis Day & Elizabeth his wife Born 8ᵇʳ ye 1st,
   1708.

Francis son of Wᵐ Dollard & Margaret his wife Baptised March
   13th, 1708–9.

Henry son of Henry Dickes Baptised February ye 25th, 17—.

James son of James Dollard Baptised April ye 15th, 171-.

Grace Daughter of John Davis Baptised June ye 3rd, 17—.

Elizabeth Daughter of Daniel Design by Mary his wife Baptised 8ᵇʳ ye 26th, ——.

Elizabeth Daughter of Francis Day Baptised March 12, ——.

Francis son of Fra. Day by Elizabeth his wife Born ye 20th of Feb'y, ——.

John son of Henry Dike Born March ye 26th, 1716.

Uriah and Hester son and Daughter of Edwᵈ and Rachel Bettes Bap. August 14th, 1709.

Jane Daughter of George Baizey Bapᵗ August ye 24th, 1709.

Hannah a negro girl of Mʳˢ Alice Butts Born April ye 22nd, 1709.

Hagar a negro girl of Madᵐ Sarah Brays Born Jan'y ye 1st, 1709.

Elizabeth Daughter of Henry Bardrick Baptised 8ᵇʳ ye 29th, 1710.

Anselm son of Jnᵒ Bailey Juʳ Baptised April ye 8th, 1711.

Peter son of Richᵈ Brooker Bapᵗˢᵈ April ye 8th, 1711.

Jane Daughter of Thomas Bassett Bapᵗˢ April ye 29th, 1711.

Peter a negro boy belonging to Madᵐ Sarah Bray Born May ye 31st, 1711.

Simon a negro boy belonging to Mʳˢ Alice Butts 7ᵇʳ 16th, 1711.

Francis son of Nathaniel Brothers Born February ye 16th, 1711.

Gedion son of Edward Bettes Baptised August ye 3rd, 1711.

Anne Daughter of Wm. Bourn Jur. Baptised March ye 1st, 1712.

Rebecca Daughter of Tho. Barns Baptised March ye 1st, 1712.

Constantine son of Henry Bardrick Baptised March 15th, 1712.

John son of Jnᵒ Bacon by Susanna his wife Born May ye 14th, 1711.

Hagar a negro belonging to ye sᵈ Bacon Born June ye 14th, 1711.

Sarah Daughter of Jnᵒ Bacon by Susanna his wife Born Dec. 28th, 1712.

Kit a negro boy belonging to ye sᵈ Bacon Born June 13th, 1713.

—— negro girl belonging to Mr. Tho. Butts Born in July, 1713.

Tabith Daughter of Jnº Bailey by Mary his wife, Bap. August 4th, 1713.

Antapass Daughter of Richard Brooker Baptised Decemᵇ ye 13th, 1713.

Ceasar a negro belonging to Dʳ Burbidge Born ——, 1713.

Paul a negro belonging to Madam Sarah Bray Born April 20th, 1713.

Francis Daughter of Wᵐ Bourn Jr. Baptised Aug. 8th, 1714.

Peter son of Thomas Butts Gent. by Catherine his wife Born 7ᵇʳ ye 1st, 1714.

Dick a negro belonging to ye sᵈ Butts Born March ye 1st, 1714.

Davy a negro belonging to ditto Born ye 24th of April, 1715.

Ursula Daughter of Tho. Bassett Born 7ᵇʳ ye 15th, 1715.

Lucy Daughter of Thomas Bailey Born August ye 28th, 1715.

Daniel a negro boy belonging to Wᵐ Bassett Esq. Born May 18th, 1716.

John son of Samm. Bugg Born ye 5th of May, 1715.

John son of Rob. Burbidge by Mary his wife Born Aug. ye 26, 1714.

Francis son of Jnº Epecen bap. ye 17th of Aprill, 168–.

John son of Sirilla Ellison bapᵗ ye 17th Day of February, 168–.

Jane Daughter of Hugh Esrott bapᵗ ye 29 day of June, 169–.

Mary Daughᵗ of Thomas Elliott bapt. ye 23 —— of Novemᵇ, 16—.

An Daugᵗ to Hugh Esrott born ye 17th of Oct., 168–.

Mary Daugᵗ to Hugh Esrott born ye 29 of Jan., 1687–8.

Jno. son of Thomas Elmor & Mary his wife bapᵗ ye 10 July, 1698.

Will son of Peter Elmor & Rebecka his wife bapᵗ ye 10 July, 1698.

Mary Daugᵗ of Jnⁿ Evans and Mary his wife bapᵗ 29 August, 169–.

Pall son of Jnº Eperson baptised the 25 Feb'y, 1699–1700.

Peter son of Peter Elmore by Rebecca his wife bapt. the 9th of June, 1700.

John son of Will. England bap^t the 29 Sept^r, 170–.
Tho. son of Tho. Elmore bap^t the 29 Mar., 170–.
Harris son of Peter Elmore Born the 5 July, 170–.
Elizabeth Daute. of Wm England bapt. ye 22 Nov., 1702.
Mary Daute. of Richd Evans baptised ye 28 March, 170⅔.
John son of Wm Eppeson baptised the 19 Sept., 1703.
Mary Daut. of Tho. Elmore bapt. ye 20 Aug^t, 170–.
Elizabeth Daut. of Peter Elmore bapt. ye 17 Sept., 1704.
Bathiah Daugh^t of Peter Elmore bapt. 11 of May, 1707.
Elizabeth Daughter of Jn° Epperson bap^t June ye 13th, 1708.
William son of Thomas & Elizabeth Epperson Bapt. ye 20th of
    June, 1708.
Mary Daughter of Peter Elmore Born 8^{br} ye 17th, 1715.
Joseph and Benjamin sons of Robt Allen Born April ye 12th,
    1711.
Francis Daughter of Jn° Apperson born December ye 3rd, 1706.
Elizabeth Daughter of Jn° Apperson Born April ye 27th, 1708.
Anne Daughter of Jn° Apperson Born March ye 19th, 1710–11.
James son of James Alford Born February ye 7th X'nd April
    12th, 1713.
Henry son of Wm Apperson Born March ye 29th, 1713.
Samuel son of Wm Allin Baptised September ye 20th, 1713.
Judith Daughter of Francis Amoss Baptized January ye 24th,
    1713.
John son of Jn° Apperson Ju^r Born Feb. ye 4th X'nd Mar.
    21st, 1713.
Drury son of Robert Allen Born April ye 6th X'nd May ye 2nd,
    1714.
Nanny a negro belonging to Mr Richd Allin Born 7^{br}, 1711.
Ned a negro belonging to ye s^d Allin Born June ye 20th, 1713.
Richard a negro belonging to Jn° Aldredge Born in September,
    1713.
Higins son of John Axford Baptised 7^{br} ye 19th, 1714.
Phil a molatto belonging to Mr Richd Allen Born Aug. ye 15th,
    (1698) 1698.
James a molatto belonging to Ditto Born October ye 3rd (1704)
    1704.
Jack a negro belonging to Ditto Born April ye ———, 1704.
Warren son of James Alford Baptised August ye 28th, 1715.

Elizabeth Daughter of Wm Apperson Born ye 17th of 7^{br}, 1715.

Mary Daughter of Joseph & Anne Ashling Born Jan'y ye 12th, 1715.

Mary Daughter of Jn° Apperson Born February 26th, 1715.

Frances Daughter of Tho. Apperson Born Baptised April 1st, 1716.

Sue a slave belonging to Jn° Aldredge Born in April, 1716.

Elizabeth ye daughter of Charles Fleming & Susanna his wife bapt. ye 28th Oct., 168–.

James Forgeson son of Robert F——— his wife bap. ye 8th day of March, 168–.

Mary daughter to Edward Finch bap^t ye 1st of April, 168–.

Joseph son to Joseph Foster & Elizabeth his wife bapt. ye 8th day of April, 168–.

Negros belonging to Capt. Joseph Foster one named Bebdana borne ye 20th of August, 1686.

One named Jenne borne ye 30th of Jan'y, 168¾.

One named Sara born ye 20th of Febr'y, 1684–5.

One named Nane borne ye 28th of Aprill, 168–.

Eliz. Daug^t to Capt. Joseph Foster & Eliz. his wife bap^t ye 27 of Sept. & born ye 1st, 1689.

Luce Daug^t of Joseph Foster Gent. by Eliz. his wife born the 5 October, 1697.

Negro Doll born the 20 October 1692, Negro Will born ye 1st of September, 1697, both belonging to Capt. Joseph Foster.

Henry son of Edwd Finch bapt. the 15 day of February, 169–.

Barbary dau^t of Wm Freeman baptised 5 July, 170–.

Peter negro belonging to Charles Fleming borne ye 24th of June, 1703.

Robin & Billy negros belonging to Cha. Fleming born ye 12th of June, 1704.

James son of John Finall bapt. ye 17th February, 1702.

Hannah Daughter of Wm Fergison bap. ye 3 March, 1704–5.

Sarah a mulatto belonging to Major Field born ye 12 March, 1705.

Dorus a negro belonging to Major Field born ye 23 March, 1705–6.

Eliz^a Daughter of Tho. Fuzzell bap^t ye 17 July, 1708.

Doll a negro girl born in May, Tamar a negro girl born in 8ᵇʰ, both belonging to Chaˢ ——, 170-.

Moll a negro girl belonging to Madam Field bapᵗ ——, 170-.

Elizabeth Daughter of John Fennell baptised March the 3rd, 170-.

Judith Daughter of William Forgeson baptised July the 4th, 1708.

Negros belonging to Mʳˢ Alice Field:
    Peter, Musca-doras, Mary, Phillis, Anne, Elizabeth, Adult, Baptized January ye 2nd, 17—.

Joseph son of Coll. Joseph Foster & Eliz. his wife Born October ye 29th, 169-.

Sarah Daughter of Thomas Fuzell baptised April ye 10th, 17—.

Jnᵒ son of Jnᵒ Foster Gent. by Jane his wife Born ye 10th day of June, ——.

Betty a negro girl belonging to Sarah Fleming Born Mar. ye 4th, ——.

Phebe a negro girl belonging to Madᵐ Alice Field Born March ye ——, ——.

Toby a negro boy belonging to Madᵐ Alice Field Born April ——, ——.

Landa a negro belonging to Capt. Jnᵒ Foster Born July ye ——, ——.

Mary Daughter of John Ferrill Born May ye 1st, ——.

Hannah a negro being Born April ye 8th belonging to ——, ——, which was given to the said Sarah by her Father ——.

Primas a negro belonging to Madᵐ Alice Field, ——.

Martha Daughter of Tho. Fuzell Born ——, ——.

Jacob a negro belonging to Capᵗ Foster Bo——, ——.

Susanna Daughter of Wᵐ ——, ——.

Sarah Daughter of Jnᵉ Fennell Born April ye ——, 1715.

Sarah Daughter of Henry Clark Born Febr'y ye 13th, 1715.

John son of Edward Finch Born March 20th, 1699.

BIRTHS AND BAPTISMS.

Jnᵒ sone to Richard Gillam Bapᵗ ye 25th day of August, 168-.

Peter sone to Samuel Gentry Bapᵗ ye 10th of Aprill, 1687.

Eliz. daug. to Nich. Gentry Bapᵗ 29 day of August, 1689.

James sone to James Garrett Bapt. ye 15 of July, 1690.

Eliz. daug. to Richd Gillam Bap. ye 5 of Oct., 1690.

Forrist sone of Edward & Jane Greene bap. July 17, 1698.

John son of Peter Goodwin Bapt^s the 25 Dec^r, 1698.

Judith Daughter of Will Gunnell Bap^t ye 5 February, 1699.

William son of Richard Gillum by Margaret Bapt. 26 March, 1699.

Nicholas son of Nicholas Gentry Baptised ye 30 May, 1699.

Elizabeth daugh. of Tho. Granger Baptised ye 21 Jan'y, 1699–1700.

Edwd son of Edward Garland born the 20th May Bapt. 8 July, 1700.

Mary Daugh. of Edwd Green baptised ye 11 August, 1700.

Joseph son of James Garrard baptised the 24th November, 1700.

Judith Daugh. of Judith Garrard baptised ye 24 November, 1700.

Elizabeth daugh. of Peter Goodwin baptised the 2 Febr'y, 1700.

Samuel son of Benj: Goodman baptised the 27 Aprill, 170–01.

Robt son of Thomas Glass Jur. baptised the 25 May, 1701.

Anne Daugh. of Will. Gunnell baptised the 12 Octo., 1701.

Margaret Daugh. of Richard Gillum baptised the 2 November, 1701.

Mabell daugh. of Nich^o Gentry baptised the 13 Dec^r, 1702.

Rich^d son of Richd Gillam baptised ye 1st day of Aprill, 1705.

James son of Edwd Green baptised 7^{br} ye 23, 1705.

Francis Daughter of Jno Googer born ye 8 7^{br}, 1697.

Jacob son of Jno Googer born ye 10 8^{br}, 1700.

Lucy Daughter of Jno Googer Born ye 8 7^{br}, 1705.

Sarah negro belonging to Jno Googer born ye 8 May 1705.

Jenny a negro girl belonging to Jno Googer born 20 Feb'y, 170–.

Anne Daughter of Jno Galing Baptised Febr'y the 4th, 170–.

Susanna daughter of Jno Graves & Eliz. his wife born X^{br} 17th, 170–.

Matthew daughter of Jno Galling Baptised Feb'y ye 9th, 170–.

Charles son of Alexander Goodin Baptised May ye 28th, 17—.

Matthew son of John Graves Baptized October ye 23, 1710.

James & John sons of Wm Green Baptised Febr'y ye 13th, 1710.

James son of Jn° Guillam Baptised Jan'y ye 27th; Born Decem. 11, 1711.

Thomas son of Alex^r Goodin Baptized June ye 8th, 1712.

Tyler son of Tho. Garrat Baptised Feb'y 14th, 1713.

Agnes Daughter of John Guillam Born Feb'y 20th X nd **March** 21st, 1713.

Honour Daughter of Jn° Gauling Born June ye 4th, ——.

Jane Daughter of Jn° Green by Sarah his wife ———, ——.

John son of Jn° Guillam Born March ye 5th, ——.

Judith Daughter of Wm Crump Baptised March ye 9th, 1715.

Judith a negro girl belonging to Mr Wm Clopton Born Jan'y ye 26th, 1715.

Sarah Daughter of Henry Clark Born Febr'y 13th, 1715.

John ye sone of John Hight & —— his wife bap^t ye 3 day of September, 168-.

William ye sone of John Hight & —— his wife baptised ye 28 day of October, 1686.

Robert ye sone of Frances Hester & —— his wife baptised ye 10 day of October, 1686.

Rachel daughter of Edward Huchens & Rebecca his wife bapt. ye 24 day of October, 1686.

Robert son to Robert Harman was baptised ye 20th day of June, 168-.

Will son to Will Hughes baptised ye 18th day of Sept^{ber}, 1687.

Will son to Will Houle bapt. ye 4th day of March, 1687-8.

Jn° son to Luke Howard bapt^{sd} ye 13th of February, 1686-7.

Jn° son to Will Hughes bap^t ye 23rd of Aprill, 1689.

Mary Daughter to Jn° Helton Born on the 2nd of February, 1691.

Eliz. daughter to Francis Hill bap^t ye 3rd day of June, 1688.

John son to John Hight bapt. ye 16th day of Septem. 1688.

John son to Thomas Hart bap^t ye 24th of Octo. Natt ye first, 1689.

Mary daughter to Fran. Hester bapt. ye 1st of March, 1689.

Charles son to Edward Howchens bap^t ye 17th of Aug^t, 1690.

Eliz. daug^t to Wm Hughs bap^t ye 19th of Octo., 1691.

Sambo negro boy of Rowland Horsly Born ye 15 of Aug. 1691.

Eliz. daug' to Wm Howle bap' ye 28 of June, 1691.

Charles son to William Hughs bap' 18 of Oct., 1691.

Richard Haynsworth and Marg' Dynd wid. married the 19th Jan'y, 169–.

Rob' son of Richd Hood & Eliz. his wife born ye 14 Febr'y & bap' 10 July, 1698.

Elizabeth daughter of Wm Harris bap' November the 27, 1698.

Geo. son of John Hilton by Eliz. bap' the 27 Aug', 1699.

Rob' son of John Hight bapt. Aug' 20th, 1699.

Mary dau' Peter Hanna baptised 29th July, 169–.

Thomas son of Thomas Hart baptised the 6 May, 1694.

Phebe a daughter of Jn° Hollaway baptised the 16 May, 1697.

Eliz. dau' of Richd Haynsworth bap' the 11 Aug', 170–.

Anne Dau' of Edwd Harris baptized 24 November, 1700.

George son of William Harris bapt. the 13 Aprill, 1701.

Richard son of Robert Harper bap' the 4 May, 1701.

Elizabeth dau' of Phillip Henson bap' the 25 Dec', 1701.

Anne dau' of Jn° Hilton bap' the 14 June, 170–.

Eliz. dau' of Jn° Hughes bap' ye 21 March, 17—.

John son of Wm Harris baptised the 28 Mar., 170–.

William son of Jn° Hill bap' the 25 Aprill, 17—.

David son of Willm Haynes bap' ye 8 Aug', 1703.

Richard son of Richd Haynsworth bap' ye 17 Octo., 1703.

Bridgett dau' of Jn° Hilton bap' ye 20 Dec., 170–.

Benj. son of John Harris by Anne born ye 5 June, 170–.

Elizabeth Daug^ht of Tho. Harris baptised the 14 day of May, 170–.

Agnes dau' of Fra. Hill Jr. bap' ye 13 Aug', 17—.

Jn° son of ——— Howle Jr. bap' ye 15 June, ——.

Ruth Daughter of Jn° Hilton bap' ye 11 Aug', ——.

George son of Jn° Hilton born ye 30 of July, ——.

James son of Sam' Hill ———, ——.

Ann ———, ——.

John son of Wm Hardcastle Baptised March the 3rd, 1707.

Jane daughter of Jn° Hughes Baptised March the 25th, 1708.

Elizabeth daughter of Jn° Hilton Born June ye 25th, 1696.

John son of Philip Hinson Baptised Aug' ye 1st, Born June ye 3rd, 1708.

Jane Daughter of Thomas Hendeson Baptised March ye 5th,
    1708–9.

Jn° son of Jn° Helton Born August ye 29th, 1709.

Elizabeth Daughter of John Hubert Bap^t 9^{br} ye 20th, 1709.

Francis son of Fr. Hill Ju^r Baptised Jany ye 12th, 1709.

Rich^d son of Robt Harris Baptised March ye 4th, Born Jan'y
    21st, 1709.

Anne Daughter of Jn° Howle Bap^t July ye 23rd, 1710.

Elinor Daughter of Jn° Hughes Baptised Aug. ye 6th, 1710.

Anne Daughter of Matthew Hardden Baptised Jan'y ye 14th,
    1710.

Hannah Daughter of Wm Hardcastle Baptised 7^{br} ye 7th, 1711.

William son of John Hughes by Sarah his wife Born Jan'y ye
    1st, 1711.

Mary Daughter of Wm Hight Baptised Jan'y ye 27th, born X^{br}
    ye 06, 1711.

Robert son of Jn^v Howle Born April ye 14th & Baptised May
    ye 11th, 1712.

Mary Daughter of Jn° Helton Born June ye 1st, 1712.

John son of Richd Haynesworth Born Jan'y ye 9th, Baptised
    July ye 27th, 1712.

Peter son of Francis Hill Baptised March ye 1st, 1712.

W^m son of Jn° Hitchcock Born Febr'y 10, Baptised March 15,
    1712.

W^m son of Wm Hardcastle Born June ye 21st, 1714.

Mary Holt servant born at Capt Alex^r Walkers of a white
    woman and a mulatto man was born Jan'y ye 10th, attested
    by certificate from ye clerk of Wi!lmington Parish, 1698.

Judith Daughter of Jn° Howle by Eliz^a his wife born 8^{br} ye 24th,
    1714.

Mary Daughter of Robt Harper Born August ye 7th, 1714.

Michael son of James Hook Baptised April ye 24th, 1714.

Francis Daughter of Jn° Helton Baptised April ye 24th, Born
    March 18th, 1715.

Thomas son of James Henderson Born Jan. ye 17th, 1715.

George son of Stephen Housman Born Jan'y ye 29th, 1715.

George the son of George Joanes & Jane his wife Bap^t ye 5 day
    of Decem^{br}, 1686.

Thomas ye sone of Edwd Johnson Eliz.— nat ye 5 of May & bap^t ye 30 of ye instant, 1680.

Eliz. daughter of Edwd Johnson Eliz.— nat ye 7th of July and baptised ye 6th of August, 1682.

Penelope Daughter of Edwd Johnson Eliz. na— ye 4 day of Agost & bapt. ye 17 of ye instant, 1684.

Rachell Daughter of Edwd Johnson and Eliz. his wife n^t ye 8 of Dec^r & bapt. ye 2 of Jan'y, 1686-7.

Eliz. Daughter of Richd Joanes & Debora his wife Baptised ye 15 day of March, 1680.

Jn° son of Richd Joanes & Debora his wife Baptised 15 of Jan'y, 1683.

Mary Daughter of Richd Joanes and Debora his wife Baptised 16 of Jan'y, 1685.

Eliz. Daughter of John Joanes Baptized ye 30 day of May, 1688.

Robt son of Robt Jarratt & Mary his wife Bapt. 16 Aug^t, 1698.

Jn° son of Robt Jenings Born Sept. 2 and Bapt. the 23 of the same, 1698.

Rebecka Daughter of Edwd Johnson Born the 8 ———— and Baptised the 11 November, 1698.

Anne dau^t of Wm Johnson by Sarah Baptised 16 Aprill, 1699.

Elizabeth dau^t of Jn° Jenkins by Hanna Baptised 7th May, 1699.

Eliz. dau^t of Tho. Jackson Baptised the 9 Decem^br, 1694.

Tho. son of Anthony Johnson baptised the 9 Dec^br, 1694.

Thomas son of Thomas Jackson by Mary Born the 1st June, 1699.

William son of William Johnson baptised the 31 August, 1701.

Benjamin son of Edwd Johnson borne the 17 August, 1701.

William son of Robt Jenings baptised the 5 July, 1702.

John son of John Johnson baptised ye 22 Novem^b, 1702.

Sarah dau^t of Tho. Jackson baptised ye 14 Nov^b, 1703.

Benj. son of Wm Johnson baptised Aprill 18, 1705.

Massie Johnson of John Johnson bapt. ye 5 Febry., 1705.

Anne Daughter of Mich^el Johnson baptised ye 12 Febry., 1705.

John son of John Jones Junr bapt. 30th May, 1706.

2

Prisanna a negro girl belonging to ———, 17—.

Collins son of William Johnson Baptised February ye 4th, 170-.

Anne Daughter of Jn° Jones Born October the 13th, 170-.

Agnes Daughter of Michael Johnson baptised 2d April, 1708.

Rob' son of Jn° Johnson Baptised the 2d of April, 1708.

Lane son of Orlando Jones by Martha his wife Born June ye 15th, 1707.

Sarah Daughter of Michael Johnson Bapt. Oct° ye 12th, 1707.

Mary Daughter of John Jackson Bap' Febry. ye 9th, 1709.

Sarah a negro girl belonging to M' Rob' Jarratt born ———, 1708.

Jacob son of Alex. Johnson born September, 1708.

Frances Daughter of William Jackson bapt. 8br ye 15, 1710.

Cicely Daughter of Wm Johnson baptised Decr ye 3d, 1711.

Sarah Daughter of John Jackson baptised Novemb ye 13th, 1711.

Richman son of Alex. Johnson baptised April ye 27th, 1712.

Thomas son of Wm Jackson by Anne his wife baptised May 3d, 1713.

Anne Daughter of Jn° Jackson baptised ye 4th of October, 1713.

Jack a negr. belonging to Jos. Joy Born May ye 1st, 1712.

Jessie a negr. belonging to Ditto Born Febry., 171-.

Richard son of Jn° Jones Born ye 6th of March, 17—.

Thomas son of John Johnson Born 7br 11th, 1714.

Anne Daughter of William Jackson Bap' February ye 18th, 1714.

John son of John Jackson Born June ye 14th, 1715.

Francis Daughter of M' Orlando Jones by Martha his wife was born August the 6th, 1710.

Rob' son of Rob' King bapt. ye 11th of March, 1687–8.

Alexander son to Rob' King bapt. ye 19th of Decem', 1689.

Elleoner Daughter of Henr Keeble bap' the 30 October, 1689.

Mary dau' of Tho. King by Mary his wife bapt. the 11 June, 1689.

Peter son of Tho. King baptised the 7 October, 1694.

Rebecka dau' of Jn° Kimbriell Jur by Eliz. born ye 10 August, 1699.

Bulkley son of Jn° Kimbriell senr by Marg' natin Nov. 19, 1699.

John Kimburrow son of Jn° Kimborow Juʳ bapt. 21 Dec., 1701.

Henrey son of Henʳ Keeble baptised the 11 January, 170½.

Major son of John Kimburrow baptised 29 ——, 170¾.

Màry dauᵗ of Jn° Kimburrow Juʳ ye 30 Jany., 170¾.

Joseph Killy A. B: child Born the Beginning of March, 1706–7.

Julius son of James Crump Born ye 5th of 9ᵇʳ, 1715.

Will a negro boy belonging to Stephen Crump born Jany. 12th, 1715.

one negro boy named Jack belonging unto Mr Richard Little-page born the 26th day of November, 1686.

Jane daughter to Richard Lamb bapᵗ ye 8th of January, 1687–8.

Jn° son of Jno. Lewes bapt. ye 27th of Febry., 1686–7.

Negroes belonging to Mʳ Jn° Lightfoot on called Jack born ye 1st Feb., 1686–7 and on negro boy called Will born ye 20th of August, 1690.

Martha daugh. to John Laneford bapᵗ ye 9th day of August, 1688.

John son to John Lawson bapᵗ ye 8 day of May, 1690.

Richᵈ son to Robᵗ Lanceston bapᵗ ye 15 of March, 1690–1.

Negroes belonging to Mʳ Jon Lightfoot one called Jenny born July ye 3rd, 1692.

one called Beck borne Septemᵇ ye 8th, 1694.

one called Matthew born March ye 25th, 1680.

Elenor dauᵗ of John Lawson & Judith his wife bapᵗ 10 July, 1698.

Alice Daughter of John Lightfoot Esq. & Anne his wife borne the 25 Sepᵗ and baptˡˢ the same day, 1698.

Abraham son of John Lewis plantʳ bapᵗ novem. the 27, 1698.

Mary Daughter of Wᵐ Lake by Mary baptis. the 16 Aprill, 1699

Peter son of Will. Lake baptis. the 19 Septʳ, 1697.

Will son of Wᵐ Leeke baptis. the 15 July, 1694.

David son of John Lewis bapᵗ the 5 May, 1695.

Richard son of Jn° Luck baptis. the 24 Septᵇʳ, 1699.

John son of Geoᵉ Lowill by Eliz. baptiz. the 15 October, 1699.

Charles son of Geoᵉ Lowill baptis. the 16 February, 1700.

Jane dauᵗᵃ of Willᵉ Leake born the 11th January, 1700–1.

Negro children belonging to Mʳ John Lewis at Chemokins viz: Hanna borne November 6 eses Phill borne June, 1689.

John borne July 1691—Anne borne Octo^r, 1694.

Isbell borne October 1697, Peter borne July, 1699.

Serv. borne March, 1702, Mary borne Aug^t, 1694.

Henry borne July, 1699, Bob borne January, 170½.

Will borne Augt 1698, Jane born October, 1694.

Tom borne Sept'ber, 1697, Mary borne December, 1699, and Tamar borne December, 1701.

Rich^d son of Wm Leake bap^t the 13 Decem^b, ——.

William son of John Lewis baptiz. ye 22 Nov^r, 17—.

Sarah dau^{tr} of Geo. Lowill baptiz. 31 Jany., 1——.

Edward son of Nich^o Lewis baptiz. ye 29 October, 1——.

Mary & Grace negroes belonging to Coll. Lightfoot baptis. ———, 1—.

Sue a negro belonging to Co^{llo} Lightfoot born in the year 17—.

Allie a negro belonging to Co^{llo} Lightfoot born in the year 17—.

Andrew a negro belonging to Co^{llo} Lightfoot ———, 17—.

Charles a mulatto belonging to Co^{llo} Lightfoot D^o ———, ——.

Sarah a mulatto born in the year Do.

Negro children belonging to Capt Rich. Littlepage:

Sarah a negro girl born ye year ——b^r, 1703.

Jenny born December, 1704.

Nanny born November, 1704.

Pompey born Sep^{tr}, 1706.

Cesar born September, 1706.

Mary daughter of Jno Luck bapt. 14 7^{br}, 170-.

Mary daughter of Nich^o Lewis baptis. Jan. ye 16th, 1708-9.

Elizabeth daughter of Capt Richd Littlepage Born Decem. 11, 1703.

Frances daughter of Capt Richd Littlepage Born Octo^r ye 2nd, 1705.

Alice Daughter of Capt Richd Littlepage Born Jany. ye 14th, 1707-8.

Sam a negro belonging to Capt Littlepage Born June ye 20th, 1708.

Samuel son of Jno Luck Baptised September ye 13th, 1709.

Rich^d son of Capt Richd Littlepage Born March ye 21st, 1709-10.

Watt a negro belonging to Mad^m Mary Lightfoot Born June ye 10th, 1709.

Buffoe was born March 7th, Harry was born May ye 20th, Hannah was born July ye 10th, all belonging to Mad^m Lightfoot, 1711.

Jack a negro was born 7^{br} ye —— 1708, Robin was born October 18th, 1709, Faller was born Feb. ye 10th, 1711, Will was born March 13th, 1711, negroes belonging to Mr Sherwood Lightfoot.

Richard a negro child belonging to Capt Richd Littlepage Baptised August ye 14th, 1711.

Hannah Daughter of Betty one of Mad^m Lightfoots negroes Xnd 9^{br} ye 17th, 1711.

Betty Peters wife a negroe belonging to ye s^d Lightfoot Xnd 9^{ber} ye 17th, 1711.

Negroes belonging to Mr Goodrich Lightfoot Registered:

Tomson a negro born in ye year 1705.

Edward Bretty born in ye year 1705.

Mrs Juda a negro girl born in ye year 1707.

Frank a negro born in ye year 1707.

Evans born in ye year 1709.

Rebecka born in ye year 1711.

Angelico Daughter of Nich^o Lewis Born March ye 20th & bapt. April ye 27th, 1708.

Anne Daughter of Mr Goodrich Lightfoot Born 7^{br} ye 22nd, 1708.

Mary Daughter of Mr Sherwood Lightfoot Born September ye 9th, 1707.

Frances Daughter of Mr Sherwood Lightfoot born October 31, 1708.

John son of Mr Sherwood Lightfoot Born November ye 13th, 1711.

Sue a negro girl belonging to Mr Sherwood Lightfoot Born July ye 27th, 1712.

John son of Mr Goodrich Lightfoot Born Febry. ye 7th, 1711.

Sue a negro girl belonging to Mr Goodrich Lightfoot Born June ye 20th, 1712.

Edmond son of Richd Littlepage Gent. Born May ye 16th, 1714.

Easter a mulatto belonging to ye s^d Littlepage Born March 10th, 1711–12.

Rich^d a negro belonging to ye s^d Littlepage Born June ye 12th, 1714.

Peace a negro belonging to Capt Richd Littlepage Born 7^{br} ye 10th, 1713.

Goodrich son of Mr Goodr^h Lightfoot Baptised Febry. ye 14th, 1713.

———— Daughter of Gwin Lewis Born Mar. ye 17th, Baptis. April ye 25, 1714.

Buck a negro belonging to Mr Tho. Lightfoot Born June 6th, 1714.

Sherwood son of Sherw^d Lightfoot Born May ye 1st, 1714.

Alice negro belonging to D^o Born July ye 12th, 17—.

Mary ye Daughter of Thomas Moreman & Eliz. his wife bapt. ye 29th day of Aug^t, 1686.

Robert son of Jno Mochi & Mary his wife baptised ye 24 day of Octob^{er}, 1686.

Gedeo ye sone of Gedeon Macon his wife natt the 20th of June & bapt. ye 22 June, 1682.

Ann ye daughter of Gedeon Macon & Martha his wife natt ye 15 day of Decem. bap. 2d Feby., 1685.

Sarah a negro girl belonging to Mr Gedeon Macon borne ye 29th day of Jan'y, 1682.

Will a negro boy belonging to Mt Gedeon Macon born ye 2d day of Febry., 1683.

Elizth daughter of Robert Morris & Rebec^a his wife baptis. ye 13th day of Decem^{br}, 1685.

Eliz. daughter to Pillomore bap^t ye 25th of December, 1687.

Will son to Robert Morris bap^t ye 1st d. of Aprill, 1688.

Peter sone to Stephen Moore born ye 24th of Jan'y, 1683.

Henry sone to Nicholas Mills bap^t ye 10th of Aprill, 1687.

Will sone to Thomas Moss bapt. ye 17 of February, 1688-9.

Will sone to Tho. Macheke bap^t ye 10 day of Octo., 1689.

Tho. son to Ric^h Martin bap^t ye 10 day of Octo., 1689.

Andrew son to Thos Moorman bap^t ye 4 day of Novem^r, 1689.

Mary Daughter to Edward Morriss bap^t ye 30 day of Jan'y, 1689-0.

Pellom sone to Pellom Moor born ye 4 of Febry. & bap^t ye 13th of March, 1689-0.

Eliz. dau^t to Jno Massey bap^t ye 27 of Sep^r, 1691.

Mark son to John Macoy bap^t ye 7 Decem^{br}, 1690.

Martha daug. of Tho. & Mary Michell baptis. July the 17, 1698.

Thomas son of Willm Martin & Mary his wife bap^t 10th July, 1698.

John son of Jno Martin natin. ye 8th Ap^l 1697, bap^t 10th October, 1698.

Judith Daughter of John Mask born ye 14th April and baptized the 10th July, 1698.

Mary daughter of John Moore baptized the 11th November, 1698.

Richd Nicholas son of Rich^t Madlin by Susana bap^t April 10, 1699.

Jno son of John Murron bapt. ye 25 June, 1699.

Nicholas son of Nicholas Meriwether Gent. by Eliz. his wife born the 11th July and baptized the 6 Augt following, 1699.

Charles son of Robt Morris by Eliz. bap^t ye 27 Aug^t, 1699.

John son of Jno Moore bap^t ye 13 Dec^e, 1699.

Mary dau^t of Will. Martin ———, 16—.

William son of Gedeon Macon Gent. born the 12 Nov., 169-.

Anne Daugh. of Nich^o Meriwether Gent. bap^t the 15 July, 169-.

Marlmeduke son of Pelthani Moore bap^t the 9 June, 16—.

Robt son of Robert Morris bap^t the 9 June, 16—.

Amy Daug^h of Edward Morgan bap^t the 9 May, 16—.

Daniell son of Micha^{ll} Johnson bap^t ye 16 May, 1699.

Margaret Daug^h of Wm Millington Ju^r bap^t 5 Novem^{br}, 169-.

Thomas son of Edwd Machen by Anne bap^t Nov. 5, 1699.

Frances Daug^t of Wm Major bap^t the 19 Nov^r, 1699.

John son of Step. Michell Ju^r natin the 19 Dec^r, 1698.

Mary Daug^h of James Moore baptiz. the 7 March, 1699–1700.

Mary Daug^h of Jno Mask bap^t the 31 Ma^e, 1700.

Cassanora Daug^h of Pelham Moore bap^t the 7 Aprill, 1700.

Peter son of Thomas Masse bap^t the 14 Aprill, 17—.

Thomas son of Richd Melton bap^t the 28 ———, 17—.

Robert son of Edwd Morgan bap^t the 14 July, 170-.

Nicholas son of Geo. Moor bapt. the 21 July, 17—.

——id son of Thomas Mims Ju^r born the 1st January, 17—.

——— the Daug^h of David Machen born the 22 of December, 17—.

Moll mulatto slave belonging to Cap' Nicholas Meriwether born the 2d of November, 1699.

Stephen son of Stephen Michell Ju' born the 24 December 1699.

Rebeca dau' of John Moore baptis. the 2 Febry., 1700–1.

Robert son of Will⁰ Martin baptis. the 13 Aprill, 1701.

William son of John Mask born the 6 May, 1701.

George son of John Medlock Ju' baptis. ye 3 June, 1701.

Sarah Daugʰ of Danˡˡ Mackgert baptised the 3 May, 1702.

William son of Pelham More baptised the 7 May, 1702.

Mary Daugʰ of Richⁿ Melton baptiz. the 10 May, 1702.

Geo. son of Geo. Marr baptized the 18 March, 1701–2.

John son of Wᵐ Major baptiz. the 17 May, 1702.

Richard son of Richᵈ Macdlin baptiz. the 5 July, 1702.

Negro children belonging to Mʳ Gedeon Macon, viz:

Nann born July, 1692, Moll born the 6th Novemᵇʳ, 1695.

Merrea born Jany., 1695, Phill born ye 17 Jany , 1696.

Isack born Jany. ye 28, 1697, Sarah borne Sepʳ, 1698.

Will borne Novʳ ye 25, 1700, Liddia borne ye 1st Apʳ, 1701 and Trefana borne the 24 December, 1701.

William son of Jnᵒ Medlock baptised the 19 July, 1702.

Timothy son of Jnᵒ Mask borne ye 20 June, 1702.

Elizabeth Daugʰ of James Moore baptiz. the 2 Augᵗ, 1702.

Sarah Daugʰ of John Madox baptis. ye 27 Sepᵗ, 1702.

Elizabeth Dau' of Tho. Marcey baptis. ye 6 Novʳ, 1702.

Frances Dau' of Edwⁿ Moore baptis. ye 13 Dec., 1702.

William son of Mʳ Gedeon Macon & Martha his wife borne the 11 Novʳ, 1693.

John son as above borne the 17 Decʳ, 1695.

James son as above borne the 28 October, 1701.

Jude dau' of Tho. Moore baptiz. 23 May, 1703.

Elizabeth daugʰ of Nicholas Meriwether Gent. by Elizabeth his wife borne the 20 June and baptised the 3 July following anno., 1703.

Robert son of Jnⁿ Marrow baptiz. the 18 July, 1703.

Elizabeth daugʰ of Step. Michell born the 20 Febry, 170⅔.

Anne dau' of Jnᵒ Moore baptiz. ye 10 Octoᵇ, 1703.

Thomas son of Jnᵒ Medlock Ju' baptized 21 Novemᵇ, 1703.

Thomas son of Wᵐ Major baptis. the 28 Novemᵇ, 1703.

William son of Geo. Merideth baptiz. 19 Dec. 1703.

Bathia dau[t] of James Martin baptiz. 27 Febry, 170¾.

Elizabeth dau[t] of W[m] Martin baptised the 21 May, 1704.

——— Daug[h] of Geo. Moore bap. 24 ———, 1704-5.

Rob[t] ——— Maddox bapt. 24 Febry, 1704-5.

Marg daugh. of Geo. Massie bap[t] 6th Aprill, 1705.

Anne Daug[h] of Step[n] Michell Jun[r] bapt. 20 Jan., 1705.

Geo. son of Jn[o] Martin bap[t] 24 March, ———.

Unity Daug[h] of James Martin bapt. 24 March, ———.

Edward ye son of James Nich[us] & Elizabeth his wife baptised ye
    7 day of Nov., 1686.

W[m] son to James Neeves bap[t] ye 4 of this instant Oct., 1691.

James sone of James Neeves baptiz. September the 25, 1698.

Isabell dau[t] of James Nuckolls baptiz. the 14 Nov., 1697.

James son of James Nuckolls baptis. the 30 June, 1695.

Bouth son of Rob[t] Napier & Marg. his wife borne ye 1st of Oct[r],
    1692.

Frances daug[h] of Rob[t] Napier & Mary his wife borne Febry. ye
    5th, 1694-5.

Rob[t] son of Rob[t] Napier & Mary his wife borne 7[br] ye 16th,
    1697.

Katherine Daughter of Rob[t] Napier & Mary his wife borne 8[br]
    ye 12th, 1700.

Eliz[r] Daughter of Rob[t] Napier & Mary his wife borne 10[br] ye
    25th, 1704.

Tho. son of James Neaves bap[t] Mar. 18th, 1704-5.

Walter son of W[m] & Susanna Norris born ye 21st X[br], 1707.

Mary Daughter of Edward Nash Baptised June ye 24th, 1711.

Thomas son of W[m] Nickles Baptised July the 26th, 1713.

Micheal son of Michal Nash baptised July 18th born ye 17th of
    June, 1714.

Mary Daughter of Edw[d] Nash by Mary his wife Born June ye
    29th, 1715.

Amesen Daughter of Martin Martin bap[t] 6th of Apri[ll], 1706.

Anne Daughter of Charles Massie bap[t] 20th Aprill, 1707.

Susanna Daughter of Jn[o] Maddox bapt. 19th, 8[br], 1707.

James son of M[r] Thomas Massie Bap[t] May ye 16th, 1708.

Phillis Daughter of Stephen Moon Ju[r] Bap[t] June ye 13th, 1708.

Thomas son of Thomas Mims Born Febry. ye 15th, 1707-8.

Anne Daughter of Martin & Sarah Martin Bap^t Aug. ye 9th. 1708.

Henry son of Jno Martin & Sarah his wife Baptised August ye 18th, 1708.

Anne Daughter of James Martin & Rebecca his wife Bapt. Aug. ye 18th, 1708.

Mary Daughter of Step. Michell Ju^r & Mary his wife Bapt. Aug. ye 22d, 1708.

Edward son of Joseph Morris Born ye 5th day of 8^{br}, 1708.

Judith & Anne Daughters of Saml Mosse X^{ned} Febry. ye 7th, 170¾.

David son of Wm Martin Baptised March ye 6th, 1708–9.

Bess a negro girl belonging to Jno Moore Born April ye 20th, 1705.

George a negro boy belonging to ye s^d Jno. Moore Born May ye 24th, 1707.

James son of Thomas Mosse Baptised March ye 13th, Born Jany. 27th, 1708–9.

Anne Daughter of Mr Jno Meuks Bapt. May the 14th, Born April 15th, 1709.

Sampson & Will negroes belonging to Wm Millinton Born April ye 30th, 1709.

Elizabeth Daughter of Jno Moore Born August ye 25th, 1690.

Stephen son of Step. Moon Ju^r Born October ye 12th, 1705.

James son of Jno Moore Born March ye 23rd, 169¾.

Jno son of Jno Moore Born September ye 28th, 1706.

Martha Daughter of Jno Moore Born Febry. ye 5th, 1708–9.

Elizabeth Daughter of Charles Marssie Born 9^{br} 5th & Bapt. X^{br} ye 4th, 1709.

Martha Daughter of Thomas Mitchell Born Sept. ye 22d, 1697.

Thomas son of Tho. Mitchell Born Jany. ye 3d, 1701.

Archelas son of Tho. Mitchell Born ye 9th of Febry., 1703.

Millinton son of Richd Manly Baptised Februa^{ry} ye 9th, 1709.

Jno son of Mr Jno Meux Born June ye 5th, 1707.

Mary a negro belonging to Mr Jno Meux Born February ye 11th, 1709.

Mary ye Daughter of John Martin Born April ye 19th, 1709.

Dick a negro belonging to Jno Martin Born June ye 15th, 1705.

Hanah a negro belonging to Jn° Martin Born May ye 2d, 1708.

Betty a negro belonging to Jn° Martin Born April ye 3d, 1709.

———ras a negro belonging to Reb^{cs} Martin Born Jany. ye 22d, 1705.

Valentine son of Martin Martin Baptised June ye 18th, 1710.

Anne Daughter of Lionel Mims Baptised June ye 18th, 1710.

Benj. son of Tho. Mims Baptised June ye 13th, 1710.

Peter son of Peter Moon Baptised ye 15th day of 8^{br}, 1710.

Stephen a negro boy belonging to Stephen ——— Senr Born Aug. 17th, 1710.

Elizabeth Daughter of Tho. Moore Baptised Jany. ye 8th, 1710.

Susanna Daughter of Edward Morris Baptised Jany. ye 8th, 1710.

Evan son of Stephen Mitchell Born Jany. ye 16th, Baptised Feb. 18th, 1710–11.

——— ——— 171–.

Richard son of M^r Jn° Meux Baptised March ye 31st, ———.

Thomas son of Jn° Martin Baptised Jany. ye 13th, ———.

Will sone to Jn° Oslin born of An his wife and bapt. ye 18th of March, 1687–8.

Sam son to John Oslin bap^t ye 18th of Oc^t, 1691.

John son of Jn° Ottey Born July ye 19th, 1713.

Mary Daughter of Jn° Otey Born July ye 17th, 1715.

John son of Stephen Moon Baptised Jany. ye 13th, 1711–12.

Robin a negro belonging to Mr Tho. Massie Born Ap^{ll} ye 3d, 1708.

Matthew son of Cornelius Matthews Born 8^{br} ye 5th, 1711, Bap^t Ap^{ll} 13th, 1712.

Joel a negro belonging to Cha. Massie Born July ye 5th, 1709.

Peter a negro belonging to ye s^d Massie Born December ye 24th, 1711.

Susanna Daughter of John Martin Born May ye 20th, 1711, Bap^t July 27th, 1712.

William son of Daniel Mackhany Born July ye 15th. 1712.

Jenny a negro belonging to M^r Jn° Meux Born October 7, 1711.

Richard son of Richd Meanly Born September ye 17th, 1712.

Katherine a negro belonging to ye s^d Meux Born October, 1711.

Elizabeth Daughter of Peter Moon Bapt. December ye 14th, 1712.

Sarah Daughter of Thomas Mims Born May ye 19th, 1712.

Lucy Daughter of Edward Moore Born February ye 4th, 1712.

Michael son of Jno Madoxs Baptised May ye 31st, 1713.

Valentine son of Stephen Mitchell Jur. Baptised 7^br ye 27th, 1713.

Charles son of Jno Morriss Baptised Decem^br ye 13th, 1713.

Rebecca Daughter of Jno Martin Born August ye 18th, Bapt. Febry. 14th, 1713.

Robert Moore son of Jno Moore Born April ye 17th, 1713.

Jack a negro boy belonging to Jno Moore Born July 7th, 1712.

Sarah Daughter of Jno Moore Born February ye 6th, 1713.

Joyce Daughter of Tho. Moss Baptised April ye 4th, 1714.

Thomas son of Wm Moss Baptised April ye 11th, 1714.

John son of Thomas Martin Baptised April ye 18th, 1714.

Billy a negro belonging to Capt James Moss Born Jany., 1709.

Jack a negro belonging to ye s^d Moss born in October, 1713.

James son of Thomas Moore by Elizabeth his wife Born Febry. ye 7th, 1713.

Charles son of Charles Massie Born October ye 13th, 1714.

Stephen Chappall a Parish child bound to ye s^d Charles Massie was born in May, 1705 and Baptised in June, 1712.

Pompey a negro belonging to ye s^d Chas Massie Born Feb^ry ye 10th, 1713.

Sarah a negro girl belonging to Edw^r Moore Born Jany, 1713.

Mary the Daughter of William Plant and Eliz. his wife baptised ye 11th July, 1686.

Edward the sone of Edward Pinick & Elizabeth his wife baptized ye 15th day of Aug., 1686.

Mr George Poindexter sen^ror negroes born one call Harciffirs yo 2d day of July, 1681.

  one negro called Polliphemus a boy born ye 15th day of August, 1681.

  one negro girl called Arianite born ye 20th day of July, 1682.

one negro gils called Joseline born ye 5 day of May, 1686.

Richard son of Susanna Pines born ye No^r 22d, Baptised ye 30th of this same instant 1676, one negro boy borne Septem^{br} ye 31st, 1682.

Charles son of George Person and his wife Baptised ye 1st day of February, 1685–6.

Sara daug. to John Parks Junr bap^t ye 8th of Aprill, 1688.

James sone to Susanna Piram bap^t ye 24th of Aprill, 1687.

Anne daugh. to Will Plant & Eliz. his wife bap^t ye 3d day of January, 1688–9.

W^m sone to Tho. Patteson bap^t ye 30th day of January, 1689–0.

Eliz. Daugh. to Capt Matt. Page by Mary his wife Na^t ye 6th of Jany. bap^t ye 16th, 1689–0.

Negros belonging to Capt Matt. Page born as followeth:

Sall born ye 1st of July, 1678, Sue born ye 5 of Augst, 1678.

Gregory born ye 8th of Oc^t, 1678, Massy born July ye 3d, 1686, Kate born Oct. 22, 1682.

Beck bo. No. ye 2d, 1682, James bo. Jan. 17. 1682, Polle bo^n Oc^t ye 20th, 1683.

Madam bo^n Mar^{ch} 7, 1684, Beauty bo^n March 17, 1684, Weny bo^n March 27, 1685.

Daniell bo^n Apr^{ll} 16, 1686, Hannah bo^n July 8, 1686, Pegg bo^n Apr^{ll} ye 24th, 1687.

Epon bo^n May 25, 1687, Tom bo^n July 12, 1687, Dick bo^n ye Decem. 15, 1688.

Sam bo^n Augt 5, 1689, Bety bo^n Oct. 21, 1689, at ye Qr^t as followeth:

Doll bo^n Feb. 7, 1683, Matt bo^n June 21, 1685, Betty bo^n Oct. 8, 1685.

Margaret bo^n Apr^{ll} 29, 1687, Jeny bo^n Decem. 1st, 1688, Frank bo^n June 6th, 1688–9.

William son to William Pullam Nat. ye 3 August bap^t ye 3 of Sept., 1690.

Th^o son to Thomas Pontin bapt. ye 21st of June, 169–.

one negro belonging to Mrs Susan Poindexter born ye 1st day of Febry, 169¾.

Susana Poindexter buryed the 15 July, 1693.

Anne Daugh. of Hump^e Parish and Mary his wife bap^t 4th Sept. 1698.

Anne Daugh. of Willᶜ Perkins by Eliz. his wife bapᵗ 12 March, 1699–0.

Elloner dauᵗ of Robᵗ Pasly by Eloner his wife bapᵗ 26 March, 1699.

Rowland son of John Pecke by Jane bapᵗ the 25 June, 1699.

Eliz. Daugh. of Gabril Pickring bapᵗ the 12 Decemᵇʳ, 1696.

Will son of Edwᵈ Penick, bapt. the 25 August, 1694.

John son of Eliz. Pedley bapᵗ the 30 June, 169–.

James son of Willᵐ Pullum baptis. the 2 May, 1690.

Sarah Daugh. of David Pattison baptis. the 24 March, 1699–1700.

Benj. son of Willᵐ Pullam baptis. the 31 March, 17—.

Susanna Daugh. of Tho. Poindexter Born the 6 Febry., 169–.

Eliz. Daugh. of Mʳ Thomas Poindexter born the 14 February, 1699–1700.

Willᵐ son of Tho. Ponton baptiz. the 12 May, 1700.

Jane Dauᵗ of Henry Parish born 22 Dec., 1699, baptz. 21 July, 1700.

Joseph son of John Peace baptis. the 13 October, 1700.

Frances dauᵗ of John Park Juʳ baptis. the 16 Febry., 1700–1.

Henᶜ son of Humphrey Parrish baptis. the 27 Aprill, 1701.

James son of James Pyrant baptis. the 27 Aprill, 1701.

Anne dauᵗ of Wᵐ Perkins baptis. the 4 May, 1701.

William son of Peter Plantine baptis. the 1st October, 1701.

Anne Daugh. of David Pattison baptis. the 2 November, 1701.

Elizabeth & Mary daughters of Mio Prerdd baptiz. 15 March, 170½.

Sarah Daugh. of Tho. Poindexter borne ye 12 May, 170–.

Anne Daugh. of Wᵐ Pullam baptis. ye 22 Novᵇ, 1702.

Susannah dauᵗ of Jnᵒ Peace bapt. the 21 Jan., 170–.

Wᵐ son of James Pirant baptis. ye 28 March, 1703.

Judith daughter of Jeremyah Peirce baptis. 24 July, 1703.

John son of Charles Person baptiz. Sept. 19, 1703.

Frances & Kate negroes belonging to Mr. Geo. Poindexter bapt. Febry. 4th, 1704–5.

Francis son of James Perry bapᵗˢ ye 13 Jany., 1705.

David son of David Pattison born ye 14th 8ᵇʳ, 1705.

Judith Daughter of Mᵉ Geo. Poindexter born ye 14 Jany. & baptized ye 8 Jany., 1705.

Margaret Daughter of Robt Pasly borne ye 25 June, 1706.

Aniss Daughter of Robt Pasly born ye 17 X^{br}, 1691.

Mary Daughter of Robt Pasly born ye 25 8^{br}, 1693.

William son of Ro. Pasley born ye 26 July, 1696.

Robert son of Ro. Pasley born ye 16 8^{br}, 1701.

Solomon son of Robt Pasley born ye 4 9^{br}, 1703.

William son of Wm Perkins baptis. ye 25 Aug^t, 1706.

Jane a negro belonging to Co^{ll} Parke born X^{br}, 1705.

Anne Daughter of —— Prior begot o. ye 5 Jany., 1706–7.

Hannah Daughter of Nicho. Perday baptised 6 April, 1707.

John son of Mr John Parke Jun. bap^t 19th July, 1707.

John son of Geo. Pattison baptised 12th 9^{br}, 1707.

Thomas son of Tho. Pattison Baptised Febry. ye 4th, 1707.

Anne Daughter of Robt Peasley Baptis^d Nov. ye 21st, 1708.

Thomas son of David Pattison Baptised January ye 13th, 1708–9.

Anne Daughter of William Perkins Born January ye 26th, 1708–9.

Phillip son of Mr Geo. Poindexter & Mary his wife baptised Decr ye 26, 1708–9.

Edward son of Thomas Pattison Baptised ye 13th of June, 1710.

Anne Daughter of Henry Porter baptised Feb^{ury} ye 25th, 1710–11.

Robert son of James Perry Baptised September ye 30th, 1711.

Judith Daughter of Wm Perkins Baptised Jany. ye 27th, Born Dec. ye 15th, 1711.

Joseph son of Jno Parish Baptised Septem. ye 20th, 1713.

Frances Daughter of Wm Pierson Baptised Decem. 13th, 1713.

Elizabeth Daughter of Edward Patison Bap^t March 21, 1713.

Charles son of —— Person Baptised Augt 8th, 1714.

Philip a negro girl belonging to Mr Jno Parke Born July 12th, 1713.

Thomas son of David Pattison Born Decem. ye 13th, 1708.

Charles son of ye s^d David Born May ye 6th, 1711.

Jonathan son of ye s^d David Born June ye 6th, 1713.

Frances ye Daughter of ye s^d David Born Decem. ye 19th, 1715.

Susanna ye Daughter of Jane Purdie Born April 25th, 1716.

Jane Daughter of Edward Pattison Born May ye 12th, 1716.

Elizabeth Daughter of Wm Pryer Born May ye 7th, 1716.

Mary Daughter of Geo. Poindexter Jur. born 7^{br} ye 5th, 1715.

James & John sons of Richd Littlepage Gent. by Frances his wife born July ye 14th, 1714.

Peg a negro girl belonging to Mad^m Barbara Levermore Born ——, 1703.

William son of Nich^c Lewis by Eliz. his wife Born March ye 22d, 1715.

Mary a negro girl belonging to sig^r Jno Lewis Born May ye 15th, 1715.

John a negro boy belonging to ye s^d Lewis Born June ye 18th, 1715.

Matthew a negro boy belonging to Mr Sherwood Lightfoot born 8^{br} 1, 1715.

Farr a negro boy Born 8^{br} ye 8th belonging to do., 1715.

Bely a negro boy belonging to Capt Richd Littlepage Born 9^{br} ye 9th, 1715.

Elizabeth Daughter of Owin Lewis Born Febr^y 6th, 1715.

George a malato belonging to Mad^m Eliz. Littlepage Born Dec^{br} ye 29th, 1715.

Judith daughter of Richd Littlepage Gent. Born July ye 31st, 1715.

Mary ye Daughter of John Roper Junior & Susan his wife baptized ye 11th day of Aprill, 1686.

James the sone of Thom^s Rice & Marie his wife baptized ye 4 day of Aprill, 1686.

Elizabeth Daughter of John Randall & his wife baptized ye 13 day of June, 1686.

Will sone of Thomas Renall & Mary his wife baptized ye 5 day of Decem^b, 1686.

Phillis Daughter of Will Rost & Eliz. his wife baptiz. ye 24 of January, 1685-6.

Thomas sone to Elinor Realy servant to Mr Sam. Firth born ye 26 of Decem., 1686.

Mary daughter to Jno Roper sen^r bap^t ye 25th of August, 1687.

Alice daughter to Jno Raylee bap^t ye 27th day of November, 1687.

Rich^d son to Will Ross bap^t ye 3d of March, 1687-8.

Mary daughter to Jn° Roberts bap' ye 1st d of Aprill, 1688.

Thom. son to Thomas Rice bap' ye 24th day of June, 1688.

Edward son to Thomas Rice bap' ye 17 of Apr", 1690.

Judith daugh' to Thomas Renalls bap' ye 19 of July, 1688.

Susanna daug' to Jonas Renall bap' ye 21 of Decem", 1690.

Eliz. daugh' to Robert Rickman bap' 22d day of Febry., 1690–1.

Eliz. daugh' to Tho. Renalls Bap' 15 of March, 1690–1.

John son of Tho. Reid & Marcey his wife Bap' the 18 Septem", 1698.

Ruth Daughter of Wm Rost baptiz. 6 of Nove. 1694.

Lydia Daugh' of Wm Rost baptiz. 11 of November, 1694.

Jn° son of Will. Raxford baptiz. the 9 Dec', 1694.

Mary dau' of Tho. Reid baptiz. the 15 July, 1694.

Jane daug' Thomas Reynolds baptiz. the ——, ——.

Leticia dau' of Tho. Renolds baptiz. the 4 April, 1697.

Phillip son of Tho. Reynolds by Mary baptiz. 15 October, 1699.

Anne dau' of Jn° Roper bap' the 18 Febry., 1699.

Alice dau' of Tho. Reid baptiz. the 29 September, 1700.

Jane daug' of John Roper baptiz. the 1st December, 1700.

Henry son of Geo. Rhodes baptiz. the 5 January, 1700–1.

William son of William Ross baptiz. the 15 June, 1701.

Elizabeth daugh' of Jn° Rayle Baptiz. the 17 May, 1702.

Marcy dau' of Tho. Reid baptiz. the 5 July, 1702.

Rebecca dau' of Jn° Roper baptiz. the 20 July, 1702.

Mary dau' of Cha' Roades baptiz. the 7 Febry., 170²₃.

William son of Wm Reynolds bap' 12 May, 1706.

William son of Jn° Roper baptised April the 2d, 1708.

William son of Robert Richardson baptized Sep' ye 28th, 1708.

Anne Daughter of Rob' Richardson baptised Sep' ye 26th, 1708.

Elizabeth Daughter of Wm Reynolds Baptised ye 7th 9^br, 1708.

William son of Evan Ragling Jun' Born May ye 1st & bap' ye 29th, 1709.

Judith Daughter of James Raymond Baptised April ye 9th, 1710.

Elizabeth Daughter of Richd Ross Baptised December ye 17th, 1710.

3

John son of Evan Ragling Junr Baptised March ye 13th, 1710.

Joseph son of Jno Rooper Born 8^{br} ye 13th, Baptised Jany. 6, 1711–12.

Edmond son of Robt Richardson Baptised June ye 1st, 1712.

Bathsheba Daughter of Wm Reynolds Born 8^{br} ye 12th, 1711.

William son of Richd Ross Baptised 8^{br} ye 12th, 1712.

Isaac son of Thomas Raglin Baptised August ye 2d, 1713.

Elizabeth Daughter of Robt Richardson Born August ye 2d, 1713.

Lucy Daughter of Wm Reynolds Born April ye 17th, 1714.

Charles son of Charles Richardson Born May ye 20th, 1714.

Thomas son of Joseph Roe Born July ye 1st, 1714.

Anne Daughter of Richd Ross Born Jan'y ye 25th, 171–.

Elizabeth Daughter of James Raymond Born 7^{br} ye 11th, 1714.

Henry son of Robt Richardson Born June ye 3rd, 1715.

Jacob son of Thomas Raglin Born October ye 22d, 1715.

John son of James & Unity Raymond Born Sep^t 10, 1717.

W^m son of Ditto Born Octo^r 10th, 1719.

John son of Ditto Born Aug. 10th, 1720.

Rebecca ye daughter of Richard Snoroe & Mary his wife Bapt^{ed} ye 1st day of Aug., 1686.

Elizabeth ye Daughter of Jno Savory & —— his wife Baptized ye 17 day of October, 1686.

John ye sone of David Smith & Elizabeth his wife Baptised ye 24 day of Octob^r, 1686.

Mary ye daughter of Robert Sporill & Ann Butterfield Bap^t ye 20 day of Septemb^{er} being aged according to ye testimony of Mr. Thom. Mitchell & others 4 years the 5 of Oct^o, 1686.

Susannah ye daughter of Thomas Spencer & Ann his wife Baptiz. ye 3 day of Nov^{br}, 1686.

Will ye sone of Will Stone & Mary his wife Baptiz. ye 15th of January, 1682.

John ye sone of Ditto & Mary his wife Baptised ye 15th of January, 1685.

Negros of Thom. Spencer one negro borne being a genhu ye 19th of Decem., 1665.

one negro boy born the 10th of August, 1674.

Elizabeth Smith daughter of Geo. Smith & Mary his wife bap^t Oct^o ye 29, 1673.

Mary daughter to Ann Spain bap^t ye 23rd of January, 1687–8.

Eliz. Daugh^t to Robert Spurlock bap^t ye 1st d of Aprill, 1688.

James sone to Thom. Stanly bap^t ye 15th of Aprill, 1688.

Susanna daughter to Thom. Smith & Mary his wife bap^t ye 16 of Aprill, 1688.

Henry son to Jno Snead bap^t ye 8th day of May, 1687,

George sone to Robert Speare bapt. ye 23d day of Septem^r, 1688.

Mary daugh^t to Timothy Serwoll bap^t ye 3d day of January, 1688–9.

Rebecca Dau^t to Thomas Sneade bap^t ye 3d day of Jany., 1688–9.

Jno son to Tho. Renalls bap^t ye 18 day of Febry., 1684.

Andrew son to Andrew Spradlin bap^t ye 21 of Novem^b, 1689.

Thomas son to Thomas Stanly bap^t ye 23 of Novem^b, 1689.

John son to Henry Scruggs bap^t ye 25 day of May, 1690.

William son to John Snead bap^t ye 9 of Novem^b, 1690.

Marg^t daug^t to William Ston bap^t ye 25 of Jany., 1690.

Tho. son to Thomas Spencer born ye 5 of Sep^t, 1689.

Negros belonging to ye s^d Spencer: Nan bo^n 10 of Decem^b, 1685, Tom bo^n Oc^t 5, 1687.

Rich^d son to Richd Skiner bap^t ye 15 of Feby, 1690–1.

John son to Tho. Stanly bap^t ye 11 of Oct^o, 1691.

Allex. son to Alexander Strainge bap^t ye 18 of Oct^o, 1690–1.

Eliz. daugh^t of James & Eliz. Stringer bap^t July 17, 1698.

Will son of Jno Sandwich & Mary his wife bap^t 10 July, 1698.

John son of John Strong bap^t the ——— 13 Nov^r, 1698.

Mary Daughter of Geo. Sheperson Baptiz. 13 Nov^r, 1698.

David son of Tho. Smith Gent. by Mary his wife born the 1st March and baptised the 3d March, 1698–9.

Frances dau^t of Robt Spurlock by Rebecka wife bapt. March 12, 1698–9.

Sam^{ll} son of Sam^{ll} Stegall by Jane his wife bap^t March 26, 1699.

Margaret dau^t of Richd Skiner by Mary bap^t ye 6 August, 1699.

John son of Jno Stiles baptiz. the 31 Jany., 1698–9.

Judith Dau⁺ of Allex: Straing bap⁺ the 6 December, 16—.

W^m son of Will Sanders baptized the 14 November, 1694.

Jn° son of James Stringer baptiz. the 9 Decem^b, 1694.

Eliz. Dau⁺ of Absalom Smith baptiz. the 19 Decem^b, 1697.

John son of Geo. Shepherdson baptiz. the 25 July, 1697.

Charles son of Natha Smith bap⁺ the 9 May, 1697.

Sarah Dau⁺ of Wm Sanders baptis. the 23 May, 1697.

William son of Thomas Smith Gent. by Mary his wife born the 25 March, 1686.

Thomas son of Mr Smith as above born the 11 October, 1669.

Major son of Mr Smith as above born the 12 March, 169⅔.

Mary dau⁺ of Mr Smith as above born ye 7 Aug⁺, 1696.

Michael son of Allex. Strainge by Anne bap⁺ 22 Octo., 16—.

Martha Dauter of And^e Spradlin by Anne bap⁺ November the 12, 1699.

Edwd son of Robert Speere by Ruth bap⁺ 19 Nov^r, 1699.

James son of Geo. Speere baptis. 19 Nov^r, 1699.

Thomas son of James Sanders by Sarah bap⁺ 19 Nov^r, 1699.

Salomon son of Tho. Simons bap⁺ the 31 Decem^b, 1699.

Anne dau⁺ of Absalom Smith baptis. the 31 March, 1700.

Mary dau⁺ of John Sanders baptiz. the 14 Aprill, 1700.

Thomas son of William Sanders baptiz. the 11 August, 1700.

William son of Will Stevens baptiz. the 29 Septem^br, 1700.

John son of Nathaniel Smith baptiz. the 20 Oct°, 1700.

Will^e son of John Strong baptis. the 5 Jany., 1700–1.

John son of Nath⁺ Smith born the 17 Sept^b, 1700.

Rebecca daugh⁺ of Rob⁺ Spurlock baptis. the 4 May, 1701.

James son of James Smith born the 14 Febry., 1700–1.

John son of ames Sanders baptiz. the 5 October, 1701.

John son of Rob⁺ Speere baptis. the 25 Decem^b, 1701.

Elizabeth dau⁺ of Allex. Strainge baptiz. 5 Apr^l, 1702.

Elizabeth daugh⁺ of Tho. Smith Gent. by Mary bor. March the 28, 1701.

Susannah dau⁺ of Wm Sanders baptiz. the 24 Febry., 170⅔.

Jude dau⁺ of Rob⁺ Spurlock baptis. ye 2 May, 1703.

George son of Jn° Strong baptis. 23 May, 1703.

Mary dau⁺ of Nath^ll Smith baptis. 17 Octo., 1703.

Anne dau⁺ of Geo. Speere baptis. 30 Octo., 1703.

Jn° son of Geo. Sheperdson baptis. the 21 Novem^b, 1703.

Alice dau' of James Sanders baptis. ye 5 March, 170¾.

Ruth dau' of Rob' Speere baptis. ye 14 May, 1704.

Anne daugh' of Allex Strainge baptis. ye 11 June, 1704.

Anne dau' of Tho. Skropbe baptis. ye 15 October, 1704.

Richard son of Rob' Spurlock bap' ye 29 Apr., 1705.

Mary Daughter of Wm Sanders bap' ye 13th May, 1705.

Robert son of Robert Spear bapt. ye 20 Jany., 1705.

Hannah Daughter of Richd Scrugs bap' 11 Febry., 1705.

Elizabeth Daughter of Rob' Spear bap' ye 24 March, 1705-6.

James son of James Smith bap' 25 Aug., 1706.

Robert son of Alex. Strange bap' ye 5 Jany., 1706-7.

Robert son of Rob' Spurlock bap' ye 11 May, 1707.

William son of Mr Wm Smith born May, 1707.

Frances Daughter of Nathaniel Smith baptised Mar. ye 4th, 1707.

Hannah Daughter of James Saunders Baptised May ye 19th, 1708.

Moses son of Sam^ll Stegall & Elizabeth his wife Bap' 7^br ye 5th, 1708.

William son of Jn° Scruges Born the 28th of July, 1708.

Major son of Wm Sanders & Elizabeth his wife X^nd X^br ye 25th, 1708.

Samuel son of Cap' Jn° Scott Baptised Febry. ye 6th, 1708-9.

Robert ye son of Will Tornes and Sarah his wife baptized ye 12th day of August, 1686.

Susanna daughter to Thom. Tiler bap' ye 23d of Jany., 1687-8.

Robert son to Rob. Thomson bap' ye 24 of Aprill, 1687.

Henry sone to Sam. Thomas bap' ye 16 of Sept', 1688.

An daug' to James Tate bap' ye 29 of August, 1689.

Sara & ———— daughters to Wm Turner born ye 7th of Sep', 1689.

John son to William Tally bap' ye 24 of Octo., 1689.

Rob' son to James Pate born ye 27 of Febry. & bap' ye 27 of March, 1691.

Sara daughter to John Tiler bap' ye 18 day of May, 1690.

Edmond son to Edwd Tony bap' ye 25 of May, 1690.

David son to Rob' Thomson bap' ye 4th of Sep', 1690.

Geo. son to Sam. Thomas bap' ye 26 of octo., 1690.

Hannah daugh' to Geo. Turner na' Jany. 14, bap' Febry. ye 4, 1690–1.

Francis son to Henry Turner bap' ye 22d of March, 1690–1.

Susannah daugh' to Charles Turner by Mary his wife bap' ye 30th of octo^br natt. ye 1st of ye instant, 1692.

Hannah daughter of Charles Turner by Mary his wife born ye 9 day of November, 1694.

John Taylor buried July the 16, 1698.

Sarah daug^h of Ja° & Mary Taylor bap' July the 17, 1698.

Tho. son of Shurle Tisdale and Elizabeth wife bap' the 7 Aug', 1798.

Rob' son of Geo. Turner and Judith his wife bap' the 7 Aug', 1698.

James son of James Teute baptiz. the 11 Novem^br, 1698.

Hannah daug' of Rob' Thompson baptiz. the 22 Januy., 1698–9.

Anne dauth. of Tho. Tharp by Anne his wife bap' the 11 June, 1699.

Rob' son of Tim. Terrill baptiz. the 25 Decem^br, 1697.

Will son of Will Talle baptiz. the 19 Septem^br, 1697.

John son of John Taylor baptiz. the 5 Jany., 1695.

Mary daut^h of James Tate baptiz. the 20 Aprill, 1694.

Susanna dau' of Rob' Thomson bap' the 25 Febry., 1696–7.

Joseph son of Timothe Terrill born 16 Nov^r & bap' 31 Dec^r, 1699.

Mary dau' of Jonathan Tomson bap' the 28 Jany., 1699.

Anne dau' of John Tyler bap' the 17 March, 1699–1700.

Anne dau' of Will Talle bap' 17 March, 1699–1700.

Pennenah dau' of Geo. Turner bap' the 21 July, 1700.

Eliz. dauter of Shurley Tisdale baptiz. the 24 Novem^br, 1700.

Usan dau' of James Teate baptized ye 5 Jany., 1700–1.

Martha dau' of Rob' Tomson bapized the 31 Aug', 1701.

Elizabeth dau' of Tho. Tharp bapt. the 31 Aug', 1701.

Susannah dau' of Wm Talle baptiz. the 15 Mar., 170½.

Issabella dau' of Tho. Tudor baptiz. the 19 Aprill, 1702.

Elizabeth dau' of Jonathan Thomson baptiz. 19 Aprill, 1702.

William son of James Teate baptiz. the 12 Apr', 1702.

Mabell Daugh' of Richd Thurman baptiz. May 24, 1702.

Will, son of Geo. Turner bap' ye 17 Jany., 170⅔.

Sarah daug' of William Turner baptised the 21 Febry., 170⅔.

Mary daug' of Tho. Tinsley baptis. ye 9 Febry., ——.

Eliz. daug' of Cornett Tinsley baptis. ye 4 Apr', ——.

John son of John Tyler baptiz. ye 4 July, 1703.

Elizabeth daut. of Geo. Turner Ju^r bap^t 13 Febry., 1704.

William son of Will Turner baptized ye 9 Apr', 1704.

Phillip son of Richd Thurmand baptiz. ye 21 May, 1704.

Elizabeth daugh' of Wm Turner bap^t 18 March, 1704-5.

Mary ye Daughter of James Taylor & Elizabeth born 11 Aug., 1705.

Anne Daughter of Mitche^{ll} Tucker bapt. 6 April, 1707.

Mary Daughter of —— Tucker bap' 29 X^{br}, 1707.

William son of James & Elizabeth Taylor Born Mar. ye 7th, 1707-8.

Alice Daughter of Tho. Tisdale Baptised Sep^t the 19th, 1708.

John son of William & Hannah Thompson Born Sep^t ye 21st, 1708.

Anne Daughter of Alexander Tony Baptised March ye 13th, 1708-9.

Thomas son of Thomas Tudor Baptised May ye 18th, 1709.

Jonathan son of Jonathan Tompson Baptised July ye 3rd, 1709.

Anne Daughter of Henry Turner Baptised March ye 4th, 1709.

George son of James Taylor by Elizabeth his wife Born March ye 20th, 1709-10.

Sarah Daughter of James Turner Baptised Febry. ye 18th, 1710.

Elinor Daughter of Thomas Tuder Baptised 7^{br} ye 30th, 1711.

Charles son of Henry Turner Born Jany. ye 25th & Baptised April ye 20th, 1712.

Honor Daughter of Alex. Tony Born Febry. ye 20th Baptised May ye 4th, 1712.

Elizabeth Daughter of James Taylor by Elizabeth his wife Born 7^{br} 26th, 1712.

Anne Daughter of James Turner by Judith his wife Baptised X^{br} 7th, 1712.

Agnes & Elizabeth Daughters of Michael Tucker Born June 2d, 1714.

Charles son of James Turner Born 8^{br} ye 10th, 1714.

John son of Henry Turner Born July ye 10th, 1714.

Christian Daughter of James Taylor by Eliz. his wife Born June ye 10th, 1715.

Agnes Daughter of William Turner Born December ye 10th, 1715.

Elizabeth Daughter of Jn° Turner Born January ye 1st, 1715.

Mary Daughter of Ed. Tony Born Jany ye 8th, 1715.

Francis Daughter of James Taylor by Eliz. his wife Born Jany 26th, 1716.

Susanna Daughter of James Taylor by Elizabeth his wife Born 9^br 8th, 1719.

Elizabeth ye Daughter of Jn° Urssery & Mary his wife baptis. ye 29 day of August, 1686.

Mattise a negro boy borne ye 15th day of May belonging to Jn° Vaughan, 1684.

Sarah daughter to Jn° Vekett bap^t ye 23rd of octo., 1687.

Dina a negro girl borne ye 22d day of June belonging to Jo^n Vaughan, 1692.

    & a negro boy named Witt borne ye 25 day of May, 1693.

    & a negro girl named betty borne ye 24 day of Aprill, 1696.

John sone of Mr Jo^n Vaughan borne ye 25 day of Novem^b, 1695.

Judith Dau^t of Amer Via baptiz. the 11 Aprill, 1699.

Sarah Dauter of Willm Vaughan baptiz. the 27 May, 1694.

Frances Dau^t of Will^e Vaughan baptiz. the 24 Septem^b, 1699.

Abraham son of Abraham Venables baptiz. the 27 Aprill, 1701.

Margaret Dauter of Amer Via baptiz. the 3 Aug^t, 1701.

William son of Jn° Vaughan baptiz. the 2 November, 1701.

Elizabeth Daut^r of Jn° Upshew baptiz. the 25 December, 1701.

Mary Dau^t of Amer Via baptiz. ye 27 Febry., 1703¾.

Sarah Dau^t of Jn° Upshew baptiz. ye 15 octo., 1704.

Tryphena Dau^t of Jn° Upshear baptiz. 13th Aprill, 1707.

Phillis a negro girl belonging to Mad^am Squires Born June ye 13th, 1709.

John son of Richard Scruggs Baptised Augt ye 21, 1709.

Elinor Daughter of Alex. Strange Baptised Jany. ye 14th, 1709.

Anne Daughter of Math^w & Hannah Simes Baptis^d Jany. ye 29th, 1709.

Robert son of John Spears & Margeret his wife Born 8^{br} 4th, 1709.

Mary Daughter of James Smith Baptised Aprill ye 23d, 1710.

Ruth Daughter of Robt Spear Baptised June ye 4th, 1710.

Elizabeth Daughter of Eliz. Sprosen A. B. child Xnd ye 18th of June, 1710.

Anne Daughter of Jno Sanders by Eliz. his wife bap^t July 2d, 1710.

Frank a negro girl Registered november ye 15 belonging to Geo. Simeon, 1709.

William Stone ——— William Stone ——— october, 1710.

Sarah Daughter of Capt John Scott Baptised 8^{br} ye 1710.

Lucy a negro girl belonging to Mr Tho. Sharp Born March 8th, 1710.

Frances Daughter of Wm Sanders Baptised April ye 8th, 1711.

Sarah Daughter of James Sanders Baptised April ye 8th, 1711.

Jno son of Jno Spear Baptised Novem^{br} ye 4th, 1711.

Mary Daughter of Jno Scott Gent. Born February ye 17th, 17011-12.

Susanna Daughter of Wm Spragin Born Mar. ye 22d & Bap. April ye 27th, 1712.

Honor Daughter of Alex. Tony Born Febry. ye 20th, Baptised May ye 4th, 1712.

Mary Daughter of Tho. Strange Born June 28, Baptised August ye 3d, 1712.

Anne Daughter of Wm Spurlock by Anne his wife Baptised 9^{br} 16th, 1712.

George son of Jno Sanders Baptised March 22d, 1712.

Alice Daughter of Robt Speare Baptised April ye 19th, 1713.

George son of Samuel Smith Baptised August ye 23rd, 1713.

Amey Daughter of Wm Spragin Born ye 7th of August, 1713.

Stephen son of James Sanders Baptised Jany. ye 24th, 1713.

Jane Daughter of Jno Scott Gent. by Judith his wife Bap^t Feby. 7th, 1713.

Agnes Daughter of Wm Sanders Baptised Augt 8th, 1714.

Davis son of Hen. Scrugs Born June ye 20th, 1715.

Drury son of Wm Spurlock Born June ye 13th, 1715.

William son of Jno Spear Born August ye 11th, 1715.

John son of Jno Sanders Born ye sixth day of 7^{br}, 1715.

Janet Daughter of Alex. Strange Ju^r Born Decem^b ye 10th, 1715.

—— of Samuel Smith Born 1715.

Will sone of James Wite & —— his wife bap^t ye 20 day of octo^{br}, 1685.

Mary daughter to Samuell Waddy was bap^t ye 20th day of June, 1687.

Martha daughter to Samuell Weaver bap^t ye 7th day of August, 1687.

Josias son to Will Williams bap^t ye 16 d. of octo., 1687.

Eliz. Daugh^t to Jno Webb bap^t ye 8th of Aprill, 1688.

Negroes belonging to Mr Mark^c Warkman: one named Nell born ye 3d of May, 1682.

and one boy named Robin born ye 25th of October, 1684.

and one girl called betty born ye 19th of May, 1685.

Eliz: daughter to Samuell Waddy bap^t ye 24 octo., 1689.

Richard son to Theophelus Wattson bap^t ye 21 of Novem^b, 1689.

Mary daughter to Thomas Wadlin bapt^t ye 19 of Decem, 1689.

Henry son to James Wade bap^t ye 30 day of January, 1689–0 .

Jane daugh. to Will Williams bap^t ye 8 of June, 1690.

James son to Jn^n Webb na^t 25 of June bap^t ye 19 of Oc^t, 1690.

Eliz. daug^t to Sam: Weaver bap^t ye 14 of Decem^{br}, 1690.

Frances daug^t to Charles Wilford the 15 of March, 1690–1.

Ruth dau^t to Thomas Winfield bap^t ye 18 of oc^t, 1691.

Eliner dau^t of Jose Webster & Rebecca his wife bap^t 14 Aug^t, 1698.

Mary dau^t of Edwd Walton baptis. the 4 December, 1698.

Rebeccah Dau^t of Robt Walker baptis. the 22 Jany., 1698–9.

James son of James Woods by Elizabeth bap^t the 10 Aprill, 1699.

John son of Sam^{ll} Wener by Eliz. his wife baptis. ye 27 Aug^t, 1699.

Anne Dau^t of Jacob Ward Cla^e bap^t ye 5 Jany., 1694–5.

Francis son of Jacob Ward Cfe baptis. the 26 Decem^b, 1695.

Thomas son of Theophelus Watson bap^t ye 7 October, 1694.

Mary Dau^t of James Wade baptis. the 17 October, 1697.

Jane Dau^t of Jno Webb bap^t the 11 June, 1697.

Mary Dau^t Theophelus Watson baptis. the 11 June, 1697.

John son of John White baptis. the 30 May, 1697.

William son of Will Waddell baptiz. the 28 Apr^l 1694.

John son of John Webb bap^t the 20 April, 1694.

Will son of John Webb bap^t ye 17 Sept^{mbr}, 1694.

John son of Jacob Winifrey baptis. the 24 Sep^t, 1699.

Luke son of Robt Wild by Mary bap^t the 22 octo., 1699.

Elizabeth Dau^t of Fran. Willis born the 29 Jany., 169-.

Nathaniell son of Fran. Willis born the 8 May, 1697,

Judith Dau^t of Francis Willis baptiz. Novem. 19, 1699.

Mary Dau^t of Thomas Ward baptiz. the 26 November, 1699.

David son of David Walker baptiz. the 25 Febry., 1699–1700.

Mary Dauter of Tho. Winfield baptiz. the 25 Febry., 1699–1700.

Jno son of Wm Wetherford by Susannah bap^t the 9 June, 1700.

John son of Jno Waddell by Mary borne the 27 octo., 1697.

Frances Dau^t of John Waddell Ju^r by Mary born 8 Febry., 1696–7.

Phillis a negro girl belonging to Mr Henry Wyatt borne the 6 of Aug^t, 1700.

Agnis Daut. of Charles Waddell baptis. the 22 Sept., 1700.

Sarah Daughter of James Wade baptiz. the 24 Nov., 1700.

William son of Edwd Walton baptiz. the 25 Decem., 1700.

Judith Dauter of Samuell Waddey baptiz. the 5 Jany., 1701.

Thomas son of John Waddell Jur. baptiz. the 27 July, 1701.

Charles Willford and Sarah his wife made oath before Nicho. Merriwether Gent. and one of his Maj^{ties} Justices of the Peace for New Kent County that Robt son of the said Charles and Sarah was born the 6th day of September, 1687. Frances dauter of the said Charles and Sarah was borne the 16 Febry. 1690 and Charles son of the aforesaid Charles and Sarah was born the 26 of August, 1692, all wch is certified by the said Merriwether.

W. CLOPTON, CC^l Reg^r.

Joseph son of Joseph Webster born ye 9 Aug^t, 1701.

Jane Dau^t of Jacob Winfrey baptiz. the 25 Decem., 1701.

Mary dau^t of Fran. Willis born the 17 Decem., 1701.

Sarah dau^t of Chas Waddell baptiz. the 5 Aprill, 1702.

Isack son of Wm Winston baptiz. the 12 Aprill, 1702.

Wentworth son of Jno Webb born the 5 baptiz. the 31 May, 1702.

Elizabeth Dau^t of Tho. Wingfield baptiz. ye 12 July, 1702.

John son of Theoph^{ls} Watson baptiz. the 19 July, 1702.

Nane negro belong. to Mr Henry Wyatt bor. ye 23 July, 1702.

William son of Wm Wetherford baptiz. the 7 Febry., 170⅔.

Marea negro girl belonging to Jno Willson born the 18 day of April, 1703.

Francis son of Dan Wilkinson baptiz. ye 17 octo., 1703.

Rebecka dau^t of Simon Woode baptiz. 21 Nov., 1703.

Thomas son of Edwd Walton baptiz. ye 20 Febry., 170¾.

Mary dau^t of John Webb baptiz. ye 19 Ma^h, 170¾.

Jacob son of Jacob Winfrey baptiz. ye 14 May, 1704.

Charles son of Chas Waddell baptiz. ye 14 May, 1704.

Pridgen son of Wm Waddell borne the 4 July and baptiz. the 18 Aug^t, 1704.

Anne Daughter of Fra. Willis bap^t 5 10^{br}, 1702.

Eliza Daughter of Jno Williamson bap^t June ye 17th, 1705.

Dinah Daughter of Fra. Willis born ye 30th Sep^t, 1705.

Peter a negro belonging to Jno Wilson born ye 18th, 9^{br}, 1705.

Susanna Daughter of Ch. Winfrey bap^t 3d March, 1705–6.

Tom a negro belonging to C. Winfrey born ye 15 Aug^t, 1705.

Doll a negro belonging to Ch. Winfrey born ye 14 Aug^t, 1703.

Sarah a negro belonging to C. Winfrey born ye 4 June, 1706.

Peter negro son of Doxy belonging to Mrs Wyatt born ye 7 November, 1704.

Mary Daughter of Jno Winfrey bap^t ye 19 May, 1706.

Sarah daughter to Samuell Yowell bap^t ye 4th d. of March, 1687–8.

Sarah dau^t to Sam^{ll} Yoell and Judith his wife bap^t 7 of Aug^t, 1698.

Ruth dau^t of Sam^{ll} Yeoell baptiz. ye 31 March, 1700.

Elizabeth dau^t of Sam Yeoell baptiz. the 12 Aprill, 1702.

Anne dau^t of Jno Yeomas baptiz. the 7 May, 1702.

Mary dau^t of Jno Young baptiz. ye 14 May, 1704.

George son of Thomas and Ann Wilkinson was born Augt 5, 1693.

John son of Tho. and Ann Wilkinson was born May 3, 1698.

George son of Tho. and Ann Wilkinson was born Augt 5, 1693.

John son of Thos and Ann Wilkinson was born May 3, 1698.

Anne Daughter of Wm Waddell born ye 9 June, 1691.

Elizabeth Daughter of Wm Waddell born ye 24 Febry., 1692.

John son of Wm Waddell born ye 24 Aug^t, 1697.

Hannah Daughter of Wm Waddell born ye 16 Aug^t, 1699.

Frances Daughter of Wm Waddell born ye 2 May, 1706.

Joseph son of Charles Waddell baptiz. 16 Febry., 1706-7.

Elinor Daughter of Jacob Winfrey bap^t 6 Apr^l. 1707.

George son of James Waddell bap^t 20th July, 1707.

Elizabeth Daughter of Edwd Walton Junr Xnd Febry. 7, ye 4th, 1707.

Hannah a mulatto of Jno Wilson Born April ye 28th, 1708.

James son of Wm Wilson Baptised February ye 4th, 1708-9.

Elizabeth Daughter of Jacob Winfrey Baptised April ye 10th, 1709.

Susana Daughter of Charles Waddill Bapt^d May the 29th, 1709.

Noel son of Mr Wm Waddill Born June ye 1st, 1709.

John son of Edwd Walton Junr Born ye 8th day of 7^{br}, 1709.

Mary Daughter of Philip Webber Born 8^{br} ye 4th, 1709.

Charles son of Jno Word Bapt^d May ye 14th, 1710.

Anne Daughter of David Walker Baptised June ye 4th, 1710.

James son of Jno Waddill Baptised June ye 25th, 1710.

Henry son of Jacob Winfrey Baptised February ye 4th, 1710.

Mary ye Daughter of Anthony Waddy Baptised May ye 21st, 1711.

John son of James Waddill Baptised July ye 1st, 1711.

Jacob son of Wm Waddill Baptised November ye 7th, 1711.

Annis Daughter of Philip Webber Baptised 9^{br} ye 11th, 1711.

Mary Daughter of Geo. Walton Baptised 8^{br} ye 23d, 1711.

Frances Daughter of Cha. Waddil Baptised April ye 18th, 1712.

Abel son of Robt Wood Born May ye 27th, 1712.

Alice Daughter of Jno Warrin Born July 16th. 1711.

Susanna Daughter of Jno Walters Born Febrary 19th, 1712.

Mary Daugh^t of Antho. Wade Baptised May 4th, 1711.

Johanna Daughter of Jno Warren Baptised May 17th, 1713.

Robin a negro belonging to Jno Whitlock Born 8^{br} ye 30th, 1706.

Dick a negro boy belonging to ye s^d Whitlock Born 8^{br} ye 28th, 1708.

Betty a negro girl belonging to ye s^d Whitlock Born May ye 3d, 1710.

Frank a negro boy belonging to ye s^d Whitlock Born March ye 4th, 1712.

Sue a negro girl belonging to Charles Winfrey Born 7^{br} ye 20th, 1713.

Presh a negro belonging to Cha. Winfrey Born 7^{br}, 1710.

Mary Daughter of Jno Waddill Baptised September 27, 1713.

Anne Daughter of Geo. Walton 7^{br} ye 13th, 1713.

Anne Daughter of Wm Waddill Ju^r Baptised Jany. 24, 1713.

Augustin son of Philip Webber Born 7^{br} ye 14th, 1713.

Anne Daughter of Wm Walker by Elizabeth his wife Born 7^{br} 26th, 1714.

Anthony son of Antho. Waddy by Sarah his wife Born X^{br} ye 14th, 1714.

Tandy son of Solo. Walker Born ye 13th, 1714.

Elizabeth Daughter of Jno Williamson Born Jany. 24th, 1714.

John son of Lewis Watkins Born 8^{br} ye 27th, 1714.

Edward son of Lewis Watkins Born Jany. ye 3d, 1714.

Elizabeth Daughter of Charles Waddill Born March ye 31st, 1715.

Moll a negro belonging to Jno Whitlock Born July ye 2d, 1715.

Elizabeth Daughter of Wm Walker Baptised Augt ye 28, 1715.

Jane Daughter of Geo. Walton ———, 1715.

MARRIAGES.

Thomas Buttler & Margery Crue Married ye 1st day of March, 1685-6.

Robt Borer & Eliza^b Row married the 22 November, 1698.

James Blackwell Ju^r & Mary Glenn marr^d the 18 Apr., 1699.

John Brown and Mary Whorton were married ye 4th of January, 1708-9.

Edward Bettes and Rachel Jackson were married ye 4th day of March, 1708-9.

John Bailey and Mary Jackson were married ye 29th of December, 1709.

John Bacon and Susanna Parke were married ye 4th day of July, 1710.

Benjamin Berell and Elizabeth Atkison were married March ye 21st, 1711.

Robert Burbidge and Mary King were married Augt ye 11th, 1711.

Wm Brown and Mary Vaughan were married Decem^r ye 28th, 1711.

Thomas Butts Gent. & Catherine Maclagehe was married ye 2d of Apr., 1713.

Rowland Blackburne and Anne Glen was married Febry. ye 6th, 1713.

Mr Hutchens Burton and Susanna Allen was maried March ye 31st, 1719.

Tho. Basset & Lidia Houl were married February 25, 1719.

Robert Crump & Martha Powell married ye 20 Jany., 1700–1.

Thomas Cotterell and Martha Hacher were married May ye 25th, 1709.

James Crump and Venicia Bostick were married July ye 14th, 1709.

Edwd Coyle and Mary Brown were married 7^br ye 21st, 1710.

Walter Clopton and Mary Jarret were married 7^br ye 4th, 1711.

Robert Clopton and Sarah Scott were married December ye 18th, 1711.

Robt Cade and Susanna Crump was married 7^br 17th, 1713.

David Clarkson and Elizabeth Jackson was married 9^br 18th, 1713.

Richard Clough and Anne Poindexter was married June ye —, 1718.

William Clopton Junr and Joice Wilkinson was married Jany. 27th, 1718.

BIRTHS, MARRIAGES AND DEATHS.

Elizabeth the wife of Benj. Crump Departed this life July the 21st, 1770, in the 26th year of her age.

Benj. Crump & Susannah Parke was married May the 21st, 1771.

Christian son of Benj. Crump & Eliz. his wife was born Augt 27, 1763 & died the 20th of March, 1764.

Lucy Daughter to aˢ born Febry. the 9, 1765.
Mary do. born March the 17, 1769.
Havilah son of do. Born April the 8, 1769.
Caty brown daughter of Benj. & Susanna Crump born March the 17th, 1772.
Jonn Parke son of Benj. & Susanna Crump was born Mar. 28th, died Apr. 5, 179–.
——— Departed this life April 5th, 1709.

MARRIAGES.

Augustin Hulett & Hannah Lane married ye 10th day of Jany., 1685–6.
Thomas Henderson & Sarah Wilkeson married 10th November, 1698.
Rob¹ Harris & Eliz. Turner married — october, 1699.
William Haynes and Litticia Cade married —— the 8th Augᵗ, 1703.
Robert Howle & Francis Bassett were married Decemʳ ye 9th, 1708.
George Hunt & Elizabeth Poindexter were married 6ᵇʳ ye 24th, 1709.
John Howard of St. Paul's Parish & Jane Howle were married July ye 11th, 1711.
James Henderson & Jone King were married March the 19th, 1714.
Michael Harfield & Grace Alford were married Feb. 14th, 1726–7.
Martin Martin & Sarah Hix married the 10th Febry., 1698–9.
Thomas Mims Jur. & Mellyan Martin married the 10th Febry., 1698–9.
Thomas Masse & Mary Walker married the 23 March, 1698–9.
George Marr & Jane Mills married the 27 Septᵇ, 1799.
Thomas Meeks & Margery Watkins maᵉᵈ 24 Decemᵇ, 1699.
Jnº Medlock and ——— married the 27 Aprill, 1701.
James Martin and Rebecca Bell married the 16th Febry., 170½.
Lineal Mims & Anne Martin marryed ye 2d Jany., 1706–7.
Daniel Murfield & Rachel Coker of St. Paul's Parish marryed ye 22 of July, 1708.
Peter Moon & Eliz. Smith married November ye 24th, 1709.

Thomas Martin & Mary Tucker married December ye 1st, 1709.

Wm Moss & Eliz. Martin was married November ye 20th, 1711.

Wm Morriss & Tabitha Walker was married Febry. 12th, 1712.

Richard Martin & Hannah Turner was married August 13th, 1718.

MORRISS FAMILY.

James Morriss Bricklayer son of James Morriss Carpenter who came in Virginia with Coll. Ludwell Gent. and was chief workman in the City of Williamsburg, and was an Englishman Born, who married Eliz. Moss near to the s^d City and became and Inhabitant: and there Departed his Life on the 19th Dec^r, 1717, and his wife Eliz. on 10th Nov^{br}, 1719, which may be found on record. They had two sons, the elder John a Carpenter who married one of the Braces in Hamton and had one daughter who was called Mary. The s^d John was born 14th Nov., 1706. The other son was named Ja^s a Bricklayer above mentioned who was born the 4 Nov. at 1 o'clock in the morning and baptised the 3d of Dec., 1710, and married Mary Vaughan daughter to Henry Vaughan of James City County and became an Inhabitant of Ja^s City County, in St. Pèter's Parish in a short time and had several children namely : John who Dy^{ed} in York County & Buried in Williamsburg churchyard. James who is now 27 years old & Clk. & Ch. & Vestry in the s^d Parish and was born the 4th December, 1735, at 11 o'clock at night in York County near to the Capitol landing Bridge the other children are recorded in this Parish in another Book. By the Rev. —— Mossom Rector these names are —— Henry —— ckah De^e, Sarah, Mary, Henry William ye younger —— James Morriss Bricklayer Departed this life the 30th November, 1760. His wife Departed this life 2nd day of Decem^r, 1760.

JA^s MORRISS, Clk. Ch. Vestry.

MARRIAGES.

Edward Nash and Mary Williamson were married June ye 20th, ——.

William Nayler & Sarah Mimes were married 8^{br} ye ——, ——.

Michael Nash and Catherine Renn was married 7^{br} ye 1, ——.

Andrew negro boy belonging to Sam[ll] Overton born the 29 day of March, 1700.

John Reynolds and Mary Woode was married Decem. ye 30th, 1708.

Charles Richardson and Elizabeth Plant was married August 31, 1709.

Edward Renn & Catherine Chappell were married April ye 1st, 1711.

Rob[t] Richardson & Jane Green was married Febry. 22, 1710–11.

Thomas Randolph of Henrico and Judith Fleming was married octo. ye 16th, 1712.

BIRTH.

Thomas son of Ann & Epaphoditus Howle was born in the middle of the summer at break of day.

MARRIAGES.

Richard Snowe & Mary Banks —— married ye 30 day of Decem[b], 1685.

Henery Scruggs & Ann Grose —— married ye 25 day of Jany., 1685–6.

Thomas Simons & Johana Moore married ye 26 June, 1699.

John Stone & Rebecca Amoss married ye 21 Jany., 1704–5.

John Spears and Margaret Austin were married Decem[b] ye 7th, 1708.

John Sheller and Johanna Munk were married Jany. ye 20th, 1708–9.

Matthew Simes and Hannah Mitchell were married March ye 3d, 1708–9.

William Spurlock & Anne Toney were married June 15th, 1709.

John Scruggs and Judith Porter were married August ye 4, 1709.

John Sanders and Elizabeth Waddill were married August ye 7, 1709.

John Smith of Henrico Co. & Cicely Amoss were married 7^{br} ye 22d, 1709.

William Stone and Elizabeth Dennett were married Jany. ye 20th, 1709–10.

John Simson and Sarah Spurlock was married July ye 24th, 1712.

Tho. Sanbige and Fra. Chappell was married Febry. 20th, 1712.

Charles Turner and Mary Cox Married ye 12 day of August, 1695.

Henry Turner and Mary Baker were married January ye 6th, 1708–9.

Wm Turner and Dorthy Whitlock were married April ye 20th, 1726.

George heath and Mary Oakley where marryed April 14, 172–.

Married on Saturday evening myself and my wife, I lov^d fun George Jackson.

POINDEXTER FAMILY.

Jno Vaughan and Sara Poindexter married ye 5th day of Novem^b, 1686.

A Register of George Benskis Poindexters children :

Geo. B. Poindexter was married to Frances Lightfoot July 17th, 1760.

Edwin son of Geo. B. Poindexter & Frances his first wife was born January 10th, 1762.

Robert son of ditto was born February 23d, 1765.

George son of ditto was born March 29, 1767.

James son of ditto was born January 7th, 1770.

Lightfoot son of ditto was born October 20th, 1772.

Armisstead son of ditto was born May 14th, 1775.

His second marriage was with Sarah Parke March the 20th, 1777.

Susannah Daughter to Geo. B. & Sarah Poindexter was born May 3d. 1778.

Parke son of ditto was born March 12th, 1779.

Frances daughter of ditto was born September 10th, 1781 & Departed this life September 17th, 1785.

Recorded by the hand of Geo. B. Poindexter himself who is now in the Fifty first year of his age.

May 18th, 1790.

MARRIAGES.

Charles Willford & Sara Ellis ———— 15th day of May, 1686.

Joseph Webster & Rebecca Baughan ———— 18th day of July, 1686.

Mr Jacobb Ware & Susanna Adams ———— Febry. ye 3d, 1790-1.

Jacob Winfrey & Eliz. Alford Married Novr 3, 1698.

Arthur Winchester & Mary Butler Marryed Jany. ye 21st, 1704-5.

Thomas Whorton Jur. & Honor Harris were married 7^{br}, ye 29th, 1709.

John Warrin of Wayinoak & Susanna Spurlock were marr^d 8^{br} ye 13, 1709.

George Walton & Sarah Roper were married February ye —, 1710-11.

Robert Wood & Mary Alford were married october ye 21st, 1711.

Lewis Watkins & Margaret Stone was married Jany. ye 6th, 1711-12.

Jno Woolams & Sarah Henderson married December, 1711.

Jn^u Webb & Mary Martin was married Febry. 12th, 1712.

William Walker & Elizabeth Clopton was married Jany ye 19, 1713.

Thomas Weaver & Judith Strange was married June ye 29th, 1715.

Edward Webster & Judith Newman alias Jones was married 27 october, 1743.

REGISTER BOOK.

William Russel.
William Heath.
William Massie.
Beverley Crump.
Carter Poindexter.
Armistead Russel.

DEATHS.

Israell Austin departed this Life ye 29th of Febry., 1687–8.

Giles Andrewson deceased ye 23d of Febry., 1687–8.

George Adams departed this Life August ye 26th, 1709.

Sarah Askew departed this Life Jany. ye 16, 1709–10.

William Alford Departed this Life Febry. ye 11th, 1709–10.

Jn° Alford Senr Departed this Life March ye 14th, 1709–10.

Margaret ye wife of Thomas Anderson Departed this Life Jany., 1710.

Elizabeth wife of Thomas Apperson Departed this Life Augt ye 22d, 1712.

Johannah wife of Tho. Ashcraft Departed this Life 7^{br} ye 25th, 1716.

Mary Holt a mulatto belonging to Mr Allin Departed this Life X^{br} 24th, 1718.

Henry Atkinson Departed this Life Febry. ye 10th, 1718.

Cipieo a negro of Mr Eben^r Adams Died the 31st day of 8^{br}, 1719.

Moll a negro belonging to William Adams Died 9^{br} 30th, 1719.

Jn° Askew Departed this Life ye 25th February, 1719.

Susannah wife of Wm Atkinson Departed this Life Jany 25, 1719.

Hannah wife of William Allen Departed this Life March 22d, 1719.

John Aldridge Deceased April 16, 1720.

Rich^d son of Mr Ebenezer Adams Deceas^d Septr 12, 1721.

The wife of Richd Ashcroft Deceas^d octo^r, 1721.

John Aperson Departed this Life May 28, 1722.

Gervis Austin Departed this Life Decr 30th, 1722.

Isaac Alford son of Jn° Alford Departed this Life Augst 21st, 1723.

Eliz. Amos Dyed wife of Fra. Amos Sept^r, ye 28, 1723.

Indian Will a slave belonging to Mr Ebene^r Adams Dyed Oc^t 18th, 1723.

Richd Allen Dyed 7^{br} ye 6th, 1725.

Nan a negro wench of Mr Eben^r Adams died 7ber ye 8th, 1725.

Hannah a mulatto woman of Richd Apperson Dyed Febry. 20, 1726–7.

Frances Alford Dyed April 27, 1726.

Jn° Alford Dyed May ye second, 1726.

Tom a negro belonging to Grace Alford Dyed May 15th, 1726.

Bowler ye son of Eben[r] Adams Dyed Novem[b] 26th, 1726.

Alex[r] son of Jn° Askew Dyed Decem[r] ye 20th, 1726.

W[m] Apperson Departed this Life April ye 8th, 1727.

Rich[d] Apperson Jun[r] Dyed Novem[r] 9, 1729.

Rose a negro belonging to M[r] Eben[r] Adams Dyed M[ch] 22, 1729–30.

Richard Brice Departed this life ye 13 day of octob[r], buried ye 14 day of octob[r], 1686.

Ann Daugh. to Jerome Brooks departed this life ye 7 of Jany., 1687–8.

Mary daugh. to James Blackwell deceased ye 20th d. of Febbry., 1687–8.

Gregory Barnett deceased ye 22d of December, 1687.

Sam Barley deceased ye 12 d. of Febry., 1687–8.

Thom. Browne deceased ye 17 d. of Decem[r], 1687.

Brett Daniell dec[d] the 14 of July, 1698.

Charles Bostock dyed ye 4 January, 1700–1.

James Bonker Cle[l] sum time minister of this Parish dyed the 10 March, 1702–3.

Rebecca wife of Charles Barker departed this life Novem[b] ye 2d, 1709.

Mary Bostrik Departed this Life December ye 7th, 1709.

Sarah ye wife of Jn[u] Bacon Departed this Life Jan[ry] ye 4th, 1709.

Joseph Beetty Departed this Life Jan[ry] ye 26th, 1709.

Amea Bairey Departed this Life Jany: ye 27th, 1709.

John Black Departed this Life Jany: ye 3d, 1709.

Jn° Brown Departed this Life Febry: ye 10th, 1709.

Hester ye Daughter of Edw[d] Bettes Departed this Life on ye 7th of 9[br], 1710.

Anne ye wife of W[m] Bourn Jun[r] Departed this Life April ye 8th, 1711.

Elizabeth Daughter of Hen: Bardrick Departed this Life Aug[st] ye 31st, 1712.

Rowland Blackbourn Departed this Life 8[br] ye 20th, 1713.

Elinor wife of Tho. Basset Departed this Life ye 29th of 7[br], 1713.

Deborah ye wife of Sam^{ll} Bugg Departed this Life ye 14th of X^{br}, 1715.

William Brown Departed this Life June ye 12th, 1716.

Francis Barnes Departed this Life August ye ——, 1716.

Elizabeth the wife of Jno Baylie Departed this Life 7^{br} ye 12th, 1716.

Samuel Buggs Departed this Life 7^{br} ye 13th, 1716.

Mad^{am} Sarah Bray Departed this life 8^{br} ye 18th, 1716.

Capt Edward Birkett Departed this Life February ye 11th, 1716.

W^m son of Tho. Bassett Departed this Life Mar. 8th, 1716.

Jno son of Tho. Bassett Departed this Life Mar. 17th, 1716.

Elizabeth ye wife of Tho. Bassett Departed this Life April 7th, 1717.

John Broad-hurst Departed this Life Decem^{br} 18th, 1717.

Catherine wife of Mr Wm Brodie Min^r of St. Peter's Parish Departed this Life February ye 20th, 1717.

Hannah a mulatto belonging to Mr Wm Bassett, died March 25, 1718.

Mrs Alice Butts Departed this Life July ye 20th, 1718.

Stephen Bourn Departed this Life Augt ye 16th, 1718.

Edward Bretain Departed this Life November ye 9th, 1718.

Jack a negro belonging to John Bailey dyed 7^{br} 28th, 1718.

Mary a negro belonging to John Bailey died Jany: 3d, 1718.

Sarah a negro belonging to Sam^{ll} Buxstone Departed this life Febry: 19th, 1718.

Mary Bailey Departed this Life February ye 28th, 1718.

Mary the wife of Tho. Bassett Died the 18th day of 9^{br}, 1719.

Rachel wife of Ed. Bettus Died March 3d, 1719.

Sarah a negro of Mr Tho. Butts Died April 1st, 1720.

Jinney a negro of Mr Tho. Butts Died April 2d, 1720.

John Barns Died April 3d, 1720.

Dick a negro belonging to Mr Tho. Butts Died April 7th, 1720.

Mr William Brodie Minister of this Parish April 16th, 1720.

Thomas Bassett Departed this Life April 20, 1720.

Joseph Beetle departed this life Augt 10th, 1720.

—— a negro of Mr Jno Bacons Deceas^d Augt 25, 1722-3.

George Baisey died Novem^{br} 20th, 1722.

Matthew Bailey Died Novr 15th, 1722.

Jno Brooker Dyed Novr 30th, 1723.

Richd Brooker Dyed Decem^{br} ye 10th, 1723.

Gift a negro man belonging to Mad^{ame} Bassett ·Dyed Decem^{br} 13, 1724.

Susannah Bradby Departed this Life June ye 16th, 1726.

Jno Brothers Junr Departed this Life Decem^{br} ye 17th, 1726-7.

James Brooker Departed this Life Jany: 31st, 1726-7.

Marg. & Antipap Brooker was killed with thunder Ap. 18th, 1727.

John ye son of Edwd Bailey Dyed Octr ye 8th, 1727.

Ben Jarnary & Bess negros belonging to Ja. Moss Dyed in May, 1727.

Sarah a negro of Coll: David Bray' Dyed Decem^{br} ye 5th, 1727.

Jemmy a negro bellonging to ditto Dyed February ye 28, 1727-8.

Will a negro belonging to ditto Dyed February ye 20, 1727-8.

Jack a negro belonging to ditto died February ye 29, 1727-8.

Jack a negro belonging to Jno Bailey Died April 21st, 1728.

Susanna Brown Departed this Life Augt ye 2d, 1728.

Natt a negro belonging to Coll: David Bray Dyed 7^{br} ye 18th, 1728.

Paul a negro belonging to Mr Wm Bassett Dyed December 23, 1728.

Eliz. Bushell serv^t to Geo. Bradby Dyed July 18, 1729.

Peter a negro belonging to Coll. David Bray Dyed Augt 30, 1729.

Betty & Anthony negros belonging to Coll. Wm Bassett Dyed nov^r 20, 1730.

Dick a negro belonging to Col^o David Bray Dyed March 29th, 1730-1.

Jeffery Cook deceased ye 9th d. of Decem., 1687.

Thom. Cook serv^t to Geo. Alvise deceased ye 4th of Decem., 1687.

Roger Crisp deceased ye 9th of Febry: and Sara his wife dece^d ye 23, 1687-8.

Thom. Crump son to Will. Crump deceased ye 4 day of March, 1687-8.

John Craford Departed this Life ye 13 day of December, 1689.

Stephen Crump Dyed the 28 Sept: and buried the 1st October, 1700.

Frances Daughter of Wm Crump Departed this Life June ye 29th, 1708.

Mary Daughter of Wm Crump Departed this Life Febry. ye 11th, 1709.

Frances Daughter of David Clarkton Departed this Life april ye 27th, 1710.

Johanna wife of Peter Clark Departed this Life February ye 3d, 1711.

Peter Clarkson Departed this Life ye 30th day of December, 1711.

Sara Daughter of Stephen Crump Departed this Life Febry: 26th 1713.

Thomas son of Stephen Crump Departed this Life March ye 2d, 1713.

Rose ye wife of Wm Cox departed this Life april ye 28th, 1715.

Richard Cotterell Junr Departed this Life 8^br 13th, 1715.

Richard Cotterell Departed this Life March ye 16th, 1715.

Thompson a negro belonging to Major Jno Custis Died April ye 25th, 1716.

Rose a negro belonging to Major Jno Custis Died Febry: ye 21st, 1716.

Anne Clopton wife of Mr Wm Clopton Departed this Life March 4th, 1716.

Richard Collam Departed this Life March ye 12th, 1716.

Elizabeth Card Departed this Life april ye 5th, 1717.

Frances wife of Jno Cooke Departed this Life March ye 4th, 1716.

Jno Cooke Departed this Life 7^br ye 27th, 1717.

Doll a negro of Steph: Crump Died March ye 1st, 1717.

Permias a negro of Steph: Crump Died March ye 18th, 1717.

Robin a negro of Tho. Cotterell Died march ye 29th, 1718.

Thomas Cotterell Departed this Life april ye 22d, 1718.

William Cox Departed this Life ye 8th of July, 1718.

Sarah ye wife of Robt Clopton Departed this Life 8^br ye 24th, 1719.

Elizabeth Clarkson Departed this Life December ye 6, 1719.

Mary Cane Departed this Life April ye 6, 1720.

George Clarke Deceased april ye 8th, 1720.

Dick a negro of Robt Clopton Deceased april 1, 1720.

Frances wife of Richd Crump Deceased april 26, 1720.

David Clarkson Departed this Life april 15, 1720.

Nanny a negro of Walter Clopton died april 6, 1720.

Beck a negro belonging to Major Custis died March 25, 1720.

Elenor Crawley Departed this Life June ye 20, 1720.

Sarah wife of Wm Crump Deceased June 29, 1720.

Peg a negro of Major Custis Deceased June 14, 1720.

Eliz: Clarkson Deceased april 17, 1720.

a negro boy belonging to David Clarkson Died April 24, 1720.

Nanny a negro of Richd Crump Deceased april 25, 1721.

Dryas a negro of Major Custis Deceased Sep^t 11, 1721.

Dryas a negro boy of Major Custis Deceased Febry: 16, 1721–2.

Beck a negro girl of Major Custis Deceased Febry: 26, 1721–2.

Martha Crump wife of Robt Crump Dep^{td} this Life May 21st, 1722.

Dinah a negro girl belonging to Major Custis died March 1st, 1722–3.

Roger a negro boy belonging to Wm Clopton Junr Dyed Jany. 24th, 1723–4.

Gilbert Cotterell Dyed ye 25 of 8^{br}, 1724.

David son of Richd Crump Died Febry: 12th, 1724–5.

Will a negro belong to Wm Clopton Junr Dyed, 1725.

Mr Henry Collins minister of this Parish Dyed Nov. 21st, 1725.

Anne Daugh. of Mr Wm Chamberlayne Died oct^r ye 8th, 1725.

Wm Cotterell Died Febry 13th, 1725–6.

Sam a negro belonging to Mr Wm Clopton Died March 4, 1725–6.

Jenny a negro belonging to Major Jno Custis Dyed april 7, 1726.

Eliz^h Crump Departed this Life March ye 12th, 1726–7.

Gloucester a negro belonging to Mr Wm Chamberlayne Dyed Ap^l, 1726.

Thos Crump Dyed March the 1st, 1726–7.

Geo. ye son of Susannah Crump Dyed 7^{br} ye 29th, 1727.

Dick a negro belonging to Col^o Jno Custis Died april ye 10th, 1728.

Jack a negro belonging to Col^o Custis Dyed March ye 12th, 1731.

Benedict son of Rich^d & Lucy Crump was Born oct^r 18, 1739.

Edwd Dorrill deceased ye 25 d of February, 1687–8.

Jno sone to Cornelius Dabenie deceased ye 7 d of aprill, 1688.

Eliz. daugh: to Cornelius Dabenie deceased ye 4 d of aprill, 1688.

Eliz: wife of Robt Depress Departed this life sep^t 27, 1789.

John Dennett Departed this Life July ye 15th and were Buried ye 17th, 1787.

Wm Dollard Departed this Life october ye 24th, 1709.

Thom. a negro belonging Capt Wm. Dangerfield Died april ye 5, 1719.

Mary Design July 15th, 1722.

Wm. Drummond departed this Life Septr ye 20th, 1723.

Dorothy ye wife of Walter Danill Died october 5th, 1724.

Fran^c Day son of Fran^c Day Dyed Decem^b 30th, 1725.

Elisth Day Dyed Jany ye 8th, 1725–6.

Rebecca Davis Dyed April ye 27th, ——.

Dic negro of Mr Dangerfield Dyed at Dr Green ——, ——.

Hanah a negro belonging to ——— Dyed ——, ——.

Edwd Dickson Dyed August ——, ——.

David Deale Dyed July ye —, ——.

Elizabeth ye wife of George Yorke departed this life ye 13 day of Sep^t, 1686.

Eliz. Smith deceased ye 23d of Febry., 1687–8.

Francis Ellis Departed this Life November ye 30th, 1719.

Alexander Ellis Departed this Life March 6, 1719.

Ann Ellis Departed this Life March 9, 1719.

Mary Ellmore Deceased Novem^b, 1721.

Cocko a negro belonging to Peter Elmore Dyed March 30th, 1729.

Peter Elmore Departed this Life March the 26th, 1730.

John Fleming departed this Life ye 27th day of August and was Buried ye 30th of Aug^t, 1686.

James Freeman deceased ye 23d of Jany., 1687–8.

Major Peter Field obijt. xxiv Die July & Sepulherat xxix, 1707.

Thomas Fidkin Departed this Life July ye 27th Annoq. Dom., 1709.

W^m son of Capt Jno Foster Departed this Life 8^b ye 28th, 1713.

William Forgos Departed this Life 9^{br} ye 15, 1714.

Chame a negro belonging to Mad^m Shield Departed this Life Feb. ye 8th, 1714.

Thomas son of Capt Jno Foster Departed this Life ye 20th of 7^{ber}, 1715.

John son of Capt Jno Foster Departed this Life Jany. ye 5th, 1715.

Sarah Daughter of Tho. Fusell Departed this Life April 5th, 1716.

Martha Daughter of Edwd Finch Departed this Life Aug. 24th, 1716.

Presse a negro belonging to Mad^{am} Field Died 9^{br} ye 15th, 1716.

Sarah a negro belonging to Mad^{am} Field Died August ye 28th, 1718.

Mad^{am} Elizabeth Foster Departed this Life Jany. ye 8th, 1718.

Edward Finch Departed this Life ye 21st day of Decem^h, 1718.

Doxer a negro of Mad^{am} Field Died the 24th of March, 1718.

George Fox a servt. of Wm Macon Gent. Died August ye 12th, 1719.

Pompey a negro belonging to Mad^{am} Alice Field died ye 9th of March, 1719.

Jane wife of Mr Jno Forster deceased Augt 21, 1720.

Mary Daughter of Capt Jno Forster Deceased April 21, 1721.

Alice Field Departed this Life Febry. 16th, 172½.

Mary Forbess Departed this Life June ye 5th, 1726.

Wm Fewterel Died at Richd Brookers Jany. ye 15th, 1726-7.

Anthony Garman servant to Mrs Pines departed this Life ye 30 day of Sep^{tr}, 1686.

Mary wife of Thom. Glass deceased ye 20th of Jany., 1687-8.

Mr Sam^{ll} Gray minister of this Parish Departed this Life ye 25th of Decem^{br}, 1709.

Stephen Gill Departed this Life March ye 14th, 1709.

Martha ye wife of Wm Gardner Departed this Life 8^{br} ye 31st, 1714.

John Gregory was killed by a fall of a horse November ye 5th, 1713.

Richard Guilam Departed this Life Febry. ye 15th, 1713.

Wm Gardner Departed this Life 8^{br} ye 5th, 1717.

Edward Green Departed this Life on ye 24th day of February, 1718.

Mary wife of Willm Green Departed this Life March, 1719.

Jane ye wife of Forrest Green Deceased May 15, 1720.

Sarah wife of Hugh Grindley deceased March, 1720.

Martha Gauling Deceased Sep^{tr}, 1721.

Will a negro belonging to Mr Gordon Deceased Augt 17, 1721.

Charles Gore Departed this Life December 9th, 1721.

Elizth wife of Wm Guilliam Dyed March 24th, 1724-5.

Edmond Green Dyed oct^r 8th, 1725.

Jn° Gorton serv^t to James Crump Dyed Jany. ye 9th, 1725-6.

Margaret Guilliam Dyed Febry. 12th, 1725-6.

Jn° Green of K. Wm County Dyed at Doc. Greenhils Novem^b, 1726.

London a negro of Paschal Greenhill Dyed July ye 15th, 1728.

Fran^e Dau^r of Tho. Garwood Dyed october —, 1728.

Sambo a negro belonging to Hugh Grindley ——^{br} 3d, 1728-9.

Jn° Hill departed this Life ye 26th d. of January, 1687-8.

Will Harmon deceased ye 4th day of Jany., 1687-8.

Jude Harmon daugh. to Rob. Harmon deceased ye 28 d. of octo., 1687.

Sam Hopkins servant to Sam Firth deceased ye 20 d. of Feby., 1687-8.

Luke Howard deceased ye 1st d. of Feby., 1687-8.

John Hurlock obist. 24th Die of octob. anno., 1707.

William Hodkison servant of M^r Jn° Alfords some time in May, 1708.

Thomas Harris Departed this Life March ye 20th Anno. Dom., 1708-9.

Francis Hill Junr Departed this Life December ye 26th, 1709.

Jn° Howle Senr Departed this Life Jany. ye 4th, 1709.

Samuel Hill Departed this Life Jany. ye 24th, 1709.

Mary and Bridget Daugh^{rs} of Jn° Helton Departed this Life Jany. 27th, 1709.

Elizabeth Hill Wid^w Departed this Life Febry. ye 10th, 1709.

Thomas Henderson Departed this Life Febry.. 1709.

Grace Hurlock Departed this Life April ye 11th Annoq. Dom., 1710.

Mercy Daughter of Robert Harris Departed this Life April 6th, 1710.

Hester ye wife of Robt Harper Departed this Life X^{br} ye 6, 1714.

Mary Hill Departed this Life in February, 1717.

Francis Hill Departed this Life March ye 6th, 1717.

Charles Harper Departed this Life Ayril ye 3d, 1718.

Elizabeth Hillton Departed this Life April ye 18th, 1718.

Richard Harvey Departed this Life May ye 13th, 1718.

John Hancock Departed this Life June ye 24th, 1718.

Mary Hancock Departed this Life July ye 4th, 1718.

John Howle Departed this Life February ye 21st, 1718.

Rose a negro belonging to John Howle Died Febry. 12th, 1718.

W^m son of Sam^{ll} Hubart Died ye 15th of June, 1716.

Mary ye wife of Martin Hulett Departed this Life November ye 7th, 1719.

Jane ye wife of Jno Hitchcock departed this life Jan. ye 14, 1719.

Joanna Hinson Departed this Life April ye 4th, 1720.

Mary Hilton Deceased March 2d, 1719.

Jno Hilton Deceased March 7th, 1719.

Mary Harper belonging to Mr Fra. Littlepage Died March 25, 1720.

James Henderson Departed this Life Augt 15, 1720.

Eliz. the wife of Wm. Howle Departed this Life Febry. 7, 1724–5.

Jno son of Jno Hull Dyed Sep^t, 1726.

Alice Hutcherson Dyed April ye 9th, 1728.

John Englebrite buried ye 21 November, 1698.

Mary ye wife of Mr Robt Jarret obist 31st March, 1707.

Mr Robt Jarrott Departed this Life January ye 21st, 1709.

Sarah ye wife of Wm. Johnson Departed this Life 8^{br} ye 28th, 1711.

William Johnson Departed this Life Novem^b ye 6th, 1714.

Martha ye wife of orlando Jones Gent. Departed this Life May ye 4th, 1716.

Jenny a negro belonging to Tho. Jackson Died 9^{br} ye 20th, 1718.

William Jackson Departed this Life Febry. ye 10th, 1718.

Thomas Jackson departed this life april 19, 1720.

Will a negro of Mary Jackson died april 14, 1721.

Jack a negro belonging to Lucy Jones Died June 22, 1721.

Mary Daughter of Robt Jarrat Deceased Augt 19, 1721.

Sarah wife of John Jackson Febry. ye 20th, 1724–5.

Eliz^{bt} Johnson Died Febr^y 20th, 1725–6.

Eliz^{bt} Jackson Deceased on ye 7th day of June, 1728.

George Laurance departed this life the 11th day of January, 1685-6.

Jn° Longworthy departed this Life ye 19th of January, 1687-8.

Rich⁴ Lamb Deceased ye 3d of March, 1687-8.

Mʳ Richard Littlepage deceased ye 20th day of aprill, 1688.

Col° John Lightfoot Esq: obijt xxviii Die Majs circa undecim: Host: & anno Lins, 1707.

Toby a negro belonging to Sherwood Lightfoot Departed this ‚Life 8ᵇʳ ye 7th, 1713.

Jack a negro belonging to Jnᵒ Lewis Esq: Died Febry:, 1714.

Tom a negro belonging to Jn° Lewis Esq: Departed this Life april ye 23d, 1715.

Wm. a negro boy of Mʳ Thoˣ Lightfoot Died, 1715.

Elizabeth wife of Owen Lewis Departed this Life 9ʰʳ ye 4, 1716.

Kate a negro woman belonging to Esq: Jn° Lewis Died ye 24th of Xʰʳ 1716.

Terpin a negro belonging to Sher: Lightfoot Gent: Died 8ᵇʳ, 1716.

Elizabeth Daughter of Owen Lewis Departed this Life May 16th, 1717.

Judith a negro of Jnᵒ Lewis Esq: Departed this Life May 18th, 1717.

a negro belonging to Mʳ Thomas Lightfoot Died Xʰʳ ye 15th, 1717.

Richard Littlepage Genᵗ Departed this Life March ye 20, 1717.

Wm. Lucas Departed this Life 7ʰᵉʳ ye 3d, 1718.

Bug a negro boy of Mʳ Fra: Littlepage Drowned in July, 1719.

Wm. Proctor Departed this Life September, 1719.

Robert Coapland a Taylor belonging to Madam Littlepage was drowned 9ᵇʳ 3d, 1719.

Sampson a negro of Madam Littlepage was drowned 9ʰʳ ye 3d, 1719.

Elizabeth Lewis wife of Owen Lewis died march 27, 1719.

Elizabeth Daughter of Owen Lewis died april 4, 1720.

Hunt a negro of Mr. Sherwood Lightfoot Died May 5, 1720.

2 negros belonging to Mʳ Goodʰ Lightfoot Died, 1720.

Matthew a negro of Mr. Sherw⁴ Lightfoot Died Febry: 16, 1720-1.

a mulatto child of Mʳ Sherw⁴ Lightfoots Died octo., 1721.

a mulatto child of Mr Sherw^d Lightfoots not named Died Sept.,
1721.

George a mulatto of Mr Sherw^d Lightfoots Died March 28th,
1721–2.

Charles an Indian belong. to Capt Goodrich Lightfoot died octo.
9th, 1722.

Hannah a mulatto belonging to Sherwood Lightfoot died octo:
20th, 1722.

Frayzer sonn of Thos Lightfoot died March 30th, 1723.

Forester son of Jno Lucas Dyed ye 21st of Augst, 1723.

Coll. George Lyddall Died Jan: 19th, 1705.

Sam a negro belonging to Mr Sherw^d Lightfoot Dyed April
28th, 1725.

Charles a negro belonging to Mr Sherwood Lightfoot Died Ap^1
15, 1726.

Fran^e Lightfoot Died Feb^{ry} 19th, 1725–6.

Elizth Langford Died Feb^{ry} ye 7th, 1725–6.

Cuffee a negro of Mr Sherw^d Lightfoots Dyed May ye 3d, 1726.

Grace a negro belonging to Do. Dyed April 17th, 1726.

Will a negro belonging to Do. Dyed May ye 12, 1726.

Bobb a negro of Mr Jno Lang was killed with thunder Ap^1 18,
1727.

Dan^{ll} a negro of Mr Sherw^d Lightfoot Dyed Ap^1 30th, 1727.

Moll a negro belonging to Do. Dyed Augst 7th, 1727.

Wm. Lewis Dyed Augst 3d, 1727.

Mary Lillingston Dyed March 4th, 1728–9.

Maj^r Sherwood Lightfoot Dyed April 26th, 1730.

Angelica Daughter of Henry Lacy Dyed May ye 14th, 1730.

Ursula Daughter of Do. Dyed June ye 3d, 1730.

Margery ye wife — Thom. Buttler departed this Life ye 8 day
of octo^{br}, 1686.

Thom. Mask deceased ye 15th d. of February, 1687–8.

Jno Morfield deceased ye 18 d. of February, 1687–8.

Anne wife of Jno Medlock Dyed the 23 March, 1699–1700.

Wm. Mutton Departed this Life at Steph. Mitchells sen^r october ye 31st, 1709.

Daniel Mackdaniell Departed this Life Decem^r ye 15th, 1709.

James Martin Departed this Life Jany. ye 27th, 1709.

Wm. Martin Departed this Life Jany. ye 30th, 1709.

REGISTER OF ST. PETER'S PARISH.   65

Edward Morgan Departed this Life June ye 3d, 1710.

William Millington Departed this Life June ye 14th, 1710.

Thomas Mims Departed this Life April ye 28th, 1711.

Susanna Murront Departed this Life May ye 6th, 1712.

Anne wife of Capt James Moss Departed this Life March 9, 1712.

Mary wife of Stephen Moon Departed this Life March 20, 1712.

Elizabeth wife of Jn° Meux Departed this Life Augt 7th, 1713.

Stephen Moon Departed this Life Jany. ye 29th, 1713.

Dick a negro child of M^r Jn° Meux Departed this Life X^br ye 15th, 1714.

Stephen Mitchell Departed this Life May ye 6th, 1715.

John son of M^r Jn° Meux was drowned June ye 26th, 1715.

Wm. Major Departed this Life 8^ber ye 4th, 1716.

Elizabeth Daughter of Tho. Moss Departed this Life May ye 20th, 1717.

Wm. Thompson Moss Departed this Life May ye 15th, 1717.

Wm. Mallett Departed this Life September ye 7th, 1717.

Mary Daughter of Peter Moon Departed this Life 8^br 12th, 1717.

Lucy Daughter of Edm^d Moore Departed this Life Feb. 12th, 1717.

John Moore Departed this Life March 12th, 1717.

Tabitha Daughter of Wm. Morriss Departed this Life June ye 4th, 1718.

James Moore Departed this Life ye 9th of July, 1718.

Edward Moore Departed this Life August ye 2d, 1718.

Elizabeth wife of Jn° Moore Departed this Life Jany. ye 19th, 1718.

Milington Meanly son of Richd Departed this Life 8^br 6th, 1718.

Anne Daughter of Mr Geo. Massie Departed this Life 8^br 5th, 1718.

Robert Morress Departed this Life ye 15th day of Decem^br, 1718.

Margaret Madox Departed this Life Decem^br ye 31st, 1718.

John Madox Departed this Life Jany. ye 6, 1718.

Catherine ye wife of Richd Martin Departed this Life 25th 8^br, 1718.

Nanny a negro of Pelham More Died August, 1719.

Peter Massey Departed this Life December 25, 1719.

Jn° son of Jn° Martyn Deceased april ye 9th, 1720.

Peter Moon Died april ye 8th, 1720.

Eliz. Moon Died april ye 9th. 1720.

Ben a negro belonging to Steph Moon Died March 23, 1719.

Cate a negro of Mr Tho. Massie Died april 25, 1720.

Robt Morriss Deceased Decem^{br}, 1720.

Stephen Mitchell Deceased April 8th, 1720.

Madam a negro belonging to Tho. Moss Junr Dec^d July 23, 1721.

Jn° Simons a carpenter belonging to Mr W. Merriwether died
    7^{br}, 1721.

Will a negro belonging to Ditto Died Sep^t, 1721.

Sarah Daughter of Richd Meanly Died augst 20th, 1722.

Kate a negro girl belonging to Capt Massie Died June 10th, 1722.

Penny a negro girl belonging to Capt Moss Died Augst 12th,
    1722.

William Cook an orphan boy belonging to Mr Meux died Nov^r
    14th, 1722.

Sarah a mulatto belonging to Richd Ross died october 18th, 1722.

Thos Major Died nov^r 19th, 1722.

Jane ye Daughter of Richd Meanly Died Jan^{ry} 23d, 1722–3.

Elizth Daugh: Wm. Mosse Dyed october ye 8th, 1724.

Anne the wife of Jn° Macon Dyed Febry: 15th, 1724–5.

Jn° son of Geo. Marchbanks Jan^{ry} 26, 1725–6.

Pelham Moore Dyed Janry: 9th, 1725–6.

Peter a negro belonging to Edwd Moore Dyed Feb^{ry} 6, 1725–6.

Stephen Moore Dyed Decem^r ye 11, 1726.

Leason son of Step^h Mitchell Dyed Decem^r, 1726.

Fran^s Moore Dyed March ye 12th, 1726–7.

Jno Meux Dyed March ye 19th, 1726–7.

Elizth Meanly Dyed April ye 7th, 1727.

Enoss Indian Dyed at Robt Moore's Decr 15th, 1726.

Mary Mitchell Dyed april ye 2d, 1727.

John Moore Departed this Life 7^{br} ye 26th, 1727.

Nathaniell Maning Departing this Life october ye 11th, 1727.

Alice Mitchell Dyed april ye 2d, 1728.

Sarah ye Daughter Wm. Moss Dyed May ye 7th, 1728.

Jane Morriss Died May ye 8th, 1728.

Benj: Morriss Dyed octob^r 16th, 1729.

Mary Moore Dyed March ye 11th, 1729–30.

Catherine Daughter of Pelham Moore Dyed Jan^ry ye 8, 1729–30.

Mary Daughter of Edwd Nash Departed this Life June ye 30th, 1715.

Martha Daughter of Mr John Netherland Dyed 7^br 26th, 1725.

Jn° Newbey Dyed at Doc^r Greenhill's Jan^ry 1st, 1726–7.

Mary Nash Dyed April 26th, 1729.

John Ossling Junr Departed this Life Feb^ry ye —, 1709–10.

John Ossling Senr Departed this Life 9^ber ye 14th, 1710.

Robin a negro belonging to Jn° Otey Died ye april ye 16th, 1719.

William son of Jn° Otey Deceas^d Sep^t 20, 1721.

Martha Daughter of Jn° Otey Deceas^d octo^r 3, 1721.

Mary ye wife of Edwd Ossling Deceas^d June 14, 1723.

Edward Ossling Dyed Decem^r 11th, 1726.

Ann Ossling Dyed 7^ber 20th, 1729.

George Phillips departed this Life ye 29th d of March, 1687–8.

Richd Perre Deceased ye 27th d of Febru^a, 1687–8.

Jonathan Price deceased ye 8 d of May, 1687.

Jno° Poiner servant to Mr Vincent Goderds Deceased Jan. ye 6, 1688–9.

Peter Pratt serv^t to Sam^ll Avis dyed the 14 Nov^r, 1700.

John Parke Senr Departed this Life January ye 17th, 1709–10.

Jarrott Pattison Departed this Life November ye 17th, 1710.

William Pains Departed this Life April ye 28, 1713.

Rowland Pierson Departed this Life June ye 12th, 1713.

Elinor Pasly Departed this Life February ye 27th, 1713.

Mary Parke wid^ow Departed this Life 9^ber ye 17th, 1714.

George Poindexter Departed this Life march ye 12th, 1716.

Susanna Powel Departed this Life april ye 20th, 1718.

Edward Patison Departed this Life Jan^ry ye 6th, 1718.

Tom a negro belonging to Wm. Perkins Died X^br 28, 1718.

Sarah a negro belonging to Wm. Perkins Jany: 4, 1718.

Frances Penstone Departed this Life april 15, 1719.

Jane Price Departed this Life July ye 30th, 1719.

Wm. son of Thos Pinchback Departed this Life June 1st, 1722.

Thomas Pattison Dyed on Whitsunday, 1725.

John Parke Departed this Life 9^ber ye 28, 1725.

Jover a negro woman belonging to Mrs Fran^s Parke Died 9^br, 1725.

Alexander Pattison Dyed March ye 8th, 1725–6.

Jack a negro of Jacob Poindexter Dyed Decem' 3, 1726.

Jn° Pully Dyed at Rob' Weaver's Jan'' 18th, 1726–7.

Jenny a negro of Jn'' Parish Dyed Decemb' 29th, 1726–7.

Sampson a negro belonging to Charles Pearson Deceas'' Decem''', 1727.

Tom negro belonging to M' Geo. Poindexter Dyed octo' 21st, 1729.

Launcelott Ray deceased ye 24 d of February, 1687–8.

Mary ye wife of Robert Richardson Departed this Life 8'' ye 24th, 1710.

Thomas son of Jo' Roe Departed this Life 7'' ye 9th, 1715.

M'' Eliz: Roober Departed this Life 8'' ye 13th, 1716.

George Ross Departed this Life march ye 14th, 1716.

Evan Raglin Departed this Life may ye 30th, 1717.

Wm. son of Rich'' Ross Departed this Life 8'' 24, 1717.

Peter a negro of Evan Ragland Died March ye 24, 1717.

Thomas Ragland Departed this Life Feb'' 15, 1719.

Sarah wife of Henry Richardson Deceased Decem'' 6th, 1720.

Henry Richardson Dyed Septem''' 17th, 1726.

Henry Richardson Jun' Dyed Jan'' ye 2d, 1726–7.

Anne Ross Dyed Decem'' ye 29th, 1726.

Susannah ye daughter of Thomas Spencer departed this life ye 4 day of Novem'', 1686.

David Smith departed this Life ye 17th d. of January, 1687–8.

Thom. Stephens departed this Life ye 3d of Jan., 1687–8.

Will Spears Deceased ye 2d of March, 1687–8.

Mr. Rich'' Squire sometime Min. of ye P'ish obijt. xii Die December & Sepulterat ——— M''', 1707.

Frances Daughter of Natt. Smith Departed this Life ye 24th day of May, 1708.

Anne ye wife of Jn° Speare Departed this Life ye 5th day of June, 1708.

Francis Stone Departed this Life ye 5th day of June, 1708.

Ruth ye Daughter of Robt. Speare Departed this Life X'' 18th, 1708.

Susanna wife of Mr. Thomas Sharp Min' of St. Paul's Parish Departed this Life May ye 17th and were Buried in St. Peter's Parish Churchyard on May ye 19th, 1709.

Martha ye wife of John Stils Departed this Life 8^{ber} ye 4th, 1709.

Elizabeth Daughter of Jno Sanders Departed this Life Sept. ye 6th, 1712.

John Simpson Departed this Life June ye 30th, 1713.

David son of Tho. Strange Departed this Life 9^{br} 28th, 1714.

Elizabeth Stringer Departed this Life 7^{br} ye 25th, 1715.

Sarah Sanders Departed this Life January ye 25th, 1716.

John Spear Departed this Life March ye 27th, 1716.

Mitchel Strange Departed this Life April ye 20th, 1717.

James Sanders Departed this Life Febry. ye 9th, 1717.

William Sanders Departed this Life February 17th, 1717.

Alice Spear Departed this Life ye 2d of March, 1717.

Charly Spear Departed this Life ye 18th of Marc., 1717.

Sarah a negro of Wm. Stone Died X^{br} ye 2d, 1718.

Elizabeth wife of Wm. Stone Departed this Life Jany. 17th, 1718.

Anne Strange Departed this Life Jany. ye 29th, 1718.

Wm. Stone Departed this Life Jany., 1718.

Nathaniel Smith Departed this Life November ye 7th, 1719.

Ruth ye wife of Robert Speere Died March 12, 1719.

Jane Daughter of Robt Speere Died March 29, 1720.

Edward son of Robt Speere Died March 8, 1720.

Marg^t wife of James Smith Died April 11, 1720.

William Stegall Departed this Life March 19, 1719.

Mr. Thos Sharpe Minister of this Parish Departed this Life Septem^b 3d, 1720.

Jane Sullevant a serv^t woman Deceas^d Augt 25th, 1720.

Paul a boy at Sarah Saunders died July 14, 1721.

Moses Stegall Deceas^d Augt 19th, 1 to charge to Robt Wingfield, 1721.

Dinah Smith Daughter to Sam^{ll} Smith died Jany. 10th, 172½.

Johannah Shailer Departed this Life June 23rd, 1722.

Suky a negro girl belonging to Mad^{am} Sharp died Jan^{ry} 13th, 1722.

Robert Spear sen^r died Febry. —, 1722.

Mary Spear Dyed March ye 12th, 1724–5.

George son of Saml Smith Dyed June 17th, 1725.

Eliz. ye wife of Grove Sanders Dyed 7^{br} 18th, 1725.

Alex. Strange Dyed 9br ye 2d, 1725.
Elizth Sanderson Dyed Febry. 20th, 1725–6.
Wm. Sims Dyed Febry. 17th, 1725–6.
Robt Speare Dyed Febry: 20th, 1725–6.
Thos S. Anderson Dyed Febry: ye 24th, 1726–7.
Sarah Sproson Dyed Aprl 28th, 1726.
Sami Smith Dyed Febry: 6th, 1726–7.
Phillis negro belonging to Md Sharpe Dyed April 2, 1729.
Dorothy Smith Dyed march 2d, 1729–30.
John Scott Dyed october 23d, 1729.
Mrs Catherine Sharpe Dyed october 29, 1729.
Wm. son of Arther Sladyen Dyed 7ber 25th, 1730.
Henry Terakries servant to Mr Thom. Smith departed this life
    ye 4 day of Septemr, 1686.
Jno Turner sone to Henry Turner departed this Life ye 18 of
    Jan., 1686–7.
Sara wife to Henry Turner Departed this Life ye 20th d of Febry,
    1686–7.
Mitchell Tucker deceased ye 25th of Febry:, 1687–8.
Lenore Thomson deceased ye 18 d of Aprill, 1688.
Will. sone to Will. Turner deceased ye 15 d of Febry:, 1687–8.
Robert Tomson Dyed the 12 Aprill, 1702.
Anne Dauter of James Teate Dyed ye 3d Novr, 1702.
Ofan Daughter of James Teate Dyed ye 13 Apr., 1703.
Judith Thomson Departed this Life March ye 14th, 1709.
Wm. son of Wm. Timson Departed this Life February ye 12th,
    1710.
Henry Turner Departed this Life December ye 17th, 1715.
George Turner Departed this Life March ye 6th, 1717.
Thomas Tudor Departed this Life March ye 12th, 1717.
James Turner Departed this Life Jany. ye 18th, 1718.
Jams Taylor Departed this Life Jany. ye 25th, 1719.
Wm. Thorpe Departed this Life Augt 21, 1720.
Rebeca Tuder Deceased September 17th, 1721.
Richd Taylor servt to Wm. Adams Deceasd Augt, 1721.
Lucy Little Daughter of Mary Taylor Dyed Febry. 9th, 172⅔.
Jeremiah Tomlinson Dyed at Docr Greenhils oct. 29th, 1726.
Michael Tucker Dyed in March, 1726–7.

Phillis a negro belonging to Henry Talman Dyed 7^{ber} 27th, 1727.

Jenny a negro belonging to Do. Dyed 7^{ber} 28th, 1727.

Phillis a negro belonging to Eliz. Taylor Dyed Febry. 16th, 1728-9.

Sara wife to Abraham Venable deceased ye 13 day of Febry., 1687-8.

Isaac son to Abraham Venable deceased ye 13 day Febry., 1687-8.

Jno Ussory deceased ye 7th February, 1687-8.

Nohome daugh. to Amar uriah deceased ye 26 d. of March, 1688.

John Upshiere Junr Departed this Life August ye 10th, 1713.

William Vaughan Departed this Life March 16, 1719.

Jno Vaughan Dyed at Mr. Poindexters Jany. 20th, 1724-5.

Elizabeth Vaiden Departed this Life 7^{ber} ye 23d, 1730.

Mathias Wood Departed this Life ye 16 day of octo^b, 1686.

Mr. James Walters deceased ye 17th of August, 1687.

Sam. sone to Sam. Waddy deceased ye 3d of Jan., 1687-8.

Jane Daugh: to Sam. Waddy deceased ye 15 d. of Jan., 1687-8.

Jude Warran deceased ye 23d of February, 1687-8,

Jane Winfree deceased ye 29 d. of February, 1687-8.

Jn^e Warran deceased ye 2d of March, 1687-8.

Eliz. wife to Thom. Wilkinson deceased ye 6 d. of Febry., 1687-8.

Catheriane Woodrowe deceased ye 12 d of Febry., 1687-8.

Jane Daugh: of John Webb Dyed the 3 May, 1700.

John Will-Son Departed this Life on ye 23d day of August, 1709.

James son of Wm. Wilson Departed this Life June ye 30th, 1709.

Elizabeth Daughter of Jacob Winfrey Departed this Life Augt ye 23, 1709.

Jno Waddill Senr Departed this Life December ye 20th, 1709.

Samuel Weaver Departed this Life Jany. ye 25th, 1709.

Peter Warrin Departed this Life Jany. ye 30th, 1709.

Mary the wife of Tho. Ashcroft Departed this Life 20th of Febry., 1711-12.

Mary Wild Departed this Life December ye 7th, 1712.

Elizabeth Winfrey Departed this Life March ye 27th, 1714.

Anne Daughter of Wm. Walker Departed this Life 7ᵇʳ 26th, 1714.

Nanny a negro woman belonging to Mr. Wm. Waddill Departed this Life 9ᵇʳ ye 17th, 1714.

Will a negro man belonging to ye sᵈ Waddill Departed this Life Xᵇʳ, 1714.

Mary ye wife of Thomas Winkfield Departed this Life Jany. ye 31st, 1714.

Moll a negro girl belonging to Jnᵒ Whitlock Departed this Life July 26, 1715.

Deliliah Wells Departed this Life Augᵗ ye 4th, 1715.

Elizabeth Williamson Departed this Life 7ᵇᵉʳ 9th, 1715.

Agnes Waddill Departed this Life February ye 8th, 1716.

James Whitlock Departed this Life March ye 29th, 1716.

Elizabeth wife of Edwᵈ Walton Departed this Life April 5th, 1717.

Wm. Walker Junʳ Departed this Life 7ᵇᵉʳ ye 23d, 1717.

Jnᵒ Pettery a servᵗ of Charles Waddill Departed this Life 7ᵇʳ 28th, 1717.

John Wildmore Departed this Life Febry. ye 9th, 1717.

Alice Whitlock Departed this Life Febry. 7th, 1717.

Charles Winfrey Departed this Life Febry. 2d, 1717.

Mary Winfrey Departed this Life on ye 6th of May, 1718.

Wm. Walker Departed this Life September ye 12th, 1718.

Sue a negro woman of Wm. Waddills Died 8ᵇʳ ye 9th, 1719.

Charles son of Chaˢ Waddill Departed this Life April 3d, 1720.

Charles Waddel senʳ Departed this Life April 9, 1720.

John Simons servᵗ to Judith Waddell Died May ye 5, 1720.

Edward Walton Departed this Life april 27, 1720.

Eliz. Wicker Departed this Life augᵗ 16, 1720.

John son of James Waddil Deceased July 13, 1720.

James son of Jnᵒ Waddill Deceasᵈ Septemʳ 3rd, 1720.

Thomas Wingfield Deceasᵈ Decemʳ 19, 1720.

Susanna Waddill Deceasᵈ March ye 7, 1720-1.

Jack a negro of Geo. Wilkinson was drowned June 18, 1721.

Benj. son of Benj. Wicker Died Augᵗ 18, 1721.

Francis Walton Died November 27, 1721.

James Waddill Died December 28th, 1721.

John Walton Died Jany. 23d, 172½.

Rebecca Waddill Died March 3d, 172½.

Pompey a negro belonging to Lewis Watkins Dyed oct. 6th, 1723.

Jenny a negro woman belonging to Cha. Winfree Dyed M^{ch} 14, 172¾.

Bess a negro woman of Hen Wyatts Dyed 11 of November, 1724.

Sarah Daug. of Anth. Waddy Dyed Decem^r 9th, 1725.

Anth° Winston Dyed Decem^r 14th, 1725.

the Daug^h of Anth° Waddy Dyed 7^{ber} 8, 1725.

Margaret Wood Dyed Feby. 25, 1725–6.

Rachel Watson Deceased Decem^r 27th, 1726.

Mary Walton Dyed Jany. ye 7th, 1726–7.

Thos. Weaver Dyed March ye 15, 1726–7.

Mrs. Mary Weaver Dyed octo^b ye 27th, 1727.

Eliz. Weaver Dyed June ye 5, 1728.

Major Willis Dyed Augt ye 12th, 1728.

Bowler Willis Dyed october ye 8th, 1728.

Ann Watkins Departed this Life Decr 14th, 1729.

Doll a negro belonging to Geo. Wilkinson Dyed Feb. 14, 1730–1.

Rebecca Webster Died october 30th, on Sunday about noon, 1743, in the 74 year of her age.

Jn° son of Thomas Yarbrough Departed this Life Augt ye 13th, 1717.

John Yeates Departed this Life ye 16th of May, 1718.

BIRTHS AND BAPTISMS.

James son of Fra. Amoss Born 8^{br} ye 15th, 1716.

Judith Daughter of Sam^{ll} Allen Born August ye 16th, 1716.

Sarah Daughter of Francis Apperson Born ye 16th of April, 1717.

Hannah a negro girl belonging to Rich^l Allin Born May ye 8th, 1717.

Frances Daughter of John Alford Born 8^{br} ye 4th, 1717.

Julius son of James Alford Born in September, 1717.

Hannah Daughter of Wm. Allin Baptised 9^{br} ye 17th, 1717.

John son of Thomas Apperson Born April ye 1st, 1718.

Major son of Thomas Anderson Born March 17th, 1717.

Peter son of John Apperson Born Augt ye 19, 1718.

Francis son of Wm. Apperson Born ye 20th day of December, 1718.

Toby a negro of Jno Aldridge Born Jany. 6th, 1719.

Mary Daughter of Francis Amoss Born August ye 9th, 1719.

Frances Danghter of Jno Alford Born 8^{br} ye 4th, 1717.

Cuffee a negro of Jno Alford Born June ye 22d, 1719.

Elizabeth Daughter of Jno Alford Born July ye 1st, 1719.

Eliz. Daughter of Wm. Adams Born Jany: 26, 1719.

Doll a negro girl of Mr. Ebenez. Adams born March 29, 1720.

Joyce Daughter of Wm. Allen born Jany: 29, 1719.

Beck a negro belonging to Wm. Atkinson born Jany: 20, 1719.

Agathy Daughter of Jno Austin was born March 3, 1720.

Dick a negro of Jno Aldridges born June 20, 1714.

George a child belonging to Richd Allen born 10^{br} 25, 1721.

Lucy a negro belonging to Jno Alford born June 22, 1721.

Simon a negro belonging to Jacoby Aldridge born Sepr 9, 1721.

Bowler sonn of Mr. Ebenezer Adams born april 19th, 1722.

Lucy a negro girl belonging to Mr. Adams born June 1st, 1722.

Flora a negro belonging to Mr. Adams born Sep^t 18th, 1722.

Hagar a negro girl belonging to Mr. Adams born oct^{br} 21st, 1722.

Sue a negro girl belonging to Jacoby Aldridge born oct^r 2d, 1723.

Mary Daughter of Jno Austin born No^r 4th, 1723.

Hen^r son of Wm. Atkinson born March 9, 172¾.

Jno a negro boy belonging to Do. born Febry. 26th, 172¾.

Phillip son of Richd Austin born June 16th. 1724.

Wm. son of Eben^r Adams Gent. born July 4, 1724.

Unity Daughter of ——— Alford & Grace born 16 Decr at 3 morn., 1724.

Charity Daw ——— born 16 of Decem^r at noon, 1724.

Punch a negro boy belonging to Eben^r Adams Gent. born Jany. 5, 1724-5.

Alex: son of John Askew born Jany. 27th, 1724-5.

Jack a negro boy belonging to Richd Apperson born May 5, 1725.

Judah Daughter of Rob' Allen born 7^{br} 31st, 1724.

Aggey a negro girl of Mr. Richd Allen born May 27th, 1725.

Judith a negro belonging to Mr. Ebenez^r Adams born 24 Jany:, 1725.

George son of Richd Apperson born June ye 24 & Dyed ye 25, 1725.

Joe a negro boy of Mr. Eben^r Adams born Febry. 10, 1725.

Jane the Daugh' of Jno Austin born April ye 12th, Bap. 22d, 1726.

Jenny a negro girl of John Alford born Jany:, 1725–6.

Geo. son of Valentine Adams born april ye 14th, 1726.

Rich^d son of Eben^r Adams Gent. born May ye 17th, 1726.

Wm. son of Valentine Amoss born October 25, 1726.

Edmund a negro of Mrs. Elizth Allen born Febry. 26, 1726–7.

Anne ye Daughter of Robert Allen born April ye 16, 1726.

Roger a negro belonging to Jacoby Aldridge born June 27th, 1727.

Jenny a negro belonging to Eben^z Adams Gent. born Octr 14, 1727.

Anne ye Da^r of Jno & Anne Askew born Octr 29, baptiz^d Decr 3d, 1727.

Orson a negro belonging to Richd Apperson born oct^b ye 19th, 1727.

Sam a negro belonging to Mr. Eliz^a Allen born March ye 4th, 1727–8.

William ye son of John Austin born July ye 7th, 1728.

Tabitha ye Daug^h of Eben^r Adams Gent. born July ye 7th, 1728.

Jane & Susanna negros belonging to Wm. Atkinson bap' 7^{ber} ye 29, 1728.

Iris a negro belonging to Ebenez^r Adams Gent. born april 4, 1728.

Jacoby Daughter of Rob' & Eliz^a Allen born July 16, bap' No^v 17, 1728.

James a negro belonging to Mr. Ebenez^r Adams bap' April 6, 1729.

Rose a negro belonging to Mr. Ebene^r Adams born July 22, 1729.

Wm. son of John & Elizth Apperson born July 17th, bap^t Augt 10th, 1729.

Ann Daugh^t of Abram Alloway born March 20, bap^t May 17, 1720.

Sue a negro belonging to Mr. Eben^r Adams born 22 of June, 1730.

Lucy a negro girl belonging to Jacoby Aldridge born May ye 3, 1730.

Harry a negro belonging to Richard Apperson born Jany: 11th, 1729-30.

Eliz. ye Dau^r of Jno & Anne Askew born Jany. 13, 1729-30.

Giles a negro boy belonging to Wm. Atkinson born Dec. 31, 1730.

John son of Jno Baily Born ye 31st of October, 1716.

Thomas son of Tho. Baily Born February ye 12th, 1716.

Samuel son of Samuel Buxton Born March ye 10th, 1716.

John son of Tho. Butts Gent. by Catherine his wife born January ye 27th, 1716.

Catherine Daughter of ye Reverend Mr. Wm. Brodie by Catherine his wife born ye 7th day of December, 1716.

Mary Daughter of Thomas Bassett Born April ye 4th, 1717.

Lyddiall son of Mr. Jno Bacon Born, 1717.

Hannah a negro girl of Wm. Bassetts Esq: Born April ye 4th, 1718.

Samuel son of Sam^{ll} Bug Born 7^{br} ye 16th, 1717.

Benjamin son of Sam^{ll} Buxston Born 8^{br}, 1718.

John son of Jno Chandler Born Febry: ye 6th, 1718.

Abraham a negro boy of Mr. Th^o Butts Born July ye 1st, 1719.

Jack a negro boy of Mr. Robt Burbridge Born 12th of July, 1719.

David son of Thomas Bassett Born ye 7th day of 9^{br}, 1719.

Frances the Daughter of Thomas Butts Gent and Catherine his wife Born the 10th day of November, 1719.

Stephen son of Sr Stephen Brown baptiz^d January 28th, 1719.

Esther a negro of Coll: Bassett born May 4, 1720.

Jno son of Richd Brooker born July 1, 1720.

Wm. son of John Bailey born Septem^r 4, 1720.

Sherw^d son of Saml Bugg born July 8, 1720.

Dorothy & James 2 negro children belonging to Mr. Tho. Bray baptiz^d July 30, 1721.

Paul a boy of Mary Bourns sen' born May, 1721.

a negro belonging to Coll: Basset born June 26, 1721.

Paul a negro belonging to Mr. Tho: Butts born Aug', 1721.

Phillis a negro belonging to Ditto born Aug', 1721.

Edm⁴ sonn of Jno° & Susanna Bacon born Apr" 8th, 1722.

Lucy Daughter of Jn° & Ann Baily born Nov' 27th, 1722.

Billy a negro boy belonging to Jn° Brothers born Jany: 10th, 1722–3.

Jacob sonn of Sam" Bugg born Feb'ʸ 16th, 1722–3.

Judith a mulatto girl belong. to Rob' Burbridge Apr' 11th, 1723.

Peter & Sam" sons of Alice Bryant born Sep' 26th, 1723.

Phillis a negro girl belonging to Mad^m Bassett born 17th Ap", 1724.

Wm. a mulatto slave belonging to Mary Bourn born Febr'ʸ 24th, 1724–5.

George & Charles 2 boys belonging to Mr. Theo. Butts born Oct: 2, 1724.

Dorothy a negro girl belonging to Ditto born November 2, 1724.

Parke son of Jn° Bailey by Anne his wife born Mar° 6th, 1724–5.

Frank a negro belong to Coll: David Bray born March 12th, 1724–5.

James son of Edw⁴ Bailey born April 28th, 1725.

David son of Rich⁴ Beer born 27 May, 1725.

Fran° D' of Mr. Wm. Brown born March 11th, 1724.

John son of Tho. Barns born oct. ye 4th, 1725.

Anne D' of David Binns born oct. 27th, 1725.

Wm. son of Jn° Bassett born 7ᵇʳ 17th, 1725.

Sarah Daugh. of Sam' Bugg born oct. 24th, 1725.

David son of David Binns born April ye 12th & April 25th, 1726.

Jn° son of Charles Bolton was born Aug' ye 22d, 1726.

Jenny a negro girl belonging to Mad^m Basset born Aug' 12th, 1726.

Anne ye Daugh: of Jn° Bassett born July ye 17th, 1726.

Sarah ye Daugh' of Tho. Butts born Jany: 4th, 1725–6.

Bess a negro girl belonging to Ditto born Febry: 1725–6.

Drary ye son of Edward Bailey born Jany: 8th, 1726–7.

Charles & George negros belonging to Mr. Wm. Browne born June 15th, 1727.

Eliz'ᵗʰ ye Daugh' of Wm. Browne born July ye 17th, 1727.

Patty a negro belonging to Ditto born 7^{br} ye 1st, 1727.

Hannah a negro of Jn° Brothers was born 7^{br} 29th, 1726.

Martha the Daugh^t of Robt Bailey born Sep^t 10th, 1727.

Sarah Da^r of Jn° & Anne Baily born oct. 4 & bap^t oct. 29th, 1727.

Anne ye Da^r of Jn° & Susanna Bacon born oct. 29th & bapt. Decem^r 11, 1727.

Jules a negro boy belonging to Coll. David Bray born Febry. 1st, 1727–8.

Betty a negro belonging to Ditto born Decem^r ye 1st, 1727.

Anne Daugh^t of Wm. & Amy Burk born Jany. 8th & bap^t March 24th, 1727–8.

Lucy a negro belonging to Wm. Atkinson born March ye 28th, 1728.

Jenny a negro belonging to Mr. Ebene^r Adams Dyed March 29th, 1728.

Jils a negro belonging to Ditto born April ye 4th, 1728.

Sarah ye Daugh. of Tho. & Margery Barnes born Feby. 9th, bap^t Mar. 10th, 1727–8.

Isaac ye son of Isaac & Elizth Vaiden born Jany. 24th, bap^t Mar. 2d, 1727–8.

Susanna ye Daugh. of Joseph & Elizth Bradley born Febry. 18, 1727–8.

Harry a negro boy belonging to Sam^t Buxton Apr^l 4, 1728.

Beck & Chinnah negros belonging to Coll. David Bray born May 2, 1728.

Geo. a negro belonging to Mr. Wm. Bassett born Sep^t ye 2d, 1728.

Nelly, Mary & Sarah negros of Mr. Wm. Browne bap^t oct: 6th, 1728.

Child of Tho. Bassett born July ye 3d, 1728.

Edmund son of Saml & Sarah Bugg born 7^{br} 24 bap^t Novem^r 10, 1728.

Wm. son of John & Eliz^a Bottom born Augt 9th bap^t Feb. 16, 1728–9.

Xtopher son of David & Eliz^a Binns born Feby 10 bap^t Mar: 16, 1728–9.

John son of Robt & Mary Baily born March 11, 1728–9, bap^t May 11th, 1729.

Edwd a negro of Mr. Wm. Brown bap^t July 20th, 1729.

Sue a negro belonging to Thomas Barnes born Augt 14, 1729.

Enee a negro belonging to Coll. David Bray born Augt 20, 1729.

Charles son of Edwd & Fran^c Baily born Augt 28 bap^t oct. 5, 1729.

Lucy a negro girl belonging to John Baily born 7^{br} 19, 1729.

Amy a negro girl belonging to Maj^r Jno Custis Born 7^{br} ye 8th, . 1716.

Mary Daughter of Walter Clopton Born 8br. ye 29th, 1716.

Jack a Negro boy belonging to Steph. Crump Born Febry. ye 3d, 1716.

Stephen son of Robt Cade Born 7br. ye 17th, 1715.

Alice a Negro girl belonging to Maj^r Jno Custis Born Febry. 15th, 1716.

Anne daughter of Tho. Cotterell Baptised March ye 31st, 1716.

Margaret daughter of Robt Clopton Born ye 8th day of April, 1717.

Wm. son of Jno. Cooke Born February ye 23rd, 1716.

Guy a negro of Maj: Jno. Custis Born June ye 9th, 1717.

Hercules a negro of Maj^r Custis Born 8br. 5th, 1717.

Elizabeth daughter of Robt Cade Born ye 29th of April, 1717.

Will a negro girl of Jno. Conors Born ye 2d of May, 1718.

Hannah a negro girl of Robt Clopton Born Febry. ye 5th, 1717.

Anne daughter of Steph. Crump Born May ye 10th, 1718.

Susanna ye Daughter of Robt Cade Born February ye 25th, 1718.

John Son of Jno. Chandler Born February ye 6th, 1718.

Ned a Negro boy of George Crumps Born February, 1718.

Bock a Negro girl belonging to John Custis gent. Born 7br. ye 27th, 1719.

Waldegrove Son of Wm. Clopton by Joyce his wife Born November ye 19th & bap^{ed} Decem^r 22d, 1719.

Jane a negro girl of Maj^r Jno. Custis Born Xber ye 28th, 1719.

Abigal a negro girl of the sd. Jno. Custis born Xber ye 29th, 1719.

Frank a negro boy of Stephⁿ Crumps born Jany 12, 1719.

Dick a negro of Robt Clopton born Novem^r 18, 1719.

Dogg a negro of Maj. Custis born Decem^r 26, 1719.

Cassaud a daughter of Rich. Crump baptis^d Apl. ye 29, 1720.

Jeremy a negro belonging to Maj. Custis born June 25th, 1720.

Anne daughter of Wm. Clopton & Joyce his wife born Jan. 16
    & baptized March ye 15th following, 1720–21.

Nanny a negro of Richd Crump born February 8, 1720–21.

John son of Robt Cade was born Feb: 16, 1720.

Walter son of Walter Clopton born March 24, 1720–1.

Beck a negro of Maj. Custis was born March 25, 1721.

James Crump son of James Crump born Jany 23d, 1721–2.

Sue a negro boy belonging to Major Custis born Novr 25th, 1721.

Sarah a negro Girl belonging to Maj. Custis born March 23d,
    1721–2.

Jemeny a negroe boy belonging to Steph Crump born June 14th,
    1722.

W^m son of Wm. Clopton Junr & Joyce born Feby 12th she &
    Wm. bap. Ap. 29, 1721–2.

―――― a negroe girl belonging to Richd Crump born Oct. 14th,
    1722.

Dinah a negroe girl belonging to Maj^r Custis born Decr 25th,
    1722.

Frances daughter of Robt Clopton born Febry 2d, 1722.

Robt Sonn of Robt Cade born March 28th, 1723.

Lucy Daughter of Stephen Crump born 7^{br} 13, 1723.

Elizth Daughter of Jno. Chandler born Oct. 28th, 1723.

George son of Wm. Clopton Junr & Joyce his wife born Jan^y
    14 & baptiz^d ye 16 of March following, 1723.

Sarah a negro girl belonging to David Clarkson born June 29,
    1724.

Simon a negro boy belonging to Clarkson born July 1st, 1724.

Joseph & Mary, negros belonging to Wm. Chamberlain Bap.
    5 Apl., 1724.

Dick a negro boy belonging to Maj. Jno. Custis born Febry 6,
    1723–4.

Phebe a negro Girl belonging to Do. born Feb. 7, 1723–4.

Anne daughter of Wm. Chamberlain born 14th March, 1723–4.

Mary a negro girl belonging to Do. born 19 Jan^{ry}, 1723–4.

Stephen a negro boy belong to Maj^r Jno. Custis born 14 June,
    1724.

Abra^m a negro boy belong to Steph^n Crump born June 17, 1724.

Anthony son of Thos. Christian born June ye 9th, 1724.

John a negro boy belonging to Maj^r Custis born Decem^r 27th, 1724.

David Son of Richard Crump born Jan^r ye 26th, 1724–5.

John son of Josiah Coleman born Decem^r 12th, 1724.

Wm. Goodall son of Sarah Cook born Febry. 10th, 1724–5.

Jesse son of James Crump born March 3rd, 1724–5.

Judy a negro girl belong to Robt Clopton born May 17th, 1725.

Robt son of Walter Clopton was born June ye 4th, 1725.

Wm. son of Robt Clopton born Novem. ye 11th, 1725.

Temperance D^r of Wm. Crump Ju^r born May 20, 1725.

Easter negro belonging to Maj. Custis born 15 of 9er, 1725.

Jos. son of Jno. Chandler born Feb. 4 & bap^t March 6, 1725–6.

Jammey a negro boy belonging to Walter Clopton born 31st M^{ch}, 1726.

Jenney a negro belonging to Maj. Jno. Custis born 1st March, 1726.

Edward Pey son of Wm. & Elizth Chamberlain born Janry 20th, 1725–6.

Dick a negro boy of Sussannah Clarkson born April, 1726.

Frank a negro Jno. Clarkson born June, 1726.

Henry a negro boy belonging to Maj^r Jno. Custis Augst ye 1st, 1726.

Martha Daugh^{tr} of Jno. Carloss born July 7th, 1726.

Anne ye Daught^r of Mark Clark born July ye 17th, 1726.

Pompey a negro boy of Robt Clopton born Sep^t 27th, 1726.

Tomson a negro boy of Maj. Jno. Custis born Decem^r 25th, 1726.

Moll a negro girl of Do. born Decr 31th, 1726.

Will a negro belonging to Steph^n Crump born Decr 26th, 1726.

Betty a negro of Maj. John Custis born Janry, 1726–7.

Nathl ye son of Richd Crump born March ye 4th, 1726–7.

Croyoon a negro belonging to Col Custis born Jan^{ry} 1st, 1728–9.

Carried to ye back of E.

E.

John son of Peter Ellmore born December ye 6th, 1719.

Mourning England born April ye 1st, 1718.

Frances Daughter of Alex^r Ellis born May, 1720.

6

Lamar a negro belonging to Genr^{al} Ellison born May 24, 1721.

John son of Peter Elmore born Janry. 22d, 1724-5.

Peter son of Peter Elmore born October ye 9th, 1726.

Sarah Daughter of Wm. Elmore born May ye 17th, 1727.

Anne ye daughter of Thos. Evans born July ye 3rd, 1727.

Charles ye son of Thos. Edwards born Janry 26, 1726-7.

Lucy the Daughter of Wm. & Eliz^{th} Elmore born Aug^{st} 5 bap.
7^{br} 7, 1729.

Lucy the Daughter of Wm. & Eliz^{a} Ellmore.

Billey a negro boy belonging to Maj. Jno. Custis born Apl. 1st,
1727 and Dyed Apl. ye 15th, 1727.

Nanny a negro belonging to Richd Crump born March 20th,
1728-9.

Mary ye Daughter of Auther Crew born April ye 11th, 1727.

Jesse a negro of Mr. Wm. Chamberlayne born May ye 10th and
bap^{t} Aug. ye 20th following, 1729.

Nat a negro belonging to Do. born June ye 12th, 1727.

Julius a mulattoe boy belonging to Do. bap^{t} Aug. 20th, 1727.

Deverex ye son of Walter Clopton born Aug. 30th, 1727.

Sussannah ye Da^{r} of Wm. & Eliz^{th} Chandler born Oct. ye 10th
and bap^{t} Novr 12th, 1727.

Jno. son of Humphrey & Amy Chappel born Febry 14 & bap^{t}
March ye 24th, 1727-8.

Gedion ye son of James & Anne Christian born Feb. 5 & bap^{t}
March 24, 1727-8.

Ned a negro belonging to Coll. Jno. Custis born March ye 30th,
1728.

Mary Da^{t} of Jno. & Mary Chandler born March 24 & bap. Apl.
14, 1728.

Dick a negro belonging to Coll. Jno. Custis born Apr. ye 7th,
1728.

Matt a negro belonging to Ditto born May ye 28th, 1728.

Thomas ye son of Wm. & Eliz^{th} Chamberlayne born Septr 13,
1727.

Venus a negro girl belonging to Wm. Clopton Junr born March
20, 1727-8.

Robt son of Robt & Mary Clopton born July 28th bap^{d} 7^{ber} 1st,
1728.

Judith a negro belonging to Coll. Jno. Custis born Augst 1st, 1728.

Abram a negro belonging to Do. born 7^{ber} 20th, 1728.

Charles a negro belonging to Do. baptized July ye 28th, 1728.

Guy, Rich^{d}, Matthew & Sarah negroes belong^{g} to Do bap^{d} Octob^{r} 6, 1728.

Mary ye Da^{r} of Jno. & Mary Chandler born Mch. 24 bap^{d} Apl. 14, 1728.

John son of Wm. & Marcy Crump born 7^{ber} 20th bap^{d} Octo^{br} 20, 1728.

Morris a negro belonging to Coll. Jno. Custis born Feb^{ry} 20th, 1728–9.

Jenny a negro girl belonging to Ja. Clarkson born Novr 13, 1728.

Rebecca D^{r} of Mark & Isabella Clark born December 20th baptized March 30, 1729.

Joe a negro belonging to Coll^{o} Jno. Custis born Apl. 16. 1729.

Moll a negro belonging to Robt Clopton born March 31st, 1729.

Mildred D^{r} of James & Venibia Crump born Apl. 19 bap. May 18th 1729.

Lewis a negro belonging to Col^{o} Custis born Aug^{s} 10, 1729.

Robt son of Wm. & Eliz^{a} Chandler born 25 of August Baptized October 5, 1729.

Margaret Da^{t} of Walter & Mary Clopton born 7^{ber} 9th baptized Octo^{br} 12, 1729.

Kitt a negro boy belonging to Do born Octob^{r} 8, 1729.

Robbin a negro boy belonging to Richd Crump born No^{r} 22, 1729.

Sarah negro belonging to Wm. Chamberlayne bap^{t} Decr 7, 1729.

Easter a mulatto belonging to Coll^{o} Foster born the 12 of August, 1705.

Harry a negro belonging to Col. Jos. Foster born 7^{br}, 1714.

Philis a negro belonging to ye sd Col. Jos. Foster Born July, 1715.

Jony a negro belonging to ye sd Col. Jos. Foster Born May, 1716.

Thomas son of Mr. Jos. Foster Born Apl. ye 16th, 1716.

Janey a mulatto belonging to ye sd Joseph Foster Born, 1711.

Charles a mulatto belonging to ye sd Jos. Foster Born, 1712.

Jony a mulatto belonging to ye sd Jos. Foster Born Augst, 1714.

Pressle a negro belonging to Mad^m Field Born 9^{br} ye 4th, 1716.

Mary Daughter of Jno. Foster Gent. Born January ye 10th, 1716.

Anne Daughter of Thos. Fussell Born 7^{br} ye 27, 1717.

Sarah a negro belonging to Mad^m Alice Field Born December ye 6, 1717.

John & Esquire 2 negros belonging to Jos. Foster Junr born X^{br}, 1718.

Jack a negro boy belonging to Mrs. Lucy Foster Born July 2d, 1719.

Betty a negro girl belonging to Mad^m Field born 8^{br} 4th, 1719.

Susanna Daughter of Henry Finch Born ye 25th day of 7^{br}, 1719.

Judith a negro belonging to Tho. Fussell born Augt 14th, 1720.

Ludlow a negro of Mad^m Alice Fields born March 12, 1720-1.

Billy a negro belonging to Martha Finch born July 1, 1721.

William son of Wm. Forsbush born June 5, 1721.

Saless a negro of Mada^m Alice Fields born June 26, 1721.

Sue a negro belonging to the Late Deceased Madam Fields Estate born Febry. 21st, 1721-2.

Lucy Fluellin Born Sep^{br} 23d, 1719.

William son of Henry Finch born Decem^{br} 12th, 1722.

George sonn of Ann Ferguson born March 3d, 1723.

John a mulatto belonging to Jos. Forster born Ap^l 1st, 1722.

Sarah Daughter of Fra^c Fussel born oct^r 11th, 1722.

Sarah Daughter of Wm. Forbess born Jany: ye 10th, 1723-4.

Mary a mulatto girl belong to Jos. Foster Gent. bap^t 26 July, 1724.

Nan a negro girl belonging to Martha Finch born 20 Dec^r, 1724.

Stroud the son of Jno Finch born Febry. 2nd, 1724-5.

Jno son of Henry Finch born June ye 17th, 1725.

Jesse ye son of Alex. Flower was born 10^{br} 4th, 1725.

Charles son of Tarleton & Hannah Fleming born Decr 10th, 1725.

Jno son of Jo^s & Fran^c Fox born 9^{ber} ye 26, 1725 & bap^t 10^{ber} 19, 1725.

Wm. son of Mary Fielding Bap^t 1ober 19th, 1725.

Joseph son of Dan^{ll} Farell born oct^b 8th, 1725.

Edward son of Henry Finch born octo^b 2d bap^t Feb. 22, 1728.

Richard ye son of Dan^{ll} & Eliz. Farell Novem^h ye 28th, 1727.

Sarah ye Daughter of Jn° Fergison born June ye 15, 1727.

Peninnah D^r of John & Peninnah Fergison born July 24 Baptized Augt 24th, 1727.

Charles son of John & Sabra Finch born oct^r 27, 1728.

Thomas ye son of Wm. & Eliz^a Firth born March ye 5th, 1729–30.

Robin a negro belonging to Henry Finch born July 8th, 1730.

Frances Daughter of Tho. Grant born ye 14th of 8^{ber} 1716.

Edward son of Edward Green born ye 8th of March, 1717.

Alexander son of Jn° Gawlin Born ye 8th of November, 1717.

Mildrett Daughter of Thomas Grant Born August ye 29th, 1719.

Eliz. Daugh^r of Jn° Gawling born June 7, 1720.

Ellinor Daughter of Hugh & Mary Grinley born July 8th, 1722.

Wm. son of Jn° Gannaway born augst ye 31st, 1723.

Joseph son of Forest Green born July ye 1st, 1724.

Sussannah Gilbert Departed this Life 21 of 7bor, 1724.

Rich^d son of Wm. Guilliam born October 26, 1724.

Mary daughter of Hugh Grindley born 8 April, 1725.

John Son of John Green born August 17, 1725.

Elizth D^r of Jno. Guilliam born Apl. 7, 1726.

Billy a negro of Dr. Greenhills born Augst 8, 1726.

Fran^s Daugh^r of Hugh Grinley born Feb^{ry} 7th, 1726–7.

Wm. son of Thos. Green born March ye 7th, 1726–7.

Mary ye Daugh^r of James & Eliz. Goodall born Sepr 15th, 1725.

Martha ye Daugh^r of Forrest Green born Augst 17th, 1727.

Thomas ye son of James & Eliz^a Goodall born Octob^r ye 5th and bap^t No, 19th, 1727.

Geo^e a negro belonging to Mr. Paschal Greenhill born Feb^{ry} ye 2d, 1727–8.

Sarah ye Da^r of Jno. & Martha Guilliam born April 25th bap^t May 26th, 1728.

Jaunny a negro belonging to Paschel Greenhill born May 26, 1728.

Lucy a negro belonging to Ditto born Sep^t ye 12, 1728.

Fran^s ye Da^r of Thomas & Sarah Garwood born 7bor 10th, bap 7bor 27th, 1728.

Jonny a negro girl belonging to Wm. Jordian born M^{ch} 4, 1728.

Zacharias Son of Jno. & Eliz^a Green born Feb^{ry} 27 bapt. Ap^l 6, 1729.

Richard Son of John & Martha Gilliam born March 2 Bapt. Easter day following, 1729-30.

Sussann^h Da^r of Forrest & Mary Green born Jan^{ry} 16th, 1729-30.

Jack a negro belonging to Wm. Jordian born March ye 14th, 1729-30.

William son of Thomas & theodosia Goodwin Born Jan^{ry} 2nd, 1748-9.

William son of Sam^{ll} Hubbart Born 8^{br} ye 27th, 1716.

Agnes Daughter of Thomas Howle Born 4^{hr} ye, 1716.

Wm. son of John Howle Born February ye 27th, 1716.

Wm. son of Anne Howle Born February ye 24th, 1716.

John son of Jno. Howl Born ye 3rd Feb^{ry} Bap^t Novr 8th, 1718.

Judith, daught^r of Matthew Hardon Born March ye 3d, 1718.

John son of Richard Howl was born Septem^r 20 children of Edwd Harris & Elizabeth his wife viz., 1719.

Edwd son of Edw'd Harris was born Novem^r 27, 1704.

Sarah Daughter of Ditto was born January 20, 1705.

Judith Daughter of Ditto was born January 5, 1707.

John son of Ditto was born April 24, 1710.

Thomas son of Ditto was born June 14 1712.

Ussery son of Jno. Hitchcock was born June 18, 1715.

Mary Daughter of Sam Hubbard born June 28, 1721.

James son of Jno. & Katherine Hitchcock born March 16th, 1721-2.

Lucy Daughter of Sam^{ll} & Ellenor Hubbard born Jan^{ry} 1st, 1722-3.

James son of John Howl born Septr ye 7th, 1723.

Sam^{ll} son of Jno. Hall born Augst ye 30, 1723.

Mary Daughter of Jas. Hitchcok born Jan^{ry} 5, 1723-4.

Sussannah Daughter of Jno. Howle born April 2, 1725.

Jane Daughter of James Howle born 9th of 7^{bor}, 1725.

Sarah Daugh^r of Richd Head born Augst 15, 1725.

Elizth ye Daught^r of Saml Hubbert born Decem^r 21st, 1726.

George ye son of Charles Hughes born Octob^r ye 2d, 1726.

Peter a negro of Wm. Hopkins born Decemb^r 13th, 1726.

Phillis a negro girl of Jno. Howle born March ye 10th, 1726-7.

George son of George Wilton born May ye 26th, 1727.

Fran⁵ ye Daughter of Michael & Grace Warfield born 7ᵇᵒʳ 26 bapt. 9bor 26th, 1727.

Crespin Grinley ye son of Anne Heaton born June ye 6 1727 & bapt. Jan^ry 21, 1727-8.

Thos. son of Thos. & Anne Howle born May ye 5th bapt. June ye 2d, 1728.

Edward son of Edward Harris born Febry ye 6th, 1726-7.

Anne ye Daʳ of Wm. & Fran⁵ Hopkins born July 20th Bapt. Aug^st 2d, 1728.

Wm. a negro belonging to Judith Hardyman bapt. 7bor 29th, 1728.

Jeremiah son of Thomas & Lucy Hilliard born Febry 26 and baptized March 23, 1728-9.

Sam¹ son of Sam¹ & Elinor Hubbard born Aug^st 9, 1728.

Eastor a negro belonging to John Howle born Apl. 6th, 1729.

James a negro of Tho⁵ Hilliard bapt. July 20, 1729.

Annis Daughtʳ of Chas. & Eliz^a Hughs born July 21 bap. Aug^st 17, 1729.

Joe a negro boy belonging to Wm. Hopkins born 7bor 10th, 1729.

Absolom son of Jno. & Mary Howl born April 26, 1730.

Epaphroditus son of Thomas & Anne Howle born 5th March, 1729-30.

Richard Dʳ of Jno. & Anne Harris born Feb^ry 20th, 1729-30.

Eliz^a the Daughter of Edmond & Unity Harris born August 1st, 1730.

Ursula the Daughter of thos. & Tresel Henderson born Febry 23 bap^d Apl. 5, 1730.

Phillis a negro belonging to Judith Hardyman born Apl. 20th, 1729.

Sam¹ son of James & Joyce Hill born Decʳ 26th, 1730.

Mingo a negro belonging to Do. born June ye 30, 1730.

Robbin a mulatto son of Dorothy Howel born March 18th, 1739.

a negro belonging to Martin Hulett born April 2d, 1731.

Thomas son of Thomas & Lucy Hilliard born March ye 4th and baptized April ye 18th following, 1730-1.

Joe a negro boy belonging to Wm. Hopkins born Septr 10th, 1729.

Absalom of Jno. & Mary Howle born April 26, 1730.

Epaphroditus son of Thomas & Anne Howle born 5 March, 1729.

Richard son of Jno. & Anne Harris born february 1st, 1810.

Mary Daughter of Wm. Jackson Born 1716.

William Willis Johnson son of John Johnson of Blissland Parish Born January ye 3rd, 1716-17.

William son of Jno. Jackson born September ye 29th, 1717.

David son of Jno. Jones Born October ye 26, 1717.

Elizabeth Daughter of John Jackson Born 7br. ye 20th, 1719.

Mossias son of Mossias Jones & Lucy his wife born March 21, 1721.

Mary daughter of Robt Jarrat born July 10, 1721.

Frances Daughter of Jno. Jackson born July 29th, 1722.

Matthew a negro boy belong to Mary Jackson born 20 Sep^r, 1723.

David son of Robt Jarrott born December 23d, 1723.

Mary daughter of Desorex Jarrott born May 5th, 1724.

Robt son of Robt Jarratt born Decem^r 26th, 1724.

Jno. son of Jno. Johnson born March 1st, 1724-5.

Pompy a negro belonging to Deborex Jarratt born 17 June, 1725.

Archolaus son of Debrix Jarrott born Jan^{ry} 5, 1725-6.

Mary daughter of Fran^s Johnson born Feb^{ry} 9th, 1725-6.

Henrietta ye D^r of Matth^w & Susan^h Jouet born Apl. 20, 1727.

Anne ye Da^r of Deverix & Eliz^h Jarratt born Novr 13, bapt. Decr 24, 1727.

Susannah ye Da^r of Robt & Sarah Jarratt born Novr ye 16 & bapt. Jan^{ry} ye 14, 1727.

Will a negro belonging to Robt Jarratt born on Christmas day, 1727.

Wm. son of Wm. & Mary Johnson born June ye 9th & bapt. July ye 7th, 1728.

Fran^e son of Fran^e & Jane Johnson born May ye 25th, 1728.

Mary Da^r of Elizabeth Jugo born 7bor. 29, 1729.

Wm. son of Rich^d & Judith Jones born Jan^{ry} 2d bap^t Feb. 22, 1729-30.

Fanny Da^r of Devorix & Eliz^a Jarratt born Jan^{ry} 15 bap^t Feb. 22, 1729–30.

Mary Da^r of James & Jane Johnson born May 2d bapt. June 7, 1730.

Moll a negro belonging to Mary Jackson born 24 July, 1728.

Isaac son of Frances & Jane Johnson born Feb^{ry} 5th, 1729–30.

Richard son of Abra^m & Jane Johnson born Jan^{ry} 18th, 1729–30.

A negro girl belonging to Jno. Lewis Esq. Born May 25th, 1716.

Elizabeth daughter of Sherwood Lightfoot born 9bor. ye 23rd, 1716.

Betty a negro girl belonging to Mr. Tho. Lightfoot Born Mar^{ch} 31st, 1717.

Mary daughter of Mr. T: Lightfoot Born 8ber ye 2d, 1717.

John son of Jno. Lucas Born ye 29 of 7br., 1717.

Frances Daughter of Tho. Lightfoot Born 8br. ye 8th, 1717.

John son of Nich^o Lewis Born November 22, 1717.

Vead a negro belonging to Mr. Sherw^d Lightfoot Born ye 15th of Xbr., 1717.

Ross a negro belonging to ye sd. Lightfoot Born Jan^{ry} ye 2d, 1717.

Lucy a mulatto Girl belonging to Mrs. Eliz. Littlepage born 17 Xbr., 1717.

Mary a negro Girl belonging to Mr. Chas. Lewis Born April ye 15th, 1718.

George a negro belonging to the sd. Chas. Lewis Born ye 5th of May, 1718.

George a negro belonging to ye sd. Chas. Lewis Born May ye 6th, 1718.

——— a negro belonging to Jno. Lewis Esqr Born 7br., 1718,

Beky a negro Girl belonging to J^{no} Lewis Esq. Born March 17, 1718.

Hannah a mulatto belonging to Mr. Sherwood Lightfoot was born April ye 26th, 1719.

Daniel a negro born ye 30th of May belonging to ye sd. S: Lightfoot, 1719.

Ned a negro boy belonging to ye sd. S. Lightfoot Born June ye 23rd, 1719.

Dick a Negro boy belonging to ye S: Lightfoot Born July ye 4th, 1719.

Susanna Daughter of Rich⁴ Littlepage Gent. Born Jan'ʸ 22nd, 1717.

Joe negro Boy belonging to Mr. Francis Littlepage Born June ye 30, 1718.

Robert a negro belonging to Mr. Fra: Littlepage born January &c, 1718.

Nanny a negro Girl belonging to ye sd. Mr. Littlepage Born March &c, 1718.

Charley son of John Lucas Born December ye 25th, 1719.

Jno. son of Jno. Langford born January ye 8th, 1719.

Elizabᵗʰ Daughter of Owen Lewis born Decemʳ 10, 1719.

Anne Daughter of Mr. Thoˢ Lightfoot born Augˢᵗ 7, 1720.

John son of Charles Lewis Gent. was born Octoʳ 8, 1720.

Tamer a Negro of Charles Lewis Gent. born March 20, 1720.

Teney a Negro of Cha. Lewis Gent. born March 15, 1720.

Ann a Negro of Mrs. Frances Littlepage Baptis⁴ May 21: 1721.

Susanna a white child belonging to a servᵗ of ye said Mrs. Frances Littlepage baptiz⁴ May 21, 1721.

Tom a negro belonging to Mr. Sherw⁴ Lightfoot born Apl. 10, 1721.

Watts & Esther negroes of Mr. Sherwᵈ Lightfoots born Augˢᵗ 1st, 1721.

Grace a negro belonging to Mr. Sherw⁴ Lightfoot born Augˢᵗ 26, 1721.

Squire a negro belonging to Jⁿᵒ Lewis Esq. born May, 1721.

Cate a negro belonging to Ditto born May, 1721.

A mulatto of Mr. Sherw⁴ Lightfoots born 7ᵇʳ 26, 1721.

George a molatto of Mr. Sherw⁴ Lightfoots born Febʳʸ 12, 172½.

Philip Louch son of Wm. Louch born Jan'ʸ 25th, 172½.

Judith Daughter of John & Mary Labamore born Jan. 16th, 172½.

Forrester son of Jⁿᵒ Lucas born July 15th, 1722.

Lucy a malatto Girl of Shwᵈ Lightfoots born Septʳ 30th, 1722.

Frayzer Sonn of Tho. Lightfoot born March 30th, 1723.

Henry sonn of Tho. Lightfoot born March 30th, 1723.

Henry son of John Langford born Sepᵗ 20th, 1722.

John son of John Langford born Feb. 6th, 1723/4.

Susanna a negro girl belonging to Mrs. Fran⁰ Littlepage born
1722.

Mary a negro girl belonging to ye afores⁴ born May 26th, 1724.

James son of Nicho⁸ Lewis born March 9th, 1723/4.

Wm. a negro boy belonging to Mrs. Fran⁰ Littlepage born June
23d, 1724.

George a negro boy belonging to Mr. Sher⁴ Lightfoot born
Dec' 10, 1724

Cuffee a negro boy belonging to Ditto born Jan'ʸ 4th, 1724-5.

Will a negro boy belong. to Sher⁴ Lightfoot born Febry: 1st,
1724-5.

Sam a negro belonging to Ditto born March 6th, 1724-5.

Mary Lines born March 4th, 1724-5.

Mary Daug: of Tho. Lightfoot born may 24, 1725.

Mary a negro girl belonging to Mʳˢ Fran⁰ Littlepage born June,
1724.

Eliz'ʰ a negro belonging to Mad'ᵐ Littlepage bapt⁸ᵈ July 25, 1725.

Eliz Daught' of Hen: Lacy born 7ᵇʳ 20th & bap' 10ᵇ 19, 1725:

Dick a negro boy belonging to Hen: Lacy born 7ᵇᵉʳ 25, 1725.

Eliz: Daught' of Jn⁰ Langford born Jany 4, 1725-6.

John son of Walter & Margaret Leigh born Jan'ʸ 16, 1725.

Judith Daugh' of Dorothy Howell a mulatto Serv' to Mr. Sherwood Lightfoot born, 1725.

Jenny a negro of Mr. Sher⁴ Lightfoot born march 19, 1726-7.

Spy a negro belonging to Do. born Aug'ˢᵗ 2d, 1726.

Christian a negro girl belonging to Mrs. Fran⁰ Littlepage born,
1726.

Sarah a negro belonging to Do born, 1727.

Charles a negro of Mr. Sher⁴ Lightfoot born oct' ye 16th, 1727.

Poll a negro belonging to Mr. S. Lightfoot born in Decem'ʳ,
1727.

Ursula ye Daughter of Henry & Angelica Lacy born Sep' 4th
Baptized october ye 29th following, 1727.

Judith Dau' to Mad'ᵐ Littlepages mullatto Sarah born Sept'ʳ 20
Baptized November ye 5th following, 1727.

Jane ye son of Rob' & Jane Lewis was born Jan'ʸ ye 1st bap'
Jany. 13th, 1727-8.

Edward ye son of Jno. & Rebecca Langford born March 6 bapt.
May 11, 1728.

Wm. a negro belonging to Mrs. Fran^e Littlepage bapt. oct: 6,
1728.

Nancy a negro girl belonging to Maj^r Sher^d Lightfoot born August ye 8th, 1729.

Matthew negro belonging to Sher^d Lightfoot born Novr 19th,
1729.

Walter son of Walter & Margaret Leigh bap^t Decr 7, 1729.

Joyce Da^r of John & Mary Lancaster born March 6, 1729-30.

Ruth Daugh^r of Steph: & Phillis Moone born Jan^ry 9, 1713.

Mary Daughter of John Mackquery Born May ye 30th, 1716.

Cate a negro girl belonging to Mr. Jno. Meux born July, 1716.

Taylor a negro boy belonging to Capt James Moss born october
ye 8th, 1716.

Susanna Daughter of Tho. Martin Baptized Jan^r ye 6, 1716.

Phili^a Daughter of Sarah a negro belonging to Mr. Wm. Macon
born 8^br 29th 1714.

Jeny Daughter of Mall a neg: belonging to ye s^d Macon Born
April 26, 1715.

Anne Daughter of Moll a negro belonging to ye s^d Macon Born
July 1st, 1717.

Mary Daughter of Peter Moon Baptised 8^br ye 11th, 1717.

Jacob son of Stephen Moon Born 8^br ye 3d, 1717.

Thomas son of Mr. Thomas Massie Born August the 2d, 1716.

——— son of Cha. Massie Born ye 17th of Decem^r, 1710.

Betty a negro girl of Mr. Jno Meux Born ye 19th of April, 1718.

Tabitha Daughter of Wm. Morriss Born ye 2d of May, 1718.

Elizabeth Daughter of Wm. Meanlly Born March ye 2d, 1717.

Wm. son of Mr. Thomas Massie Born May the 28th, 1718.

Thomas son of Stephen Mitchell Born July ye 2d, 1718.

Thomas son of Mr. Thomas Massie Born August ye 2d, 1716.

Peter son of Charles Massie Born August ye 29th, 1718.

Robin a negro boy of Cha. Massies Born ye 4th day of May,
1718.

John son of Edward Moore by Frances his wife Born Aug^st 7th,
1718.

Tom a negro boy belonging to Edwd Moore Born July 9, 1718.

Susanna Daughter of Edwd Morgan Born March ye 8, 1718.

Mingo a negro boy belonging to Mr. John Meux Born X^{br} ye 31, 1718.

a negro girl belonging to James Mosse Gent. Born May ye 12, 1719.

David a negro belonging to Mr. Jn° Meux Born July the 14th, 1719.

William son of John Maddox Born January 11, 1719.

Thomas son of Meirtin Martyn born June 4, 1720.

William son of Stephen Moon born april 21, 1720.

James son of Wm. Martyn was born July 24, 1720.

Mary Daughter of Mr. Tho. Massie was born January 1719–20.

William son of Wm. Merriwether born Sepr 13, 1720.

William son of Tho. Martyn born April 14, 1721.

Isaac son of Richd Meanley baptiz^d april 27, 1721.

Jn° son of Edward Morgan born March 24, 1721.

James son of William Moss born July 15, 1721.

Jenny a negro of Capt Moss born August 1, 1721.

Phillis a negro belonging to Pelham More Junr born July 3, 1721.

Mary Daughter of Capt James Moss born August, 1721.

John son of Capt Tho. Massie born octo^r 3d, 1721.

David son of Cha. Massie born Sepr 3, 1721.

Lewis a negro of Mr. Jn° Meuxes born June 1st, 1721.

Sarah May Daughter of Elizabeth May born Sep^t 2nd, 1721.

Martha Daughter of Wm. Macon Gent. Born Augst 12th, 1722.

Doll a negro belonging to Do. born August 21st, 1722.

Kate a negro girl belonging to Capt Massie born May 10th, 1722.

Beck a negro girl belonging to Capt Macon born Septr 9th, 1722.

Hannah Daughter of Jn° Meanly Born Jany ye 18th, 172⅔.

Jane Daughter of Stephen & Phillis Moone born oct^r 21st, 1722.

Rachel a negro girl belong to Capt Macon born Novem^r 5th, 1722.

William sonn of William May born May 9th, 1723.

John sonn of William Meanly born March 17th, 1723.

Eliz. Daughter of James Moore born apr^l 3rd, 1723.

Jane Daughter of William Martin born March 23rd, 172⅔.

Amy Daughter of Edwd Morgan born Augst ye 17th, 1723.

Ned a negro boy belonging to Jno Mux born augst 20th, 1723.

Susanah Daughter of Thomas Martin born Sepr ye 12th, 1723.

John ye son of Wm. Moss born Novem^{br} ye 18th, 1723.

Jane ye Daughter of Richd Meanly born Novem^r 28th, 1723.

Anne Daughter of Wm. Macon Gent. born oct^r 21st, 1720.

Mary Daughter of Aforesaid born 9th day of March, 1723.

Mary Daughter of Cha. Massie born Decr 3d, 1723.

Lucy Daughter of Thos. Macon a negro belong to Mad^m Little-
    page born Feb. 13, 172¾.

Jno son of George Marchbanks born 16th March, 172¾.

Leayon son of Steph: Mitchell born May 30th, 1724.

Catherine Daughter of Pelham Moore Junr born July 2d, 1724.

Anne Daught^r of Alex: Moss born 7^{br} ye 30th, 1724.

Unity ye Daughter of Thos: Martin born Decem^r 26th, 1724.

David son of Wm. McCommick born Febry: 3d, 1724-5.

Mary Daugh^r of Wm. May born Febry: 17th, 1724-5.

Wm. son of Richd Martin born April 24th, 1725.

Fanny a negro belonging to James Moss born in May, 1725.

Susannah Daugh: of Wm. Morriss born July ye 9, 1725.

Archelaus ye son of Thos: Mitchell Junr born July 27, 1725.

Judith a negro belonging to Cha: Massie born 7^{br} ye 3d, 1725.

James son of Cha: Massie born octo^b 16th, 1725.

Susannah Daugh^r of John Meanly born Augst 30th, 1725.

George son of Geo: Marchbanks born Sept. 28th, 1725.

Judith ye Daugh^r of Stephen Moone born Augst 7th, 1725.

Jno ye son of Mr. Jas. Netherland born octob^r ye 4th, 1726.

Cate a negro belonging to Do. born Augst 22d, 1726.

Fanny a negro belonging to Do. born Decem^{br} 10th, 1728.

William son of James Nance Jany: 20, 1726-7.

Dorothy a negro belonging to James Nance bapt. July 20th,
    1729.

Wm. ye son of Wm. & Sus^n North born 15th of July bapt.
    Augst 16th, 1730.

Benj^a son of John & Sarah Netherland born 7^{br} 11th bapt. 7^{br}
    28th, 1730.

Martha Daughter of Grezel Maccomick bap^d 10^{br} 19th, 1725.

Jno son of Jno & Marg^t Martin born Novemb^r 24th & bap^d Jany:
    30th, 1725.

Batt a negro boy belonging to David McGill born Novem^r 9, 1725.

Peter a negro boy of Capt Wm. Marston born Novem^r 17, 1725.

Mars a negro boy of Pelham Moore born Febry: 13, 1725.

Abselom son of Richd Meanly born Novem^r 10th, 1725.

Wm. son of Wm. Martin & Sarah his wife Jany: 1st and bap^d Feby: 20th following, 1725.

Michael ye son of Stephen Mitchell was born March 17th And was bap^d April ye 17th, 1726.

Fran^e ye Daugh^r of Robt Morgan born July 2d, 1726.

Sarah the Daughter of Wm. Moss born Sep^t 5th, 1726.

Sarah ye Daug^r of Wm. Meanly born July 28th, 1726.

Lucy ye Daugh^r of Martin Martin born Augst 20th, 1726.

Edward ye son of Edward Morgan born Octo^{br} 1st 1726.

Nicholas ye son of Wm. Morris born Novem^{br} ye 5th, 1726.

David ye son of Robt Martin born March ye 24th 1726–7.

John ye son of James Moore born June ye 14th, 1727.

Jack a negro boy of Charles Morris born April ye 10th, 1727.

Wm. ye son of Mr. Wm. Macon & Mary his wife born Jany: 4th 1725.

Robbin a negro belonging to James Moss born in May, 1727.

Nathanael ye son of Charles Massie born Augst ye 2d, 1727.

James ye son of James Moore was born ye 13th of Nov', 1718.

Mary ye Daughter of James Moore born Febry: 1st, 1721.

Rebecca ye Daughter of James Moore born Augst ye 13th, 1725.

Henry ye son of Wm. Macon Gent. & Mary his wife born 7^{br} 1st, 1727.

Susannah ye Daugh^r of Pelham & Sarah Moore born 7^{br} 13th, 1727.

Mary ye Daugh^r of Wm. McCormick born oct. ye 18th, 1727.

Nanny a negro belonging to Tho. Mitchel born 7^{br} 25th, 1727.

Peter a negro of Ed. Morgan born Augst ye 4th, 1727.

Mary ye Da^r of Marmaduke & Hannah Moore born Sept. 19th bap^t oct. 29th, 1727.

Judith ye Da^r of Wm. & Tabitha Morris born oct. 16th, bap^t Novr 12th, 1727.

Susanna Da^r of Rich^d & Frances Martin born oct^r 17th & bap^t Nov. 19th, 1727.

Wm. son of Thos. Marston born Novem^r ye 7th & bapt^{sd} Novem^{br} 22d, 1727.

Anne ye Da^r of Tho: & Eliz^{bh} Mitchell born Jany ye 3d, bap^t March ye 3d, 1727–8.

Jenny & Venus negros belonging to Capt Tho: Massie born March ye 1st, 1727–8.

Elizth D^r of Tho. Martin born March ye 14th, 1727–8.

Stephen ye son of Steph: Mitchell born April 24th & bap^t May ye 4th, 1728.

Phebe a negro girl belonging to Wm. Marston born April ye 13th, 1728.

———— negro belonging to Richd Meux born June ye 11th, 1728.

Martha Daughter of Jno. Otey born July ye 23rd, 1717.

William son of John Otey born March 18: 1719.

Sarah Oslin Daughter of Sam^{el} Oslin born Feb^{ry} 20th, 172½,

Saml son of Sam^{ll} Ossling born June ye 17th, 1724.

Doel a negro girl belonging to Mr. Jno. Otey born 17 Mch., and bap^t July ye 22d following 1726–7.

David son of Saml Ossling born Sepr 7th, 1726.

Jesse ye son of Saml & Mary Ossling born March 31st bap^t Apl. 27, 1729.

Susan^h ye Da^r of Owen & Catherine Ohern born March 2d, 1729–30.

Lucy a negro belonging to Thomas Mosse Junr born Decem^r 19th, 1730.

Richard ye son of Arnal & Rebecca Man born Jan^{ry} 25 bap^t May 12, 1728.

Betty a negro belonging to Capt Thos Massie born Augst 15, 1728.

Lucy a negro belonging to Charles Massie born June 28th, 1728.

John ye son of John Meanly born July 6th bap^t July ye 30th, 1728.

Patty a negro girl belonging to David Mackgill born Augst 5, 1728.

Charles of Gresel Macomick born Octob^r bap^t No^r 24th, 1728.

Hannah Daugh^r of Edwd & Hannah Morgan born No. 9th, 1728 bap. Apl. 27, 1729.

Eliz^a Daughter of Wm. & Ann Morris born Apl. 8 bapt. May 11th, 1729.

Dick a negro belonging to Marmaduke Moore born Ap^l 11th, 1729.

Jude a negro boy belonging to Thos Moss Junr born July 25th, 1729.

Eliz^a Da^r of Robt & Eliz^a Morgan born Augst 12 bap^t 7bor. 21, 1729.

Wm. son of Saml & Bathia Mosse born 7bor. 19th bap^t Novr 2d, 1729.

Cesar a negro belonging to Thos Mitchel born October 15, 1729.

John son of Robt & Mary Moore born Jan^{ry} 23d bap^t M^{ch} 20th, 1729–30.

Anthony son of Pelham & Sarah Moore born Ap^l 3d bap^t May 3d, 1730.

Wm. son of Archelius Mitchel born Apl. 14, bap^t May 31, 1730.

Elizth the Daughter of Stephen & Ann Martin born June 1st & bap^t Aug: 3d, 1730.

Jemmy a negro belonging to William Marston born 15 of June, 1730.

Thomas ye son of Thos & Elizth Mitchel born July 16 bap. Aug^{sr} 30, 1730.

Joyce ye Daughter of Thos Mosse & Susanna his wife born Aug. bap^t 7bor. 6, 1730.

Eliz^a the Daughter of James Mosse baptized June ye 13th, 1730.

Cecilla Daughter of Charles Massie born October ye 3d, 1729–30.

Robert ye son of James & Agnis Moore born Decr. ye 8, 1729.

Isaac ye son of Thomas Middlebrook born Jan^{ry} ye 12th, 1727–8.

Dick a negro belonging to Edwd Morgan born May 11th, 1730.

Betty Daughter of Stephen & Margaret Moore born Jan^{ry} 21, 1729–30.

James a negro belonging to Chas. Moss born 28 Novr. 1730.

Lucy a negro belonging to John Martin born March, 1729–30.

Nanny a negro belonging to Thomas Marston born Augst 1st, 1731.

Joan a negro belonging to Do. born Novem^r ye 1st, 1732.

Cate a negro belonging to Do. born April ye 1st, 1733.

Joel son of Thos. & Mary Mekins, free negroes born Oct' 29,
     1747.

Daniel son of Do. born Aprill 17th, 1749.

Isaac Son of Mary Mekins, a free negroe woman, Aprill 19,
     1754.

Daniel, son of William Moore & Susanna his wife born ye 24
     June, 1739.

Susanna Daughter of Robert Predy Born June ye 23d, 1717.

Sarah Daughter of Wm. Perkin Born June ye 29, 1717.

Obadiah son of David Patison Born February ye 30th, 1717.

Edward son of Edwd Patison Born May ye 5th, 1718.

William son of Wm. Brior Born March ye 30th, 1719.

Julius Ceaser son of Sarah Poindexter Born May ye 31st. 1719.

Elizabeth Daughter of John Philips Born the 19th of August,
     1719.

Robert son of William Peasley was born January 10, 1719.

James son of Alex' Pattison born May 25, 1720.

Gideon son of David Pattison born July 7th, 1720.

Eliz: daughter of Matthew Pond born June 10, 1721.

William son of Jacob Poindexter born July 13, 1721.

Eliz: Daught' of Wm. Paul was born July 12, 1721.

Wm. sonn of Thos. & Eliz: Pinchback born March 8th, 172½.

Jameston son of Alex' Patterson born Oct' 4th, 1722.

William sonn of William Peasley born April 13th, 1722.

Mary Daughter of Thos. & Eliz: Pinchback born April 19th,
     1723.

Jno. ye son of Wm. Pearson born Augst ye 19, 1723.

James ye son of David Patterson born Feb^{ry} ye 10th, 1722–3.

Jacob son of Jacob Poindexter born Sep^t 25th, 1723.

Sue a negro girl belong to Jacob Poindexter born Decr., 1723.

Cuffee a negro boy belonging to Wm. Peasley born March 9,
     1723–4.

Billy a negro boy belong to Geo. Pearson Apl. 30, 1724.

Fran^s Daug' of Wm. Paul born June ye 17th, 1724.

Thomas son of Wm. Peasley born 10th of 7^{ber}, 1724.

Jones & Susannah negros belonging to Mr. Geo: Poindexter was
     baptized Jan^{ry} ye 3d, 1724–5.

Alex' son of Alex' Pattison born Jan^{ry} 30th, 1724–5.

Anne Daugh' of David pattison born March 15, 1724–5.

Hannah Daugh^r of Charles Pearson born 12 Ap^{ll} & bap^t may: 15th following, 1725.

Thos. son of Thos. Pinchback born Jan^{ry} 8th and bap^t 27th of Feb: following. 1725–6.

Henry son of Jacob & Sarah Poindexter born Feb: 16 & bap^t March 27 following, 1725–6.

Wm. Son of Nicholas Pryor born 7ber. 26th & bap^t Ap. 10th, 1725.

Sam a negro of Wm. Peasley born June 25th, 1726.

John son of Wm. Pall born Feb^{ry} ye 17th, 1726–7.

Tom a negro of Jacob Poindexter born May ye 15, 1727.

Geo: ye son of George Pearson born March 23, 1726–7.

Bess a negro of Wm. Peasley born July ye 14th, 1727.

Sam a negro of George Pearson born July ye 10th, 1727.

Negroes belonging to Mr. Geo. Poindexter born :

    Moll born Jan^{ry} ye 9, 1711.

    Tanner born in March, 1713.

    Jones born March 31, 1714.

    Lucy born Jan^{ry} 18, 1715–16.

    Bess born July, 1718.

    Sampson born in May, 1720,

    Sue born in July, 1721.

    Ned born in Augst, 1724.

    Sarah born June ye 28, 1724.

    Tom born Feb^{ry} 14, 1725.

    Isaac born Jan^{ry} ye 14, 1726–7.

    Judith born in Feb^{ry}, 1727–8.

    Jemmy born Christmas day, 1722.

Frank a negro belonging to Jacob Poindexter born March ye 14th, 1727–8.

Susannah ye Da^r of Charles & Hannah Pearson born March ye 20th & bap^t April 28, 1728.

Danl a negro belonging to Martha Pattison born Jan^{ry} 14, 1727–8.

Susan^h Da^r of Wm. & Eliz^a Pattison born July 31, 1725, bap^t May 14, 1728.

Tho' son of Jones & Eliz^a Parish born Jan^{ry} 9th, 1727–8.

Edward son of Ditto born Feb: 25, 1727–8.

John son of John & Agnes Foster born Jan^{ry} 31st bap^t May ye 14, 1728.

———— ye Da^r of David Pattison born ————.

Augustine ye son of Wm. & fran^s Pasley born June ye 9th & bap^t July 7th, 1728.

Jno. & Rebecca negro^s belonging to Jacob Poindexter bap^t 7ber. 29, 1728.

Sarah D^r of Thomas & Eliz^a Pinchback born 7ber. 4th bap^t Octob^r 20, 1728.

Elizth Daugh^r of Stephen & Jane Pepper born July 14th bap^t Augst 14, 1729.

Aggey a negro girl belonging to Jacob Poindexter born March 18, 1729–30.

Sarah Da^r of John & Mary Pearson born March ye 26, 1730.

Edward the son of Eliz^a Parish wch is now the wife of James Sims was born May the 20th, 1730.

Dick a negro belonging to Geo. Poindexter born October, 1729.

Sarah negro belonging to Martha Pattison born Octob^r 15, 1729.

Ann the Daugh^r of Wm. & Mary Pearson born Jan^{ry} ye 17, 1729–30.

Elizth Daughter of Thos & Elizth Pinchback born feb^{ry} 14th bapt Mch. 4, 1730.

Elizabeth Daughter of Anne Patteson, a free mulatto woman born July 29th, 1750.

John son of Thomas & Elizabeth Pinchback born April 28th, 1732–3.

Daniel son of Thos & Catherine Butts born 7ber. 20th, 1729.

Osilla Da^r of Fridkin Barker born April 20th, 1730.

Thos the son of Charles & Judith Bolton born June 14 bap^t Aug. 3d, 1738.

Major a negro belonging to Col^o David Bray born Feb^{ry} 20, 1729–30.

Jemmy a negro boy belonging to Catherine Broadies born Mch. 22d, 1729–30.

Ellenor Daughter of Jno. & Eliz^a Bassett born Decr ye 7th, 1729.

James ye son of Jos. Baughon born August ye 11th, 1729.

Paul a negro belonging to Col° Wm. Bassett born in Septem^r, 1729.

Lucy a negro girl belonging to Do. born April ye 4th, 1730.

Joe a negro boy belonging to Do. born May ye 10th, 1730.

Anthony a negro boy belonging to Do. born October ye 12th, 1730.

Joe a negro belonging to Coll° David Bray born March ye 3d, 1730–1.

Susanna Daugh: of John & Susanna Bacon born Jan^ry 6th, 1730–1.

Mary ye Daughter of John & Susanna Briant born Decr 11th, 1730.

Mary ye Daughter of Robt & Sarah Browning born March 6 and baptized April the 11th following, 1730–1.

Martin son of Jno. Realy Junr born Jany ye 30th 1716.

Mary Daughter of Robt Richardson by Jane his wife July 29th, 1716.

——— son of James Raymond 8^ber ye 2d, 1717.

Wm. son of Richd Ross born June 3d, 1717.

Sherwood son of Wm. Reynolds born Jany: 11th, 1716.

Thomas son of Jn° Reynolds born ye 21st of September, 1717.

Frances Daughter of Jn° Ross born 7^ber ye 28, 1718.

Agnes Daughter of Charles Toney Born ——— Bap^t June 1st, 1718.

Elizabeth Daughter of Thomas Ragland Born March 28, 1718.

Robert son of Robt Richardson Born ye 23d of July, 1719.

William son of Wm. Reynolds born Aug^st 23, 1719.

Mary Daughter of Henry Richardson was born June 22, 1720.

June Daughter of Rob: Richardson born May 30, 1721.

Theodocia Daughter of Jn° Ross born March 15, 1721.

——— son of Richd Ross was born Aug^st 4, 1721.

Ruth Daughter of Henry & Ruth Richardson born April 17th, 1722.

Susanna Daughter of James & Unity Raymond born Aug^st 10th, 1722.

John son of Thos: & Elizabeth Roper Born Novem^r 10th, 1722.

Angelica Daughter of Robt Richardson born Ap^l 30th, 1723.

Cuffee a negro belong. to James Roberts Born Apr^l 16th, 1723.

Gideon son of Eben Ragland Born March 26th, 1723.

Frances Daughter of James Roberts born oct^r ye 5th, 1723.

David son of Jno Ross born Novr 12th, 1723.

Thos. son of Skip. Richardson born June 25, 1724.

Henry son of Henry Rich^{d}son born Jany 30th, 1724–5.

Temperance Daugh^r of Jno Ross & Ann was born Novr 2d, 1716.

Nanny a negro girl of James Roberts born 16 March, 1724–5.

Elizth Daugh^r of Cha: & Elizth Richardson born Decr 20, 1711.

Hannah Daugh^r of Do. born Jan^{ry} 12th, 1717–8.

Henry son of Do. born April 2d, 1720.

Lucy Daugh^r of Do. born March 5th, 1721.

Martha Daugh^r of Thos: & Eliz: Roper born 7^{ber} 4th, 1725.

Isaac ye son of Richd Ross born March 9, 1723–4.

Anne Daugh^r of Robert & Susana Rogers born Augst 6th & bap^{tsd} octo^{br} 27th, 1725.

Susannah Daugh^r of Ship: Richardson born 7^{ber} 28, 1725.

Judith a negro of Robt Rogers born Jany. 6th, 1724–5.

Green ye son of Robt & Jane Richardson born Febry: 12th, 1725–6.

Plant ye son of Charles & Elizth Richardson born March 9th bap^t May 28, 1728.

Hector a negro belonging to Mr. Robt Rogers born May 12th, 1726.

David ye son of Jno Ross July ye 12th, 1726.

Betty a negro belonging to James Roberts born Ap^l 30, 1727.

Sarah Daughter of Robt & Jane Richardson born Novem^r 8, 1727.

David son of Jno & Mary Roper born Jan^{ry} ye 8th & bap^t 24th March, 1727–8.

Elizth ye Da^r of Thos: & Elizth Roper born Febry. 21st Bap^{ts} March 24, 1727–8.

Anne ye Da^r of Rich^d & Alice Ross born March ye 9th & bapt. May ye 5th, 1728.

Sall a negro belonging to Lancaster Roughley born April 13th, 1728.

David ye son of Robt & Sus^a Rogers born March ye 1st bapt^d March 3d, 1727–8.

James son of James & Marg^t Roberts born 7^{ber} 18th bap^t octo^b 20, 1728.

John son of Skip & Marg^t Richardson born octo^b 21st bap^t Nov. 10, 1728.

Dudley son of Wm. & Dorcas Rountree born Jany 4 bap. March 2d, 1728–9.

Johny a negro boy belonging to James Roberts born octo^r 7, 1729.

Mary D^r of Thomas & Elizth Roper born March ye 12th, 1729–30.

David son of John Raynolds born Octo^r, 1728.

Nanny a negro belonging to Lancaster Roughley born Augt 12, 1730.

Hannah ye Daughter of Robt & Jane Richardson born Decr 23, 1729.

Elizabeth Daughter of James Landers by Sarah his wife Born July ye 6th, 1716.

Owin son of Thomas Strang Born 23d of January, 1716.

Betty a negro girl of Sam^{ll} Smith Born 7^{ber} 24th, 1716.

Martha Daughter of Jno Scott Gent. Born ye 28th April, 1716.

Martha Daughter of Richd Scruggs Junr Born April 4th, 1718.

Frances Daughter of Jno Landers Born May ye 1st, 1718.

Jesse son of Jno Scott Born May ye ——, 1718.

Susan a negro girl belonging to Mr. Tho. Sharp Born ye 3d of September, 1718.

Austin son of John Spear Born ye 17th of 7^{ber}, 1718.

Joseph & Benjamin sons of Alex^r Strange Ju. Born ye 14th day of March, 1716.

Francis Daughter of Alex^r Strange Ju^r Born ye 11th day of November, 1618.

Thomas son of Thomas Strange Born ye 24th of August, 1719.

Rich^d son of Richd Scrugs & Martha his wife Born Jany. 10, 1720.

Henry son of Jno Speere Born March 4. 1720–1.

Judith Daughter of Robt Speere Junr born March 31, 1721.

Eliz Daughter of James Smith born May, 1721.

Henry sonn of Henry Scruggs born June 11th, 1722.

George a negro boy belonging to Mad^m Sharp Born Feby 16th, 1722.

Tamar a negro girl belonging to Mad^m Sharp Born Novr 26th, 1722.

John sonn of Robt Spear born Febry: 17th, 1722–3.

James son of Henry Scrugg born March 13th, 1723–4.

Frances Daugh[r] of Rob[t] Speare by Mary born M[ch] 3d, 1724–5.

Baudy a negro girl belonging to Wm. Sims 15th, 1724.

Wm. son of Sam[n] Smith born Nov[r] 27th, 1719.

Eliz[th] Daughter of Hen: Strange born 14 May, 1725.

Eliz Daughter of James Sims was born July ye 28th, 1725.

Drury Scruggs son of Rich[d] Scruggs born Feb[ry] 1, 1725.

Pompey a negro belonging to Sam[l] Bugg born Aug[st] 27th, 1726.

Mitchel son Henry Strange born Aug[st] 11, 1726.

Sam[l] son of Henry Scruggs born Sep[t] 23, 1726.

Sarah D[r] of Rob[t] Sims born Sep[t] 20th, 1726.

Charles son of Nath[l] Smith born oct[r] 3d, 1726.

Azess a negro boy of Fran[s] Sims born May ye 30th, 1727.

Will a negro of James Sims born June 30th, 1727.

Sarah ye Daughter of Michael Sherman born May ye 3d, 1727.

Jack a negro belonging to Michael Sherman born October ye 7, 1727.

Fran[s] Da[r] Jno. & Judith Sanders born April 10th bapt. May ye 12, 1727.

James & Jane son & Da[r] of Henry & Mary Strange born March ye 17th, 1727–8.

Milly ye Daugh[r] of Wm. & Eliz[th] Sledd born May ye 21st bapt. June ye 3d, 1728.

Will a negro boy belonging to Sarah Sanders born July ye 16th, 1728.

Napier a negro belonging to James Sims bapt. July 20th, 1729.

Sarah a negro belonging to Frances Sims bapt. July 20th, 1729.

Eliz[h], Jane, Rich[d] & Judith Negroes belonging to Henry Soane was Baptized Aug[st] the 31st, 1729.

Thomas the son of Rich[d] & Martha Scrugg born July 30 Baptized 7ber. 14th, 1729.

Fran[s] Da[r] of Nat[l] & Susan[h] Smith bor 7ber. 18 bap[t] Oct[r] 5th, 1729.

Eliz[h] Da[r] of Henry & Eliz[h] Scrugg born Septemb[r], 1729.

Sarah a Negro Girl belonging to James Sims born Dec[r] 8, 1729.

Edmond son of Henry Strange born Jan^ry 9th bap^t Feb. 22, 1729–30.

Agnes Da^r of Henry & Mary Scrugg born Feb^ry 25 Bap^t Easter, 1729–30.

John the son of Leman & Mary Leshange born July 31st and died October ye 8th Followinge, 1730.

Eliz^a the Daughter of John & Judith Sanders born 15 Aug^st bap^t 7ber. 27, 1730.

Sarah ye Daughter of Hannah Scrugg born May ye 27, 1729.

John the son of Author & Rachel Slayden born feb. 22d bap^t Mch. 4, 1730–1.

Susanna Daughter of Wm. Thompson by Hannah his wife Baptized July ye 1st, 1716.

Sarah Daughter of Elex^r Tony Born 7ber ye 17th, 1716.

Wm. son of Michael Tucker Born 7ber ye 17th, 1716.

Frances Daughter of James Taylor by Eliz: his wife Born Jan^ry 26th, 1716.

George son of Wm. Thompson Born March ye 13th, 1717.

Agnes Daughter of Chas Toney Born ye 9th of 9br, 1717.

Robert son of Edwd Toney by Eliz: his wife Born May 15th, 1719.

Susanna Daughter of James Taylor Born November ye 8th, 1719.

Honnour Daughter of Chas Toney was born Jany 8, 1719.

Tamer a negro of Sarah Turner born Jany 10: 1720–21.

Edmund son of Edm^d Jones was born Februrary: 8: 1720–21.

Susanna daughter of Jno. Turner born June 17th, 1721.

Tho: son of Michael Tucker born April 1, 1721.

Simson son of Mich^el Tucker born July ye 9th, 1723.

Lucy Little the Daughter of Mary Taylor born No^r 17th, 1723.

James son of Jno. Taylor born Decem^r ye 10th, 1724.

Timothy son of Edm^d Toney born April 1st, 1725.

Charles son of Jno. & Eliz^th Turner born May 26th & bapt. June ye 27th following, 1725.

Drury ye son of Michael Tucker born 7^ber 11th, 1726.

Jane ye Da^r of Jno. & Eliz^th Turner born 7^ber ye 16th & bap^t Octr 29, 1727.

Eliz^a ye Da^r of Edmund & Eliz^a Toney born Aug^st 4 bap^t No^r · ye 5th, 1727.

Sarah Daughter of Wm. & Mary Thomas born No^r 3d bap. 24th, 1728.

Sarah Daughter of Jno. & Mary Thomson born March 18th bap. Apl. 20, 1729.

Sampson a negro boy belonging to Caleb Turner born Apl. 2d, 1729.

Frank a negro boy belonging to Do. born October 1st, 1729.

Martha Da^r of Wm. & Mary Thomas bap^t Jan^ry 11th, 1729-30.

Mary Da^r of Wm. & Dorothy Turner born May 1st, 1730.

Susanna ye Daughter of Edmond & Eliz Toney born May ye ——, ——.

Martha Daughter of Wm. & Mary T—— ——, ——.

Deverex ye son of John & Eliz^a Turner ——, ——.

James son of Wm. Noughan born Feb: 5th, 1722-3.

Frances a mulatto Girl slave belonging to Wm. Boughon was born 25th of August, 1721.

Wm. a negro boy belonging to Do. born May 5th, 1724.

Jno. son of Robt Vaiden was born Octr 20th 1725.

Hannah Daugh^r of Wm. Noaghon born 25 7^{br}, 1725.

George a negro boy belonging to Ditto born Jan^ry 4, 1725-6.

Liddia a negro girl belonging to Wm. Vaiden born May ye 10th, 1727.

Isaac ye son of Isaac & Eliz^a Vaiden Jan^ry 24 bap^t March ye 2d, 1727-8.

Janney a negro belonging Isaac Vaiden born July ye 16th, 1728.

Anna Daught^r of Daniel & Mary Neere was born July 13 bap. Augst 11, 1728.

Cate a negro girl belonging to Wm. Vaiden born Octob^r 3d, 1728.

Agness Daught^r of Robt & Eliz^a Vaiden Octob^r 8th bap^t no: 17, 1728.

Wm. Shiels son Wm. & Eliz^a Naughan born Jan^ry 30th, 1729-30.

Mary the D^r of Wm. & Susanna Vaiden born July 3d bap^t July 31, 1730.

Betty negro girl belonging to Wm. Vaiden born Jan^ry 19th, 1729-30.

Angelica ye Daughter of Henry & Angelica Lacy born feb: 28, 1729-30.

Philip a negro boy belonging to Madam Littlepage born Feb. 15, 1729–30.

Arlott a negro girl belonging to Do. born June ye 1st, 1730.

Natt a negro belonging to Eliz[th] Lightfoot born Febry. ye 6th, 1730–1.

William son of Thomas Weaver Born August ye 20th, 1716.

John son of Geo. Wilkinson Born 8[ber] ye 22d, 1716.

Judith a negro girl of Cha: Winfrys Born ye 16th of March, 1716.

William son of Wm. Walker Born ye 15 of December, 1716.

Mary Daughter of Lewis Watkins Born April ye 2d, 1717.

Sam[a] negro boy of Lott Walker's Born ye 11th of 7[ber] 1717.

Thomas son of Benj[a] Wicker Born ye 11th of August, 1717.

Anne Daughter of Philip Webber born X[br] 15th, 1715.

John son of Wm. Williams Baptized February ye 16, 1717.

Tabitha Daughter of —— ——.

Sarah Daughter of Wm. Waddill Jun[r] Born 7[br] ye 13, 1718.

Selvannus son of Selv. Walker born ye 11th of Dec[r], 1718.

Joseph son of Jamy. Weaver born ye 22d of X[ber] 1718.

George son of Geo: Wilkinson Born Jan[ry] ye 27, 1718.

Sarah Daughter of Geo. Walton Born March ye 8th, 1718.

Thomas son of Thomas Weaver Born on May ye 15th, 1719.

Benj[a] son of Benj[a] Whickor Born July ye 13th, 1719.

Owen son of Mary Winkfield Born ye 23d day of September, 1719.

Able Wood Died 8br. ye 25th, 1719.

Jno. son of Charles Waddil born Decem[r] 5, 1719.

Charles son of James Waddil was born July 18, 1720.

Wm. son of Wm. Waddil Jun[r] was born Aug[st] 2d, 1720.

Jenny a negro belonging to Cha[s] Winfrey born Jan[ry]: 12: 1720–21.

Izzard son of George Wilkinson baptiz[d] March 29: 1721.

A negro of Geo: Wilkinsons born July 22d, 1721.

Anne daughter of Tho: Weaver born July 20: 1721.

James Whicker son of Benjamin Whicker born Sept[r] 21st, 1731.

Alice Walton Daughter of John Walton born Nov[r] 11th, 1721.

Jacob son of George & Sarah Walton born March 22d, 172½.

John sonn of John Waddill Born Nov[r] 20th, 1722.

Frank a negro Boy belonging to Charles Winfrey born Ap^ll 15th, 1722.

Eliz^th Daugh^r of Charles Winfree born April 3d, 1723.

A Negroe boy belong: to Hannah Waddill born Ap^ll 1st, 1723.

Eliz: Daughter of William Waddill Junr was born Jan^ry 4th, 172⅔.

Sarah Daughter of Jno. Williams born Aug^st 1st, 1723.

Billey a neg^r boy belong. to Joseph Waddill born 7br. 10th, 1723.

Anne Daughter of George Wilkinson born Novr 14th, 1723.

Susannah Daugh^r of Cha: Winfree born Aug^st 14th, 1724.

Anne Daugh^r of David Wilkinson born Aug^st 6th, 1724.

Agnes Daugh^r of Lewis Watkins born June 7, 1724.

Robt son of Robt & Fran^s Walton born Jan^ry 7th, 1717–18.

Rebecca Daugh^r of Do. born April 20th, 1720.

Joseph son of Do. born April 20th. 172½.

George son of Do. born feb^ry 6th, 1724–5.

Agnes Daugh^r of Jno. Waddill born feb: 1st & bapt: March 21st, 1724–5.

Moll a negro girl belong to Charles Winfree born M^ch 25, 1725.

Eliz^th Daugh. of Thos: Weaver born 24 of March, 1724–5.

Rich^d son of Wm. Waddill Junr born March 29, 1725.

Anne Daugh^r of Jno. Winfree born July ye 7th & Dyed Oct. 4, 1725.

Jno. son of Antho: Waddy born Octob^r 28th, 1725.

Wm. son of Geo. Wilkinson born 9^br 17th, 1725.

Anne Daugh^r of Cha: & Jane Winfree born Decr 9, 1725.

Fran^s ye Daughter of Robt & Fran^s Walton born 14th Jan^y, 1726–7.

Easter a negro girl of Anthony Waddy born June 25th, 1726.

Dick a negro of Do. —— born Aug^st ye 5th, 1726.

Peter ye son of Jno Winfree born July 28th, 1726.

Julius son of Robt Willis born June ye 8th, 1726.

Anne ye Daught^r of Eliz^th Williamson born March 17th, 1725–6.

Mary ye Daugh^r of Henry Wyatt born Sept. 20th, 1726.

Jno. son of Jno. Weaver born Decemb^r 6th, 1726.

Mary ye Daugh^r of Alex^r Watson born Ap^l 3d, 1726.

Anniss ye Daugh^r of Jno Williams born Febr^y 9th, 1726.

George son of George Walton born 19th May, 1726.

George a negro boy of Hannah Waddill born May ye 24th, 1726.

Jenney a negro of George Wilkinson Dyed April ye 10th, 1726.

Charles son of Charles Winfree born Ap¹ 29th, 1727.

Dennis son of Jn° Waddill born May ye 11th, 1727.

Martha Dʳ of Franˢ Williams born May ye 9th, 1727.

Harry a negro of Joe Whitlock born June 20th, 1729.

Elizᵗʰ Daughʳ of Robᵗ Whitchurch born Febʳʸ 2d, 1726–7.

Bowler ye son of Robᵗ & Elizᵃ Willis born Sept. 2d & bapt. Novembʳ ye 9th, 1727.

Rebecca ye Daʳ of Francis & Mary Wilkinson born January ye 16th bapt. February 14, 1727.

Judith Daʳ of Thos. & Judith Weaver born October 14 & bapt. November 26, 1727.

Thos. ye son of George & Margaret Wilkinson born January ye 2d, 1727–8.

Joe a negro belonging to Cha: Winfree born June ye 24th, 1728.

Caffee a negro belonging to Anthᵃ Waddy born 7ᵇᵉʳ ye 7, 1728.

Alexʳ ye son of Alexʳ & Foster Watson born July ye 11 bapt. Augᵗ 11, 1728.

Billy a mullatto belonging to Geoʳ Webb born July ye 25, 1728.

Sherwood son of Robᵗ & Franˢ Walton born July ye 10 bapᵗ Augˢᵗ 11, 1728.

Elizᵃ of David & Elizᵃ Wilkinson born Octʳ 28, 1718.

James son of James Whaley born July ye 19 bapᵗ Augˢᵗ 11th, 1728.

Samˡ ye son of John & Jane Weaver born July 20th bapᵗ Oct. 6th, 1728.

Jn° son of Jno. & Franˢ Winfree born Augⁿ 17th bapᵗ Augˢᵗ 25th 1728.

Mary and Joseph Negros belonging to Cha Winfree bapᵗ 7ber 1, 1728.

Mars & Jane negros belonging Joˢ Weddill bapᵗ 7 ber 29th 1729.

Martha Daʳ of Wᵐ & Sarah Waddill born Feb. 28th bapᵗ Apl. 6 1729.

Judith, Peter & Judith Ware born Decʳ 4th bapᵗ March 8, 1728-9.

Mary the Daughʳ of Robert & Sarah Whitchurch born May 31, 1729.

Frances daugh^r of Anthony Waddy born June 19th bap^t July 27th, 1729.

Dick a negro belonging to Geo. Wilkinson born July 22, 1729.

George son of Geo. & Lucy Webb born July 4 bapt. July 10th, 1729.

Rebecca a negro of Geo. Webb Baptized November 16th, 1729.

Patt a Negro belonging to Wm. Weddill born Novr 17th, 1729.

Rebecca Da^r of Stephen & Susan^h Willis born Octob^r 10 Baptized Decr ye 14, 1729.

Mary Da^r of John & Mary Waddill born No^r 27, Bapt. January ye 4 following, 1729.

Richard son of Charles & Jane Winfree born Septem^r 29, 1729.

Mary Daughter of Do. born Feb^ry 19th, 1729–30.

Mary D^r of Geo. & Margaret Wilkinson born March 3d, 1729–30.

Keen, Merriday, Lucy, Rebecca, Thomas, Negros belonging to Mr. Lancelott Woodward bap^t June 21: 1730.

John son of Fran^s & Mary Wilkinson born Apl. 19th, 1730.

Wm. ye son of Alex^a & Hester Watson born June ye 30 bap^t Augst 3d, 1730.

Jeremiah ye son of Eliz^a Word born June 13th bap^t July 19th, 1730.

Noel son Wm. Waddill Junr born Augst 17th bap^t 7ber. 27,

David a negro belonging to John Whitlock born March ye 4th, 1729–30.

Lewis ye son of George & Lucy Webb born April 19th, 1731.

Squire a negro belonging to ye sd. Webb born May ye 11th, 1731.

Ursula Daughter of Fran^s & Martha Williams born 25th Dec^r, 1729.

Toney a negro belonging to Jno. Waddill born Feb: 28, 1729–30.

Sarah ye Daughter of Lewis Watkins born Feb^ry 12, 1730–31.

Nap ———.

Elizabeth ———.

John son ———.

Devereux ———.
Sarah Daugh. ———.
Sue negro ———.
Jesse son of ———.
Pridgin Son of ———.
Thomas Connor ———.
Mary Mitchell dy ———.
Frances wife of John ———.
John son of Francis and ———.
William son of William and ———.
Ann Daughter of David and ———.
Richard son of Walter and Mary ———.
Mary wife of George Poindexter ———.
James Mosse dyed ———.
Abraham Johnson dyed ———.
William son of Nicholas and Frances Lewis ———.
Isaac son of Samuel and Mary Osling born Decem^r ———.
Francis Daughter of William and Susanna Moore Decem^r 17,
    baptized January 20, ———.
Sarah Daughter ot John and Frances New born Octob^r 19, bap-
    tized January 20, ———.
Parke and Jimmy two negro's belon. to Colo. Custis Dyed
    ———.
Frances Daughter of George and Lucy Taylor born Decem^r 18,
    baptized Janury. 20, ———.
Sarah Atkinson dyed ——— Jan'y, ———.
Ann Daughter of Thomas & Mary Truett born Decem^r 24, bap-
    tized Febry. 3, ———.
Elizabeth Daughter of Thomas and Ann Addison dyed —
    Febr'y, ———.
John son of John Bacon Junr & Ann Bacon born Novem^r 20,
    ———.
Susanna Daughter of Caleb and Elizabeth Turner born Janry.
    16. ———.
Elkanah Son of Joseph and Ann Baughan born Septem^b 17, ———.
Edmund Son of William and Elizabeth Forbis born Febry. 15,
    baptized March 10, ———.
William Son of John and Mary Hockaday born Febry. 10, bap-
    tized March 10, ———.

Susanna Daughter of George & Margaret Wilkinson born Febry. 12, baptized March 10, ——.

John Hockaday dyed ——.

Frances Negro of Benskin Marstons baptized Octo. 23, ——.

Temperance Negro belonging to John Lightfoot baptized Octo. 23, ——.

Parke a Negro belonging to Colo. Custis born Novem^r 1, ——.

T—— Daughter of Fidkin and Elizabeth Barker born Octob^r 1, ——.

T—— Negro belonging to Alexander Moss born A. D. Novem^r 5, ——.

Judith Negro belonging to George Poindexter baptized Novem^r 5, ——.

Testis: DAVID MOSSOM, Min^r.

YEAR 1734.

Fanney Negro belonging to William Atkinson born May 24.

Pompey Negro belonging to Richard Crump born May 22.

Martha Daughter of Henry and Ann Talman born March 16, baptized June 16, 1733.

Isaac Bastard son of Anne Bowles born April 9, baptized June 16.

Archelaus Son of John and Margaret Meanly born May 10, baptized June 16.

Elizabeth Daughter of Andrew and Amadca Mantiply born Feby. 15, baptized June 16.

Margaret Daughter of Robert and Elizabeth Allen born April 22, baptized June 16.

Frances Daughter —— and Hannah Turner born May 6, baptized June 16.

Mary Daughter of David and Agatha Dodd born May 4, baptized June 16.

Dilsey negro girl belonging to Col. Thomas Bray born April 30.

Moll negro girl belonging to Col. Thomas Bray born May 26.

Daniel Negro belonging to Benskin Marston born June 12.

Lucy Negro belonging to James Nance born June 14.

Ann Daughter of George Wilkinson dyed June 2.

Lucy negro belonging to Colo. John Custis born June 15.

Doll negro belonging to Robert Jarratt born July 4.

Archelaus Son of John and Ann Carless born May 24, baptized July 7.

Susanna Daughter of Archelaus and Ann Mitchell born May 16, baptized July 7.

John son of John and Susanna Roberts born June 2, baptized July 7.

Josias son of Joseph & Cassandra Crump born June 24, baptized July 21.

Robert son of Arthur and Mary Crew born May 28, baptized July 21.

Joseph Shoners Son of Joseph and Ann Price baptized July 21.

Ruth Daughter of Thomas and Ann Addison born June 6, baptized July 21.

Elizabeth Daughter of Robert and Mary Bailey born June 21, baptized July 21.

Venus Negro girl belonging to Mr. Daniel Farell born May 11.

Frank negro belonging to George Poindexter born March 31, baptized July 28.

William son of Lodowick and Elizabeth Alford born July 31, baptized August 2.

Roger negro belonging to John Apperson born June 10.

Sam negro belonging to John Howle born July 1.

Frances Bastard Daughter of Ruth Speare born March 14, baptized August 7.

Beck negro belonging to David McGill born March 22, 1733.

Solomon son of William and Frances Paisley born July 18, baptized August 11.

William negro belonging to Hargrove Sanders dyed August 5.

David son of Michael & Grace Harfield born July 8, baptized August 25.

James son of Thomas and Ann Howle born July 17, baptized August 25.

John son of Marmaduke Moore dyed August 9.

Pelham Moore dyed August 13.

Sue negro belonging to John Carless born August 22.

Conney negro belonging to John Green born July 15.

James son of John and Elizabeth Green born August 15, baptized Septem. 15.

Testis: DAVID MOSSOM, Minister.

REGISTERS.

YEAR 1734.

Christian son of William and Isabel Perkins born Decem[r] 25, baptized Feby. 16.

William son of William and Sarah Drake born January 11, baptized Feb'ry 16.

Elizabeth Daughter of Decinnah and Elizabeth Dalton born Decem[r] 27, baptized Feb'ry 16.

Valentine son of Orson and Susannah Martin born Febr'y 14, baptized Feb'ry 19.

James son of Francis and Judith Amos born Novem[r] 17, baptized Feb'ry 23.

Rachel Daughter of Alexander and Esther Watson born Janu'ry 13, baptized March 23.

Peter Negro boy belonging to Capt. Wm. Dangerfield born Feb'ry 22.

Julius Mullatto Boy belonging to Capt. Jos. Foster born Jan'ry 1, baptized March 2.

Moll Negro girl belonging to sd. Foster born Decem[r] 10, baptized March 2.

William son of John and Jane Ferguson born Janu'ry 2d, baptized March 2.

Caleb son of William and Frances Stone born Jan'ry 27, baptized March 2.

Elizabeth Daughter of John & Mary Waddill born Jan'ry 22, baptized March 2.

Peter son of David and Elizabeth Benns born Decem[r] 10, baptized Decem[r] 27.

Elizabeth Moore dy'd at John Guilliams Febry. 20.

Valentine son of Orson and Susanna Martin Dyed Febry. 27.

Roger Negro Boy belonging to John Gannaway born Febry. 10, baptized March 23.

Jane Mulatto Girl belonging to Mr. ——berlayne born Janu'ry 10, 1733.

Tom Negro Boy belonging to Mrs. ——ghtfoot born Decem[r] 20, baptized March 16.

Frances Daughter of David P—— died Novem[r] 8.

William Jones dy'd at P—— Feb'ry 28.

Jammy Negro Boy belo —— born Jan'ry 15.

Jenny Negro Girl belonging —— born Feb'ry 19.

Randolph Son of John Harris dy'd Febry. 20.

Sherwood son of John and Mary Lightfoot born Feb'ry 14, baptized March 16.

Doll Negro Girl belonging to Robt Dousing over Cha. Manning born Feb'ry 10.

Lydia Daughter of Matthew and Phyllis Pond born Feb'ry 14, baptized March 23.

Robert Negro boy belonging to Eliz^a Vaughan born Feb'ry 16.

Hannah Daughter of Marmaduke and Alice Moore dy'd Febry. 14.

Violetta Tomson died March 11, 1735.

Ann Daughter of Nathaniel and Susanna Smith born March 12, baptized March 27.

Sue Negro Girl belonging to Richard Whitlock born March 12.

Sarah Daughter of Thomas and Elizabeth Roper born Feb. —, baptized Ap. 6.

Susanna Daughter of Isaac and Elizabeth Vaiden born Feb. 6.

William Mulatto Boy belonging to William Massie born Oct. 7.

Sarah Negro Girl belonging to Thomas Pinchback born Mar. —, baptized Ap. 7.

Squire a negro Boy belonging to Capt. Jos. Foster dy'd March 26.

Will a negro man belonging to sd. Foster was drown'd Decr 24, 1734.

Benjamin Son of Francis & Jane Johnson born Mar. 13.

Frances Wife of Richard Meux dy'ed April 15.

Dinah Negro Woman belonging to Catherine Brodie dy'd April 2.

William Thomas was drowned ——.

Testis: DAVID MOSSOM, Minister.

YEAR 1735.

William son of John and Frances Dandridge baptized April 30.

Thomas son of Francis and Mary Wilkinson born March 10, baptized May 4.

Gravesend Negro belonging to Thomas Underwood dy'd March 27.

Sarah a Mulatto Girl belonging to John Waddill Junr born April 12.

1734. Cesar negro boy belonging to Thomas Marston born Decem^r 20.

1734. Sam Negro Boy belonging to Archelaus Mitchell born Feb'ry 27.

Susanna Pattison dy'd at Thomas Davis's April 20.

John Pritchard dy'd at Thomas Davis's April 26.

Charles Negro Boy belonging to Colo. John Custis born May 7.

1729. Elizabeth Daughter of William & Mary Macon born Febry. 15.

1731. Sarah Daughter of William and Mary Macon born Febry. 21.

1733. Moses Mulatto Boy belonging to Major Wm. Macon born Febry. 5.

1733. Kitty Negro Girl belonging to Major Wm. Macon born March 2.

1734. Ben Negro Boy belonging to Major Wm. Macon born March 17.

Duley Negro Girl belonging to Major Wm. Macon born May 23.

William Son of Arthur and Rachel Sladyen born April 27, baptized May 25.

Godfry Negro Boy belonging to Colo. Custis born May 10, dy'd Novr 21.

Nell Negro girl belonging to William Burk born May 8.

Mary Daughter of William and Mary Macon born April 17, baptized June 1.

Ann Daughter of Martin and Susanna Hewlet born May 20, baptized June 8.

Solomon Negro Boy belonging to Colo. John Custis born May 17.

Henry son of John and Margret Spear dy'd June 1.

Thomas son of Mack and Isabella Clarke dy'd May 2.

Mary Daughter of Isaac and Elizabeth Vaiden dy'd May 2.

Elizabeth wife of Isaac Vaiden dy'd May 12.

Davy Negro boy belonging to Colo. Thos. Bray born Febry. 21.

Nell Negro Girl belonging to Said Bray born May 7.

Nan negro woman belonging to s'd Bray dy'd Mar. 1.

Prince Negro Man belonging to s'd Bray dy'd Ap. 14.

David son of John and Elizabeth Apperson born May 27, baptized June 22.

Ebenezer Adams Gent. dy'd June 13.

Fanny Daughter of John and Jane Brothers born June 8, baptized July 7.

Esther negro girl belonging to Wade Netherland born June 13.

1734. Mary Daughter of Ann Holt a free Mulatto woman born Dec' 20, baptized June 27.

Jacob Negro Boy belonging to Sarah Moore born June 15.

Alice negro girl belonging to Colo. Jno. Custis born June 25.

Old Queen Negro Woman belonging to Colo. John Custis dy'd July 15.

Jacob Negro Boy belonging to Sarah Moore widow born June 15, baptized August 3.

Ann Daughter of James and Rachell Blackstone born June 13, baptized August 3.

Testis: DAVID MOSSOM, Minister.

YEAR 1735.

Robert son of Robert and Eliz* Morgan born Octob' 9, baptized Novem' 9.

Christian Bastard Daughter of Tabitha Meanley born Sept. 24, baptized Novem' 9, died Novem' 11.

Esther Negro girl belonging to Capt. Joseph Foster born Octob' 1, baptized Novem' 9.

Elizabeth Negro girl belonging to Lane Jones born Febry 11, baptized Novem' 9.

Joseph Lucas Mulatto Boy bound to Michael Harfield 31 years, born July 16.

Andrew Banks dy'd at Henry Lacy's Oct. 23.

Anthony negro belonging to said Lacy, born Octo. 15.

Susanna Daughter to Wm. and Susanna Moore, born Novr. 10, baptized Decr. 9.

1733. Eliza Simbler Mulatto girl bound to Wm. Waddill 31 years, born Janry. 6.

George son of William and Elizabeth Forbes, born Novemr. 11, baptized Decemr. 14.

John son of Thomas and Mary Cox, born Nov. 10, baptized Decemr. 14.

David son of Thomas and Elizabeth Martin, born Septr. 23, baptized Decr. 14.

William son of Stephen and Mary Cade, born August 24, baptized Decemr. 14.

Marmaduke Moore dy'd Decr. 3.

William son of Richard and Rebecca Guilliam, born Novemr. 22, baptized Decemr. 21.

Caesar negro man belonging to Mrs. Daniel Farrell dy'd Decr. 21.

Richard son of John and Mary Briggs, born Decemr. 2, baptized Decemr. 25.

Mary Daughter of William and Ann Wakelin, born Novemr. 20, baptized December 25.

Michael Mulatto Boy belonging to Majr. Macon, born Novr. 26.

Hugh Negro Boy belonging to Majr. Macon, born Decemr. 15.

Thomas Son of William and Sarah Binns, born Nov. 13, baptized Janry. 11.

William son of William and Susanna Vaiden, born Nov. 27, baptized Janry. 11.

John son of William and Grace Page, born Novr. 14, baptized Janry. 11.

Jeremy Mulatto Boy belonging to Mr. Wm. Brown, born Septr. 2, baptized Jany. 11.

Janny Mulatto man belonging to Mr. Chamberlayne dy'd Jany. 2.

Agnes wife of William Jones dy'd at Ste'n Crumps Decr. 31.

Jenny a negro girl belonging to Ste'n Crump dy'd Decr. 31.

Sarah a negro woman belonging to Jno. Parke dy'd Jany 12.

Ann Bastard Daughter of Hannah Griggs, born Novr. 1, baptized Jany. 18.

Valentine son of James and Agnes Moore, born Nov. 21, baptized Jany. 27.

1734. Mary Daughter of Wm. and Isabella Perkins dy'd Jany. 19.

Archer son of Matthew and Judith Johnson, born December 27, baptized Feb. 1.

Frank a negro girl belonging to Colo. Wm. Basset, born Dec. 13.

Guy a negro man belonging to Colo. Wm. Bassett, dy'd Jan. 25.

Christmas son of Thomas and Mary Meekins, born Dec. 25, babtized Feby. 13.

Fanny Daughter of John and Susanna Bacon, born Feby. 5, baptized Feby. 24.

Jane Daughter of Thomas and Ann Anderson, born Janry 15, baptized Feb. 29.

Petronella Daughter of Samuel Ann Buxton, born Jany 22, baptized Feby. 29.

Ann Daughter of George and Susanna Waddill, born Feby. 25, baptized Feby 29, died March 3.

Edmond son of Charles and Elizabeth Crump dy'd Oct. 15.

Elizabeth wife of John Strange dy'd Feb. 2.

Testis: DAVID MOSSOM, Minister.

YEAR, 1735.

Nanny negro girl belong. to Wm. Atkinson, born Jany. 1.

Naomi Daughter of Walter and Mary Clopton born Jany. 11, baptized March 21.

Mary Daughter of John and Sarah Christian, born Octo. 8, baptized March 8.

Hannah negro girl belonging to Henry French, born March 2.

Elizabeth wife of Lodowick Alford, dy'd May 29.

John and Ann son and daughter Twins of John and Ann Smith, born March 8, baptized March 13.

Ann Daughter of William and Susanna Christian, born Febry. 21, baptized March 13.

Matt mulatto Boy belonging to Jno. Lightfoot, born Jany 25, baptized August 8, 1736.

John son of William and Mary Johnson, born Feby. 5, baptized Mar. 14.

Ann Daughter of Jno. and Ann Poindexter, born Jany. 24, baptized Mar. 14.

Ann Daughter of Thomas and Susanna Moss, born Feby. 15, baptized Mar. 14.

Agnes Daughter of Cornelius and Eliza. Matthews, born Feby. 5, baptized Mar. 14.

Jane Austin dy'd, Febry.

Richard Ross dy'd March 5.

Ann wife of Jno. Gauling dy'd Octo. 27.

Hannah wife of Thomas Underwood dy'd March 18.

Punch negro man belonging to Sarh. Poindexter dy'd March 15,

1736. John son of Thomas and Lucy Hilliard born Mar. 4, baptized Mar. 28.

Mary Daughter of John and Ann Harris, born March 7, baptized April 4.

Mary Daughter of Thomas and Mary Trewit, born Febry. 27, baptized April 4.

Ann Daughter of William and Frances Hopkins dy'd April 3.

Esther negro girl belonging to Wade Netherland dy'd Mar. 27.

Dick a negro man belonging to Thomas Roper dy'd April 2.

Lucretia Daughter of Robert and Mary Bailey, born March 20, baptized May 2.

Jack negro man belonging to Robert Jarratt dy'd Mar. 29.

James son of Ambrose and Eliza Dudley, born April 2, baptized May 9.

Samuel son of William and Jane Webb, born Feby. 6, baptized May 9.

Martha Daughter of Thomas and Ann Bradley, born March 30, baptized May 9.

Mary Daughter of Philip and Eliza. Poindexter, born March 30, baptized May 9.

Will negro boy belonging to Philip Poindexter, born April 10.

Daniel Farrele dy'd May 8.

James son of James and Joyce Hill, born Mar. 5, baptized May 11.

Lucy Daughter of Edward and Hannah Morgan, born Mar. 29, baptized May 16.

Richard son of Joseph and Cassandra Crump, born April 28, baptized May 23.

Thomas son of Mark and Isabella Clark, born April 18, baptized May 23.

Sarah Daughter of Samuel and Elinor Hubbard, born Novr. 5, baptized May 23.

Susanna Daughter of David and Agathe Dodd, born April 2 baptized May 23.

Susanna Mulatto Girl belonging to Wm. Brown, baptized May 23.

William Negro boy belonging to M^{dm} Page (H. Lacy oo'r), baptized May 23.

> Testis: DAVID MOSSOM, Minister.

YEAR 1736.

William son of John and Elizabeth Green, born April 20, baptized May 30.

Charles Negro boy belonging to Thomas Addison, born April 20.

Mary negro woman belonging to Thomas Addison dy'd May 15.

John Negro Boy belonging to George Poindexter, born April 25, baptized May 30.

Peter negro Boy belonging to George Poindexter, born Sept. 15, 1735.

William Binns dy'd May 12.

Peter negro man belonging to Mary Barnes dy'd April 26.

Pat negro girl belonging to Mary Barnes, born May 8.

Nat Negro Boy belonging to Timothy Vaughan, born May 26.

James son of George and Lucy Taylor, born May 1, baptized June 6.

Edmond Bastard Son of Agnes Crump, born April 6, baptized June 6.

Watt Negro Boy belonging to John Whitlock, born May 10.

Roper negro Boy belonging to Rich'd Whitlock, born April 20.

Frances Evans Daughter of William and Frances, born July 4.

Thomas Evans son of Will & Frances, born Aug. 17.

York Negro Boy belonging to Wm. Vaiden, born April 12.

Squire Negro Boy belonging to Colo. Custis, born Febry. 20, baptized June 20.

Jenny Negro Girl belonging to Sarah Turner, born June 5.

William Son of John and Sarah Bartwell, born April 5, baptized June 27.

Rachel Daughter of Benja. and Ann Bradley, born May 20, baptized June 27.

Hannah Mulatto Girl belonging to Wm. Brown, born March 30, baptized June 27.

Thomas son of Willam and Sarah Dollard, born May 27, baptized July 1.

Nell negro girl belonging to Elizabeth Otey, born April 23.

John son of John and Jane Ferguson, born June 24, baptized July 11.

Margrett Daughter of John and Frances Mᶜdowgle, born Janry. 17, baptized July 18.

Elizabeth Daughter of George & Susana Mitchell, born July 3, baptized July 18.

Rachel Daughter Joseph and Mary Swinney, born April 14, baptized July 18.

Bella Negro girl belonging to Colo. Custis, born Janry. 15, baptized July 4.

1735. Peter Negro Boy belonging to George Poindexter, born Sept. 15, baptized July 4.

Judy Negro girl belonging to Rebecca Mosse, born July 4.

Sarah Negro Girl belonging to Jacob Vaiden, born June 23.

Daniel Negro Boy belonging to James Nance, born May 25, baptized July 29.

Agnes Negro girl belonging to Mr. Wm. Chamberlayne, born Febry. 6, baptized June 15.

Jack Negro Boy belonging to Wade Netherland, born July 1.

John son of John and Mary Tomson, born June 27, baptized August 1.

Julius son of Leman and Sarah Le'Strange, born June 9, baptized August 8.

Roper Negro Boy belonging to Richard Whitlock, born May 8.

Jane Negro girl belonging to Sarah Turner, born May 7.

Cæsar Negro Boy belonging to John Paris, born August 12.

Testis: DAVID MOSSOM, Minister.

YEAR 1736.

Fanny Daughter of John Whitlock dyed Augt. 21.

John Martin Bastard son of Hannah Allen, born August 1, baptized August 29.

Moses Negroy Boy belonging to Colo. Custis, born August 11, baptized Septr. 26.

Judith Daughter of Sam'l & Bethiah Moss, born Augt. 5, baptized Septr. 5.

Lucy Daughter of John and Ann Bowles, born Augt 5, baptized Sept. 5.

Lucy Negro Girl belonging to Robert Jarratt, born Augt 4.

Grace Negro Girl belonging to Colo. Custis, born Septemr. 1, baptized Octor. 24.

William Chamberlayne dy'd Augt. 2.

Jesse son of Richard and Martha Scruggs, born July 23, baptized Septr. 12.

Jane Daughter of John and Jane Weaver, born Augt. 3, baptized Septr. 12.

Lucy Daughter of Archelaus & Ann Mitchell, born July 18, baptized Septr. 12.

Julius Mulatto Boy belonging to Wm. Massie, born April 28, baptized Septr. 19.

Hannah Daughter of Marmaduke & Hanh. Gannaway, born July 22, baptized Septr. 19.

Patty Bryan Daughter of John and Mary Symcock, born Aug. 5, baptized Septr. 19.

Richard Son of Richard and Judith Jones, born Aug. 20, baptized Septr. 19.

Sarah Bastard Daughter of Eliza Barker, born Janry. 15, baptized Septr. 19.

Matthew Negro Boy belonging to Thos. Butts, born April 6, baptized Septr. 26.

Elizabeth Daughter of Theodorick and Elizabeth Carter, born August 22, baptized Septr. 26.

Sarah Daughter of Timothy and Eliza Sarah Vaughan, born Septr. 2, baptized Octor. 3.

Moses Mulatto Boy belonging to Majr. Macon dy'd Octo. 7.

Frances Ann Daughter of William and Eliza Vaughan, born Septr. 9, baptized Octob. 10.

Daniel Bastard Son of Mary Apperson 1734, born July 18, baptized Octor. 10.

Fanny Daughter of Stephen and Ann Martin born Augt. 2, baptized Octob'r 10.

Thomas Negro Boy belonging to John Carless born Augt. 29, baptized Octob'r 10.

Elizabeth Daughter of Abraham and Ann Alloway born Oct'r 10, baptized Oct'r 17, 1735.

Hannah Daughter of John and Magdalen Sanders born Sept'r 6, baptized Octob'r 25.

Dinah negro Girl belonging to Ralph Graves born Octo. 15.

John son of Nathaniel & Elizabeth Ragland born Octo. 10, baptized Nov'r 7.

Thomas Son of William & Sarah Drake born Octo'r 8, baptized Nov'r 17.

William Son of William and Mary Roper born Sept'r 24, baptized Nov'r 14.

Susanna Daughter of Gower and Susanna Dennis, born Octo'r 14, baptized Nov'r 14.

Venus a Negro girl belonging to Joseph Waddill, born Octo'r 25.

Venus Negro woman belonging to Joseph Waddill dy'd Nov. 1.

Elleana Daughter of Charles and Elizabeth Crump, born Octo'r 10, baptized Nov'r 21.

Alice Daughter of John & Frances Bacon, born Nov'r 22, baptized Nov'r 24, died Nov'r 24.

Ann Daughter of Maj. Wm. Macon dy'd Nov'r 9.

Testis: DAVID MOSSOM, Minister.

YEAR 1736.

Dubartas son of William and Frances Paisley, born Octob'r 28, baptized Nov'r 28.

Jemima Daughter of George and Tamar Crump, born Nov'r 3, baptized Nov'r 28.

Frances Daughter of Jonathan & Eliza Pattison, born Octob'r 19, baptized Decem'r 2.

Theophilus son of Henry and Angelica Lacy, born Novem'r 4, baptized Decem'r 5.

Thomas Negro Boy belonging to said Lacy, born Novem'r 15, baptized Decem'r 5.

James Negro Boy belonging to said Lacy, baptized Decem'r 5.

1729. Joseph Negro Boy belonging to Sarah Hopkins, born March 25, baptized Decem'r 5.

1731. Henry Negro Boy belonging to said Hopkins, born April 12, baptized Decem'r 5.

1734. Charles Negro Boy belonging to said Hopkins, born Janr'y 10, baptized Decem'r 5.

Dick Negro Boy belonging to Thomas Marston, born Septem. 1.

Richard son of Richard and Margrett Russell, born Octo'r 6, baptized Decem'r 12.

Ashcraft son of Henry and Catharine Roach, born Octob'r 29, baptized Decem'r 12.

David son of Robert and Mary Moore, born Sept'r 8, baptized Decem'r 12.

Elizabeth Daughter of Richard and Lucy Crump, born Novem'r 5, baptized Decem'r 12.

William Negro Boy belonging to Thomas Butts, born Oct'r 15, baptized Decem'r 14.

James Mulatto Boy belonging to Mrs. Eliza. Chamberlayne, born Novem'r 22, baptized May 3, 1737.

Jeremiah Hilliard dy'd at John Hilliards Novm'r 6.

Dilsey Negro Girl belonging to Frances Walton, born August 17.

Phebe Negro Girl belonging to David Mossom, born Novem'r 20, baptized Jan. 30.

Thomas Mitchell Sen'r dy'd Jan'y 6.

Susanna Daughter of Charles & Jane Winfree, born Novem'r 9, baptized Decem'r 25.

Eustace Son of Edmond and Alice Daniel, born Decem'r 14, baptized Feb'ry 6.

William Son of Orson and Susanna Martin, born Novem'r 20, baptized Feb'ry 6.

Sarah Daughter of Arthur and Rachel Slayden, born Decem'r 26, baptized Feb'ry 6.

Elizabeth Daughter of Lodowick & Susanna Alford, born Decem'r 22, baptized Feb'ry 6.

Ann Daughter of John and Judith Ragland, born Decem'r 5, baptized Feb'ry 6.

Sarah Negro girl belonging to Jacob Vaiden dy'd Dec'r 13.

Patt Negro girl belonging to Jacob Vaiden dy'd Dec'r 20.

Rachel Negro girl belonging to John Green, born Jan'ry 30.

Isabella wife of William Perkins Jun'r dy'd Decem'r 18.

Doll negro girl belonging to Charles Winfree, born Novem'r 5, baptized June 12.

Oreana Daughter of Richard and Oreana Littlepage, born Jan'y 20, baptized Feb'ry 16.

Alice Daughter of William and Susanna Mason, born Jan'ry 6, baptized Feb'ry 20.

Micajah Son of Charles and Elizabeth Case, born Jan'ry 24, baptized Feb'ry 20.

Julius Son of Henry & Elizabeth Scruggs, born Jan'ry 1, baptized March 6.

Mary Daughter of Matthew and Phillis Pond, born Jan'ry 31, baptized March 6.

Sarah Negro Girl belonging to Wade Netherland, born Feb'ry 9.

Tom Negro Boy belonging to James Nance, born Feb'ry 14.

Rachel Negro Girl belonging to Robt. Crawley, born Feb'ry 11.

John Son John and Eliza. Apperson died Feb'ry 20.

Testis: DAVID MOSSOM, Minister.

YEAR 1736.

Ann Daughter Richard and Elizabeth Meux, born March 3, baptized March 15.

Jack Negro Boy belonging to Richard Meux, born Feb'ry 1, baptized May 22, 1737.

Jamey negro man belonging to Richard Meux dy'd Octob'r 16.

Bartholomew son of John & Frances Dandridge, born Decem'r 26, baptized March 13.

Francis son of John and Mary Lightfoot, born Feb'ry 9, baptized March 20.

Frances Daughter of William and Ann Morris, born Feb'ry 21, baptized March 20.

Cuffee negro man belonging to Thomas Addison died Feb'ry 28.

Sam Negro Boy belonging to George Wilkinson, born Feb'ry 20.

Joe Negro Boy belonging to John Hutcheson, born Feb'ry 14.

1737. Jemima Daughter Martin and Susanna Hewlett, born March 29, baptized March 29, died March 29.

Benjamin son John and Frances Bugg, born Nov'r 24, 1736, baptized March 25.

Lucy Daughter of Goodrich and Sarah Alford, born Feb'ry 25, baptized March 27.

Mellicent Daughter John and Elizabeth Showers, born March 1, baptized April 3.

Judith Daughter of Francis and Judith Amos 1736, born Nov'r 15, baptized April 10.

Robin Negro boy belonging to Mrs. Tabitha Adams, born Octo'r 15, 1736.

George Negro Boy belonging to Mrs. Tabitha Adams, born March 16, baptized August 21, 1736.

Matt Negro Boy belonging to Thomas Couzens, born March 25.

Duncan Negro man belonging to John Custis Esq. died March 21.

Hannah Waddill dy'd April 7.

James Son of Richard and Susanna Tompson. born Feb'ry 18, baptized April 7.

Mary Daughter of Francis and Mary Wilkinson, born Feb'ry 19, baptized April 17.

Thomas Negro Boy belonging Thomas Pinchback, born March 13, baptized April 24.

Nathaniel Son of Andrew and Amadca Mantiply, born Jan'ry 11, baptized April 24.

John Son of William and Elizabeth Forbes, born March 26, baptized April 24.

Ann Kedley Daughter of Eliza. Chamberlayne widow, born April 10, baptized April 24.

Mary Daughter of Peter and Elizabeth Martin, born Sep'r 26, baptized April 26.

George Son of John and Susanna Parke, born April 12, baptized April 28.

Rebecca Daughter of Thomas and Elizabeth Mitchell, born March 16, baptized May 8.

James Son of John and Susanna Dollard, born March 27, baptized May 15.

Elizabeth Daughter of William and Mercy Crump, born April 14, baptized May 22.

Martha Daughter of John and Mary Waddill, born April, baptized May 22.

Phillis Negro Girl belonging to James Sanders, born March 26.

William Booth Son of Jacob Waddill dyed May 11.

Sarah the Wife of John Hall dyed March 16.

Major Negro man belonging to Alice Meredith dyed May 2.

Dick Negro Boy belonging to John James, born May 2.

1736. Frances Mulatto Girl belonging to Susanna Cooper, born March 30.

Tamar Negro girl belonging to Thomas Pinchback, born Jan'ry 25.

Ann Daughter of Thomas and Elizabeth Pinchback, born March 30.

Daniel Negro man belonging to William Massie dyed April 15.

Testis: DAVID MOSSOM, Minister.

YEAR 1737.

Joseph Son of David and Elizabeth Binns, born April 25, baptized May 29.

James son of Thomas and Ann Addison, born April 28, baptized May 29.

Sarah Mulatto Girl belonging to Charles Bolton, born March 17, baptized June 5.

William son of Francis and Catherine Martin, born Feb'ry 8, baptized June 5.

Rebeckah Daughter of Henry and Ann Talman, born April 2, baptized June 12.

Elizabeth Daughter of William and Frances Stone, born May 18, baptized June 12.

Richard Negro Boy belonging to Francis Littlepage, born March 15, baptized June 12.

Dinah Negro Girl belonging to Colo. Custis, born May 15, baptized Nov'r 5.

George Negro Boy belonging to Sarah Berry, born May 17.

Benja. Son of David and Elizabeth Roper, born April 25, baptized June 19.

Nell Negro woman belonging to Colo. Wm. Bassett died May 29.

Charles Son of Joseph and Judith Waddill, born May 9, baptized June 23.

Betty Daughter of Isaac and Frances Otey, born May 13, baptized June 23.

Elizabeth Daughter of John and Susanna Roberts, born May 19, baptized June 26.

David Son of John and Margaret Meanley, born May 26, baptized July 3.

Judith Daughter of John and Elizabeth Moore, born June 1, baptized July 3.

Charles Negro Boy belonging to Thos. Marston, born April 3.

Matt Negro Boy belonging to Sarah Moore 1736, born Jan'ry 20.

Davy Negro Boy belonging to Jacob Vaiden, born April 9, baptized Octob'r 9.

Absalom Son of Matthew and Judith Johnson, born May 30, baptized July 10.

Mary Daughter of Thomas and Mary Cox, born July 17, baptized July 28, died Aug't 5.

Isaac Son of Thomas and Elizabeth Roper, born June 30, baptized July 31.

1736. Beck Negro Girl belonging to Charles Massie, born Decem'r 21.

1736. Maggy Negro Girl belonging to Charles Massie, born Novemb'r 14.

Martin Negro Boy belonging to Charles Massie, born June 20.

Randal Negro Boy belonging to Thomas Hilliard, born July 5.

Matthew Negro Boy belonging to Sarah Moore, born January 17, baptized Aug't 7.

Lucy Negro girl belonging to Colo. Custis, born May 10, baptized Aug't 7.

Watlington Negro Boy belonging to John Whitlock, born June 14, baptized Aug't 7.

William Bas'd Son of Mary Gibbon, born June 24, baptized Aug't 9.

John Son of Anthony and Mary Cole, born July 4, baptized Aug't 14.

Thomas son of Edmond and Mary Richardson, born July 8, baptized Aug't 14.

Beck Negro girl belonging to John Lightfoot, born July 30.

William Moss Bastard son of Mary Toney, born June 28, baptized Aug't 21.

Doll Negro Girl belonging to James Blackstone, born July 12.

Jacob Negro Boy belonging to James Blackstone, born July 21.

Martha Daughter of John and Sabra Finch, born July 27, baptized Aug't 28.

Robin Negro Boy belonging to Thomas Barnes, born Aug't 21.

Testis: DAVID MOSSOM, Minister.

YEAR 1737.

Nathaniel son of John and Jane Brothers, born July 22, baptized Sep'r 11.

Caleb son of William and Dorothy Turner, born July 28, baptized Sep'r 11.

Frances Daughter of Henry and Margret Finch, born Aug't 10, baptized Sep't 11.

Unity Daughter of Thomas and Susanna Martin, born July 6, baptized Sep'r 11.

Agnes Daughter of John and Sarah Ferris, born April 20, baptized Sept'r 11.

Cloe and Esther twin Negro Girls belonging to Rich'd Littlepage, born March 27, baptized Sept'r 18.

Jane Daughter of James and Jane Johnson, born August 6, baptized Sep'r 9.

Mary Daughter of James and Ann Nance, born May 2, baptized Aug't 14.

Rachel Negro Girl belonging to Michael Sherman, born August 10.

Mary Barnes, widow, dy'd Sept'r 2.

Judith Daughter of Colo. William and Mary Macon, born August 12, baptized Sept'r 25.

Dick Negro Boy belonging to John Apperson, born August 25.

Jammy Negro boy belonging to Richard Apperson, born July 18.

Alice Daughter of Ric'd & Eliza. Whitlock, born Aug't 29, baptized Octo'r 2.

Ann and Rebecca Twin Daughters of Wm. and Ann Wakelin, born Aug't 25, baptized Octo'r 2.

James Son of George and Susanna Waddill, born Sept'r 12, baptized Octo'r 9.

Jany Negro Girl belonging to Eliza Vaughan, born Sept'r 13.

Elizabeth Daughter of Alexander & Esther Watson, born August 20, baptized Octo'r 16.

Thomas Son of Samuel & Rebecca Butler, born Sept'r 25, baptized Octo'r 23.

Peter Son of John and Agnes Apperson, born Sept'r 15, baptized Octo'r 23.

Peg. Negro Girl belonging to Colo. Custis, born Octo'r 15, died Nov'r 12.

Robert Richardson dy'd Octo'r 12.

John Son of John and Elizabeth Apperson, born August 18, baptized Octo. 30.

John Son of Theodorick and Ann Carter, born Aug't 26, baptized Octo. 30.

Elizabeth Daughter of James and Mary Morris, born Sept. 22, baptized Octo. 30.

William Son of John and Mary Hockaday dy'd Oct'r 16.

Matthew Mulatto Boy belonging to Capt. Joseph Foster, born Aug't 1, baptized Nov'r 6.

Philip Negro Boy belonging to Colo. Custis, born Aug't 1, baptized Nov'r 6.

Robert Negro Boy belonging to Ann Bayley 1734, born Nov'r 6, baptized Nov'r 10.

James Son of Walter and Million Daniel, born Octo'r 21, baptized Nov'r 27.

John Son of Edmond and Elizabeth Toney, born Octo'r 25, baptized Nov'r 27.

Nanny Negro Girl belonging to John Gannaway, born July 15.

Hagar Negro Girl belonging to John Gannaway, born Nov'r 1.

Mary Daughter of John and Frances Winfree, born Octo'r 20, baptized Dec'r 4.

Jesse Son of John and Mary Chandler, born Nov'r 4, baptized Dec'r 4.

George Son of Samuel and Eliza. Plumley, born Nov'r 12, baptized Dec'r 11.

John Son of John and Ann Poindexter, born Nov'r 10, baptized Dec'r 11.

Testis: DAVID MOSSOM, Minister.

YEAR 1737.

Elizabeth wife of John Buxton died Jan'ry 22.

Mary Daughter of William and Cassandra Clopton, born Nov'r 13, baptized Jan'y 5.

Lucy Negro Girl belonging to Charles Pearson, born Oct'r 4.

—— Negro Boy belonging to Capt. Jos. Foster, born Aug't 1, died Aug. 7.

George Son of George and Lucy Taylor, born Decem'r 11, baptized Jan'ry 7.

Jemima Daughter of John and Frances New, born Nov'r 26, baptized Dec'r 25.

Ann Daughter of William and Sarah Ragland, born Nov'r 25, baptized Jan'ry 8.

Beck Negro Girl belonging to John Lightfoot died Dec'r 15.

Jack Negro Girl belonging to John Whitlock, born Jan'ry 7, died Jan'ry 13.

Dugall Son of John and Frances Mcdougle, born Sept'r 9, baptized Jan'ry 20.

Elizabeth Daughter Joseph and Sarah Parkinson; born Decem'r 15, baptized Jan'ry 15.

John Son of Nathaniel and Elizabeth Ragland died Jan'ry 14.

Rebecca Daughter of Robert Vaiden died Jan'ry 10.

Mary Daughter of Edward and Sarah Jones, born Decem'r 24, baptized Feb'ry 5.

Greenwich Negro man belonging to the Rev'd D. Mossom died Feb'ry 17.

Sarah Daughter of William and Mary Battin, born Jan'ry 2, baptized Feb'ry 19.

Jane Daughter of John and Elizabeth McGregor, born Jan'ry 15, baptized March 5.

Mary Daughter of John and Ann Bowles, born Feb'ry 14, baptized March 12.

Jeremiah son of Robert and Mary Bailey, born Jan'y 24, baptized Mar. 12.

Peter Negro Boy belonging to Sherwood Lightfoot, born Feb'ry 17, baptized July 2.

John Buxton died Feb'ry 7.

Nathaniel son of Nathaniel and Susa. Smith, born Jan'y 2, baptized March 19.

Chunk Negro Woman belonging to Colo. Custis died Mar. 15.

Michael Negro Boy belonging to Colo. Custis, born Feb'ry 20, baptized June 11.

Samuel son of William and Susanna Mason, born Jan'ry 28, baptized March 21.

George mulatto Boy belonging to Maj. Jos. Foster, born Jan'ry 23, baptized March 23.

1738. John son of John and Mary Brown, born March 1, baptized March 31.

Jane Daughter of Richard and Lucy Crump, born Feb'ry 14, baptized March 31.

Lancy Negro Boy belonging to Colo. Custis, born March 10, baptized June 11.

Martin son of Martin and Susanna Hewlet, born March 26, baptized April 23.

Elizabeth Daughter of John and Elizabeth Barkwell, born Feb'ry 7, baptized April 23.

Sam Negro Boy belonging to James Nance, born April 12.

1737. William Lucas mulatto Boy belong. to Mich'l Harfield, born Aug't 25.

George Son of Philip and Elizabeth Poindexter, born March 16, baptized April 23.

John Son of William and Mary Perkins, born April 3, baptized May 7.

David Negro Boy belonging to Jacob Vaiden dy'd April 24.

Isaac Son of Theodorick & Temperance Martin, born March 2, baptized May 14.

Testis: DAVID MOSSOM, Minister.

YEAR 1738.

Rachel Negro girl belonging to Elizabeth Farell, born Jan'ry 23, baptized April 23.

Elizabeth negro girl belonging to Mr. Thos. Arnott, baptized May 20.

Moses Negro Boy belonging to Mrs. Elizabeth Farell, baptized May 21.

George Negro boy belonging to William Atkinson 1737, born Septem'r 15, baptized May 21.

Rebecca Daughter David and Elizabeth Wilkinson 1737, born Decem'r 14, baptized May 21.

Judith Daughter of Eustace and Jane Studskill, born April 16, baptized May 21.

Frances Daughter of John and Frances Bacon, born April 24, baptized May 21.

Silvanus son of Peter and Ann Massie, born April 8, baptized May 26.

Spy Negro Boy belonging to Charles Winfree, born March 30, baptized July 23.

William son of Charles and Jane Winfree, born May 19, baptized May 26.

Robin Negro Boy belonging to Colo. Thomas Bray, born May 2.

William son of William and Elizabeth Vaughan, born April 28, baptized June 4.

Hezekiah son of John and Joyce Spear, born April 27, baptized June 4.

Roger Negro Boy belonging to James Roberts, born May 25.

Patty Daughter of Cornelius and Elizabeth Matthews, born May 11, baptized June 11.

Mary Daughter of Richard and Margrett Russell, born April 28, baptized June 11.

Mary Daughter of Benjamin and Mary Spencer, born May 30, baptized June 18, died June 20.

Mary wife of Benjamin Spencer died June 12.

Martha Daughter of James and Ruth Gilliam, born April 26, baptized June 25.

Sarah Negro Girl belonging to Mrs. Elizabeth Otey born June 5.

Luce Negro Girl belonging to Capt. Edwin Dangerfield born June 5.

Abraham Negro Boy belonging to Alice Meredith born Decr 10, baptized July 2, 1737.

James Son of Samuel and Sarah Osling born June 20, baptized July 16.

Oct. 20. George Bastard Son of Ann Holt a free mulatto woman born Oct'r 20, baptized July 23, 1737.

Benjamin Negro Boy belonging to George Poindexter born Feb'ry 25, baptized July 23.

James Son of John Weaver died June 16.

David Negro Boy belonging to Thomas Couzens born April 13.

Hannah Daughter of William and Mary Johnson born July 10, baptized Fe'y 16.

Isham Mulatto Boy belonging to Wm. Brown baptized Augt. 13.

Mary Daughter of Charles and Sarah Amoss born July 3, baptized Sept. 3.

Aaron Son of George and Sarah Gowan born June 9, baptized Sept. 3.

Frances Daughter of Peter and Elizabeth Davison born Jan'ry 5, baptized Sept. 3.

Thomas Son of James and Elizabeth Sanders born Augt. 7, baptized Sept'r 10.

Sabra Daughter of Henry and Catharine Roach born Augt. 8, baptized Sept'r 10.

Judith Daughter of Charles and Sarah Manning born May 3, baptized Sept'r 10.

George Son of George and Mary Heath born Augt. 26, baptized Sept'r 17.

Stephen Mulatto Boy belonging to Mr. Willm Brown born Sept'r 13, baptized Octo. 8.

Mary Daughter of Henry Scruggs died July 8.

Edward Son of Henry Scruggs died July 15.

Henry Son of Henry Scruggs died Sept'r 8.

John son of Christopher and Ann Nordan born Augt. 8, baptized Octo'r 8.

Joseph Son of Michael and Susanna Sherman born June 26, baptized Sept'r 4.

Testis: DAVID MOSSOM, Minister.

YEAR 1738.

Will Negro Boy belonging to Jonathan Pattison born Augt. 29.

Ketarah Daughter of James and Ann Nance born July 21, baptized Augt. 16.

Nan Negro Girl belonging to Richard Apperson born July 18.

Lucy Mulatto Girl belonging to Mr. William Brown born June 12, baptized July 29.

John MacGregor died Augt. 4.

Lucy Negro Girl belonging to Mr. Edwin Daingerfield dy'd Augt. 16.

Sarah Hopkins dy'd Jan'ry 29, 1737.

Francis and James Twin sons of William and Frances Hopkins born Feb'ry 27, 1737.

Phil Negro Boy belonging to William Hopkins born April 24.

George Poindexter dy'd July 6.

James Mulatto Boy belonging to Mr. Wm. Massie baptized Octo. 8.

Ann Daughter of Benjamin and Ann Bradley born Augt. 9, baptized October 8.

Mary Daughter of Isaac and Frances Otey born August 24, baptized October 8.

———— of Richard and Rebecca Gilliam born August 29, baptized Octob'r 8.

Mary Daughter of Thomas and Elizabeth Martin born August 6, baptized Octob'r 8.

Batt Negro Boy belonging to John Custis Esq' born Sept'r 28.

Katee Rabley Daughter of Timothy & Sarah Vaughan born Sept'r 13, baptized Octob'r 15.

Judy Negro Girl belonging to Wm. Ragland born Sept'r 10.

Sarah Daughter of Thomas and Mary Cox born Sept'r 14, baptized Octob'r 22.

Fanny Negro Girl belonging to Richard Whitlock born Octob'r 1.

Elizabeth Negro Girl belonging to Mary Turner born July 7, baptized Nov'r 5.

Richard Son of William and Elizabeth Pearson born Octob'r 3, baptized Novem'r 5.

Mary Daughter of Archelaus and Ann Mitchell born Sept'r 19, baptized Nov'r 5.

Joseph Son of Israel and Elizabeth Austin born Sept'r 22, baptized Nov'r 12.

Ann Daughter of John and Ann Harris born Octob'r 15, baptized Nov'r 12.

Thomas Son of Richard and Elizabeth Meux born Octob'r 17, baptized Nov'r 12.

Ann Daughter of William and Sarah Drake born Octo'r 22, baptized Nov'r 19.

Robert Son of Joseph and Cassandra Crump born Nov'r 1, baptized Dec'r 3.

Nathaniel Son of Nathaniel and Elizabeth Ragland born Nov'r 8, baptized Dec'r 3.

John Son of Charles and Sarah Woard born Octo'r 22, baptized Dec'r 3.

Suffaliston Daughter of John & Elizabeth Byrd born Nov'r 1, baptized Dec'r 3.

Martha Daughter of Arthur and Rachel Sladyen born Nov'r 8, baptized Dec'r 17.

Henry Son of William and Frances Paisley born Decem'r 17, baptized Dec'r 18.

Thomas Son of William and Elizabeth Forbes born Decem'r 5, baptized Jan'ry 21.

John Son of Richard and Elizabeth Whitlock born Decem'r 14, baptized Feb'ry 4.

Jane Daughter of George and Susanna Mitchell born Jan'ry 21, baptized Feb'ry 25.

Elizabeth Wife of the Rev'd David Mossom dy'd Jan'ry 28.

Richard Son of Jonathan and Elizabeth Pattison born Jan'ry 28, baptized March 4.

Shadrach Son of William and Sarah Waddill born Sept'r 6, baptized March 4.

Daniel Son of John and Elizabeth Haslewood born Dec'r 26, baptized March 4.

Mingo Negro Man belonging to John Paris dy'd Feb'ry 26.

Peter Elmore dy'd Nov'r 7.

Testis: DAVID MOSSOM, Minister.

YEAR 1738.

Ann Daughter of James and Tabitha Christian born Decem'r 14, baptized Feb'ry 18.

Isaac Son of William and Susanna Vaiden born Decem'r 11, baptized Feb'ry 18.

Mary Daughter of Christopher and Mary Ammon born Decem'r 13, baptised Feb'ry 18.

Judith Daughter of Charles and Frances Jones born Jan'ry 10, baptized Feb'ry 18.

Josias Son of William and Sarah Leake born Novem'r 1, baptized Feb'ry 18.

James son of Bernard and Sarah Taylor born Decem'r 15, baptized Feb'ry 18.

Susanna Daughter of John and Jane Weaver born Decem'r 26, baptized Feb'ry 18.

Jacob Son of Lodowick and Susanna Alford born Decem'r 12, baptized Feb'ry 18.

Thomas Son of Robert and Mary Moore born Jan'ry 2, baptized Feb'ry 18.

Ann Daughter of William and Susanna Baker born Novem'r 20, baptized Feb'ry 18.

Thomas son of John and Sabra Finch born Octob'r 27, baptized Feb'ry 18.

Mary Daughter of William and Elizabeth Ballard, born Novem'r 22.

Ann Bastard Daughter of Mary Taylor, born Novem'r 19.

Mary Dyer Daughter of Mathew and Miriam Harfield, born Feb'ry 11, baptized Mar. 18.

Martha Daughter of William and Elizabeth Gray, born Feb'ry 7, baptized Feb'ry 11, died Feb'ry 13.

1739. John son of James and Mary Morris, born Feb'ry 18, baptized March 25.

Thomas son of Edward and Mary Matthews, born Feb'ry 22, baptized March 25.

Sarah Daughter of John and Jane Pruet, born Feb'ry 18, baptized March 25.

Elizabeth Daughter of Thomas and Elizabeth Mitchell, born March 14, baptized March 25, died March 25.

Thomas son of the Rev'd David Mossom dy'd March 29.

Mary Daughter of Richard and Martha Scruggs, born Feb'ry 12, baptized April 8.

George son of Peter and Frances Apperson, born March 10, baptized April 8.

Elizabeth Daughter of James and Angelica Hanson, born March 5, baptized April 8.

Neson Negro Boy belonging to Colo. Custis, born March 14, baptized June 3.

Joe Negro Boy belonging to Colo. Custis, born March 25.

Sarah Daughter of Marmaduke and Hannah Gannaway, born Feb'ry 22, baptized April 15.

Joseph son of Gower and Frances Dennis, born Feb'ry 26, baptized April 15.

Ann Daughter of Samuel and Bethia Moss, born March 13, baptized April 15.

John son of Thomas and Susanna Martin, born Feb'ry 28, baptized April 15.

Kezia Daughter of William and Lucretia Hughes, born March 7, baptized April 15.

Frank Negro Girl belonging to Capt. John Darricott, born Feb'ry 1, baptized April 22.

Judith Negro Girl belonging to Charles Winfree, born Dec'r 15, baptized April 22.

George negro boy belonging to Capt. Rich'd Meux, born Feb'ry 5, baptized April 22.

Richard negro boy belonging to Charles Winfree, born March 15, baptized April 22.

Hannah Daughter of John and Judith Ragland, born March 26, baptized April 22.

1738. Betty mulatto girl belonging to John Waddill, Jr., born July 3.

Elizabeth Daughter of Anthony and Mary Cole, born March 1, baptized April 14.

Martha Daughter of Thomas and Rebecca Marston, born March 19, baptized April 3.

Agge negro girl belonging to Henry Finch, born March 29.

Moll negro girl belonging to James Blackstone, born March 15.

Kate negro girl belonging to James Blackstone, born April 25.

1738. Hannah negro girl belonging to Capt. Ric'd Littlepage, born Aug. 12, baptized Feb'ry 6.

Testis: DAVID MOSSOM, Minister.

YEAR 1739.

Richard son of Stephen and Phillis Brooker born Mar. 10, baptized May 6.

James Son of Matthew and Judith Johnson born April 3, baptized May 6.

Frances Daughter of David and Eliz^a Roper born March 5, baptized May 6.

Martin Son of William and Jane Webb born Dec'r 29, baptized May 6, 1738.

Mary Daughter of Theodorick and Temperance Martin born March 28, baptized May 6.

Anna Maria Daughter of John and Frances Dandridge born March 30, baptized May 18.

Richard Son of John and Mary Tomson born April 16, baptized May 20.

Ithamar Son of John and Elizabeth Green born April 8, baptized May 20.

Walter Son of William and Cassandra Clopton born April 29,
   baptized May 27,
Susanna Daughter of John and Susanna Roberts born Jan'ry
   28, baptized June 3.
Matthew Negro Boy belonging to John Whitlock born Jan'ry
   20, baptized June 10.
Thomas Moss dy'd June 11.
Joanna Negro Girl belonging to Amy Burk born May 17.
Elizabeth Daughter of Henry and Mary Burrows born March
   29, baptized June 29.
Jenny Negro Girl belonging to John Poindexter born Augt. 30,
   1738.
William Son of George and Lucy Taylor born May 1, baptized
   June 17.
Elizabeth Daughter of Mary Rock free malatto born April 23,
   baptized July 8.
Edward son of John and Susanna Dollard born May 18, bap-
   tized July 8.
Thomas Negro Boy belonging to Mrs. Tabitha Adams born
   March 15, baptized July 15, 1738.
Edward Negro Boy belonging to said Adams born Decem'r 25,
   baptized July 15, 1738.
Chiloe Negro girl belonging to said Adams born April 10, bap-
   tized July 15.
Prudence Negro girl belonging to Maj' Jos. Foster born May 1,
   baptized July 15.
John Son of Frances and Martha Williams born June 16, bap-
   tized July 15.
John Son of Anselm and Ann Bailey born June 18, baptized
   July 21.
Sue Negro girl belonging to William Vaiden born June 28.
John Son of Samuel and Elizabeth Plumley born June 27, bap-
   tized July 22.
Jane Daughter of John and Jane Smith born June 23, baptized
   Augt. 5.
John Son of John and Mary Pearson born June 27, baptized
   Augt. 5.
Betty Negro Girl belonging to Rebecca Mosse born July 23.

William Negro Boy belonging to Mr. William Winch born May 20, baptized Augt. 19.

Richard Negro Boy belonging to Robt. Clopton born June 5, baptized Augt. 19.

Joseph Negro Boy belonging to Colo. Custis born March 30, baptized Augt. 19.

Ann Daughter of Arthur and Mary Chew born July 7, baptized Sept'r 2.

John Cox Bastard Son of Elizabeth Barnes born Augt. 19, baptized Sept'r 2.

Frances Daughter of John and Mary Lightfoot born July 30, baptized Sept'r 2.

Bristol Negro Boy belonging to Elizᵃ Vaughan born Augt. 16.

Sarah Daughter of Thomas and Mary Meekins born Augt. 17, baptized Sept. 23.

Frances Negro girl belonging to Jacob Vaiden born May 17, baptized Sept. 23.

Randal Negro Boy belonging to Thomas Hilliard born July 9, baptized Sept. 23.

Lucy Negro girl belonging to John Usory, born May 15, baptized Sept'r 23.

George Benskin son of George & Susanna Poindexter, born Aug't 26, baptized Sept'r 23.

Testis: DAVID MOSSOM, Minister.

YEAR 1739.

Eaton son of James and Ann Nance, born August 21, baptized Oct. 7.

Susanna Daughter of John and Agnes Apperson, born Sept'r 2, baptized Oct. 7.

John son of Thomas and Agnes Bradley, born Sept'r 10, baptized Oct. 21.

Jack Negro Boy belonging to Edmund Richardson, born Sept'r 18.

John son of William and Ann Morris, born Sept'r 25, baptized Oct'r 28.

James son of John and Elizabeth Howle, born Sept'r 25, baptised Oct'r 28.

Stephen son of Stephen and Mary Stricker, born Sep'r 17, baptized Oct'r 28.

Joel son of William and Sarah Ragland, born Sept'r 22, baptized Oct'r 28.

Elizabeth Daughter of William and Frances Stone, born May 24, baptized June 17.

Matthew son of William and Elizabeth Vaughan, born Sept'r 13, baptized Oct'r 28.

Rebecca mulatto girl belonging to Mr. William Gray, born April 29, baptized Oct'r 28.

Esther mulatto girl belonging to Rev'd D. Mossom, born Sept'r 17, baptized Nov'r 11.

Susanne Daughter of Goodrich and Sarah Alford, born Oct'r 5, baptized Nov'r 18.

Charity Ann Daughter of David and Elizabeth Binns, born Oct'r 20, baptized Nov'r 18.

Benedict son of Richard and Lucy Crump, born Oct'r 18, babtized Nov'r 25, died August 11.

Elizabeth negro girl belonging to Ann Bailey, born Sept'r 27, baptized Decem'r 16.

Elizabeth negro girl belonging to Colo. Custis, born June 15, baptized Dec'r 16.

John son of Thomas and Catherine Tudal, born Nov'r 25, baptized Dec'r 26.

Frances Watson Daughter of Charles and Rebecca Pearson, born July 2, baptized Aug't 13.

1738. Phebe negro girl belonging to James Morris, born Jan'ry 13.

Jesse son of Benjamin and Ann Bradley, born Nov'r 26, baptized Jan'ry 6.

Elizabeth Daughter of John and Sarah Otey, born Nov'r 26, baptized Jan'ry 6.

Patty negro girl belonging to John Lightfoot, born Octo: 7.

Betty negro girl belonging to Mrs. Sarah Barry, born July 22.

1738. Lucy negro girl belonging to Philip Poindexter, born Nov'r 10.

Judith Daughter of Robert and Mary Bailey, born Dec'r 19, baptized Feb'ry 17.

John son of Samuel and Jane Apperson, born Jan'ry 22, baptized Feb'ry 24.

Elizabeth Daughter of Edmund & Mary Richardson, born Jan'ry 11, baptized Feb. 24.

Solomon son of John and Ann Bowles, born Feb'ry 9, baptized March 16.

Toney Negro Boy belonging to Colo. Custis, born Jan'ry 10, baptized March 23.

George son of George and Susanna Waddill, born Feb'ry 8, baptized March 23.

Nimrod son of John and Ann Poindexter, born Feb'ry, baptized March 23.

1740. Walter son of Walter and Mary Clopton, born Feb'ry 18, baptized March 30.

Anna Daughter of Richard and Judith Jones, born Feb'ry 26, baptized March 30.

Thomas Negro Boy belonging to Colo. Custis, born Feb'ry 2, baptized April 6.

Henry Son of Henry and Anna Talman 1739, born Dec'r 26, baptized April 8.

1739. Henry Son of Henry and Margret Barnes, born Octo'r 12.

Dilsey Negro Girl belonging to George Wilkinson, born July 20.

Lucy Negro Girl belonging to Do., born Aug't 26.

Cloe Negro girl belonging to Do., born Sept'r 4.

YEAR.

1743. Sam Negro Boy belonging to Thomas Moss born Decem'r 5.

1751. Joe Negro Boy belonging to Thomas Moss born August 6.

1753. Ned Negro Boy belonging to Thomas Moss born July 24.

1756. Betty Negro girl belonging to Thomas Mosse born October 8.

1754. Sarah Daughter of George and Ann Webb born January 3, baptized Feb. 6.

1756. Mary Daughter of George and Ann Webb born Septem'r 25, baptized Octo. 17.

1758. Bernard Son of George Webb deceased and Ann his wife born May 18, baptized June 14.

1748. Esther Negro girl belonging to David Mossom born July 3, baptized Aug. 17.

1756. John Negro Boy belonging to Samuel Apperson born July 3, baptized Aug, 15.

1757. Mary Daughter of Marianna Austin born Sept. 2.

1756. Joyce Daughter of John and Joyce Apperson born October 27, baptized Nov. 30.

1757. Elizabeth Griffin Daughter of Richard and Eliz^a Adams born Dec'r 17.

1757. Kitty Negro girl belonging to Henry Atkinson baptized Nov. 6.

1757. Katherine Negro girl belonging to Christopher Ammon born Sept. 19.

1757. Ben Negro Boy belonging to Christopher Ammon born Feb'ry 5.

1757. Jude Negro girl belonging to Christopher Ammon born Feb'ry 5.

1759. Frances Daughter of John and Joyce Apperson born March 15, baptized April 20.

1759. Robin Negro Boy belonging to John Apperson born Feb'ry 10.

1759. Richard Son of Samuel Apperson born July 25.

1759. Peter Son of Peter Apperson born Dec'r 29.

1754. William Son of John and Agnes Armistead born Jan'ry 5.

1754. Susanna Daughter of Henry and Elizabeth Atkinson born March 7, baptized Apr. 26.

1754. Mary Daughter of John and Agnes Apperson born July 30, baptized Sept. 1.

1755. Richard Son of Peter and Frances Apperson born Feb'ry 15.

1755. Fanny Daughter of John and Elizabeth Austin born Jan'ry 22, baptized Apr. 15.

1755. George Son of Christopher and Mary Ammon born Apr. 1.

1756. Peachy, John and Frances Addison's born April 27.

1756. George Son of Henry and Eliz^a Apperson born May 6.

1756. John son of Henry and Elizabeth Atkinson born May 20, baptized June 20.

1756. Kiddy Chamberlayne Bastard Daughter of Eliz^a Austin born October 24.

1757. John Son of John and Agnes Apperson born Janr. 17, baptized Feb'ry 27.

1757. William Son of Peter and Frances Apperson born March 15.

1758. Lucy Daughter of Christopher and Mary Ammon born Nov'r 27, baptized Jan'ry 1.

1758. Jane Daughter of Henry and Elizabeth Atkinson born Janr. 30.

1758. Sally Daughter of George and Lucy Adams born Feb'ry 23, baptized May 14.

1758. Sarah Daughter of Philip and Mary Austin born October 2, baptized Nov'r 19.

1758. Pattey Daughter of George and Lucy Adams born Nov'r 23.

1759. Frances Daughter of George and Betty Apperson born Augt. 5, baptized Sept. 15.

1759. Sylvanus Son of Nicholas and Mary Amos born Augt. 6, baptized Sept'r 30.

1759. Jacob son of John and Agness Apperson born Sept'r 17.

1759. James Moody Son of Henry and Eliz^a Atkinson born Augt. 23.

1760. John son of Henry and Lucy Adams born Apr. 26, baptized June 15.

1763. Frances Daughter of Henry and Eliz^a Atkinson born Jan. 10.

1767. Lyddall Son of John and Joyee Apperson born Sept. 27.

1768. Peter of George and Betty Apperson, born June 18, baptized Aug't 2nd.

1769. Mary of Joseph & Austin his wife, born Jan'y 20.

1769. Lucy Daughter of John & Joice Apperson, born April 29.

1769. Zacharias of Absalom Austin & wife, born July 5.

1770. Sarah of Peter and Sarah Apperson, born January 12, baptized February 25.

1771. Henry son of William and Frances Apperson, born Feb'ry 3, baptized April 21.

1773. Negro child belonging to Christopher Amons, baptized Jan'ry 21.

1774. Wm. of Wm. & Frances Apperson, born Nov'r 23.

A.

1779. Colo. John Armistead Departed this Life May 2.

    James Glenn Departed this Life July 4th.

1781. James Moodey Atkinson Departed (with Small Pox) aged 23 years, 17 days, Jan'y 5th.

1782. Sarah Apperson Departed this life with Dead Palsy, Jan'ry 9th.

1787. Peter Apperson Departed this Life (Pulona Feaver) July 29.

1790. Austin Hewlett Departed this Life Oct. 19.

1791. Rebecca Hewlett ———— May.

B.

1758. Eleanor Daughter of Francis and Tabitha Brown, born Sept'r 20.

1758. Tabithai wife of Francis Brown died Octo. 11.

1756. Mary Thornton Daughter of Henry and Sarah Bolton, born June 23.

1754. Rebeckah Negro girl belonging to Francis Barns baptized Aug't 3.

1754. Tabitha Daughter of Francis & Tabitha Barnes, born March 31.

1754. Gideon son of Thomas and Agnes Brothers, born May 25.

1753. William son of Peter & Martha Barnet, born Aug'st 29, baptized Sept'r 15.

1753. Sherwood Bastard Daughter of Lucy Boastman, born Jan'y 7, baptized March 23.

1755. Lucy Daughter of Wm. and Ann Bailey, born March 1.

1755. Benjamin Son of Jedediah & Elinor Bristow, born May 19, baptized June 15.

1756. James Son of Samuel and Judith Bailey, born June 27, baptized Aug't 24.

1756. Lyddal Son of Edmund and Elizabeth Bacon, born Jan'y 10.

1756. Thomas Son of Francis & Tabitha Barnes, born Feb'y 17.

1756. David Son of Thomas & Rebekah Bottom, born March 21.

1756. Mary Thornton Daughter of Henry & Sarah Bolton, born June 23, baptized Aug'st 15.

1757. Peter Son of Peter and Martha Barnet, born Dec'r 9, baptized Jan'ry 23.

1757. Rebecca Bishop Daughter of Nathan & Lucy Barnet, born March 10, baptized April 17.

1758. John son of Thomas and Mary Bowles, born Jan'ry 27.

1758. William Son of Jedediah and Elinor Bristow, born March 1, baptized Apr. 23.

1758. Martha Daughter of John and Mary Binns, born July 17, baptized Aug'st 13.

1758. Anselm son of Samuel and Judith Bailey, born July 17, baptized Aug'st 27.

1758. Mary Duke Daughter of Nathan & Lucy Barnet, born July 23, baptized Sept'r 3.

1758. Milly Daughter of William and Amy Binns, born Sept'r 12, baptized Oct'r 8.

1758. Eleanor Daughter of Francis and Tabitha Barnes, born Sept. 20, baptized Oct. 15.

1758. Littlebury son of Peter and Martha Barnes, born Nov. 27.

1760. James son of Thomas and Mary Bowles, born March 29.

1767. Daniel Son of Thos. & Frances Binns born June 19.

1767. Rebekah Daughter of Wm. Butler & Sufelistan his wife born Dec'r 11.

1768. Nelson Son of Walter & Lovy Bradley born Jan'ry 20 dyed Sep. 16, 1794.

1768. Jesse Scott of Robt. & Frances Bowes his wife born Jan'ry 22.

1769. Edm^d of Edwd & Mary Bailey born Feb. 18.

1769. Sarah Daughter of Lyddall & Ann Bacon born Apr. 17.

1769. William of Thoms. & Frances Binns born May 8, baptized June 18.

1770. Mary Furbish Brooker Daugh^r of Jno. and Rebeker Brooker born Nov. 13.

1770. William Bailey of John Bailey and Fra^s his wife born Nov. 21, baptized Jan. 20.

1771. Susannah Daughter of James & Susannah Bozman born Feb'ry 3.

1771. Eliza Ann Daughter of Edwd and Mary Bailey born Sep'r 9, baptized Oct. 15.

1771. Sally Daughter of Jno. & Eve Barkwell born Oct'r 2.

1771. John Parish Barkwell of Thos. and Eliz^a Barkwell born Nov'r 8.

1772. Absalom of Peter and Martha Barnett born Feb'ry 1.

1773. Parkes son of Edwd and Mary Bailey born Ja'ry 8.

1773. Sarah of James and Susannah Bosman born Mar. 22.

1773. Dan'l of Wm. & Sufeliston Butler born May 24.

1773. Sarah Moon of John & Rebeckah Brooker born Augt. 10.

1775. Jas. of Edwd and Mary Bailey born Saturday Augt. 12.

1773. James of Thos. & Eliza Barkwell born Sep'r 26.

1775. Thos. of Do. and do. born Dec'r 1, baptized Jany. 21.

1775. Anne of Parrobo & Fra^s Ann Boswel born Nov. 14.

1778. Polly Daughter of do. was Born June 5.

1777. Thos. Son of Edwd & Mary Bailey born Nov. 22.

1777. Martha Daughter of Parrobo & Frances Ann Boswell born May 23.

1746. Adam a Negro Boy belonging to Nancy Addison born Jan'ry 10.

C.

1757. Michael Negro Boy belonging to Thomas Coussans born April 23.

1757. Richard Negro Boy belonging to Watt Clopton born March 12, baptized June 20.

1757. Morris Jones belonging to Martha Custis born October 29.

1757. Sarah Negro girl belonging to Watt Clopton born November 16.

1756. Benjamin Negro Boy belonging to Nathan Crump born June 19.

1758. Jasper son of John Clayton Junr. born Aug'st 23.

1759. Elvira Daughter of William & Elvira Clayton born Dec'r 27, baptized Jan'ry 27, 1760.

1753. John son of Richard & Lucy Crump born Sept'r 25.

1753. Lucy Wife of Richard Crump died in Sept'r.

1753. Julius Son of James and Martha Crump born October 22, baptized De'r 2.

1753. William Son of John and Patty Crump born Dec'r 3, baptized Jan'ry 13.

1753. David Son of Wm. and Ann Corley born Jan'ry 6, baptized Feb'ry 10.

1754. Jesse Son of Charles & Eliz* Crump born Jan'ry 8.

1754. James Son of William & Eliz* Cock born March 9, baptized Apr. 21.

1754. Melvin Son of Nathaniel & Mary Crump born April 8.

1754. John Allen Son of John and Fanny Chandler born May 13, baptized June 9.

1754. Daniel son of Richard & Susan Crump, born Aug'st 13.

1755. Waldegrave son of Waldegrave & Unity Clopton, born Nov. 11, baptized Jan'ry 25, 1758.

1755. Robert son of Robert and Frances Clopton, born Feb'ry 26.

1755. Anna Daughter of Antho. & Ann Cole, born Feb'ry 4, baptized May 25.

1755. Gideon Son of James & Tabitha Christian, born April 30, baptized June 1.

1755. Ann Daughter of James & Ann Clarkson, born June 4, baptized July 30.

1755. Charles son of Nathaniel & Sarah Crump, born Sept'r 14, baptized Nov'r 30.

1756. Mary Daughter of Charles & Ann Cooper, born April 2, baptized May 16.

1756. Cecily Daughter of John & Patty Crump, born June 18, baptized July 11.

1756. Abner son of Richard & Mary Crump, born July 5, baptized Aug'st 15.

1756. Mary Ann Daughter of Benjamin & Sarah Collier, born Oct'r 4, baptized Oct'r 31.

1756. Thomas son of Richard & Susanna Crump, born Nov'r 5, baptized Dec'r 5.

1757. Elizabeth Daughter of Nathaniel & Sarah Crump, born Jan'ry 29.

1757. Sarah Daughter of Joel & Sarah Christian, born Jan'ry 19, baptized March 20.

1757. Jacob son of John & Elizabeth Carter, born Jan'ry 1.

1760. Judah Daughter of Richard Crump, born Octo'r 29.

1759. Henry son of James & Ann Clarke, born Nov'r 19.

1760. Robert son of William & Elizabeth Christian, born May 5.

1757. Jesse Bastard Son of Hannah Crump, born Feb'ry 28, baptized June 5.

1757. Susanna Daughter of William & Susanna Christian, born May 29, baptized July 10.

1757. Abner son of Robert & Frances Clopton, born July 14.

1757. Ann Daughter of James & Anne Clarke, born June 19, baptized Aug't 17.

1757. Elizabeth Daughter of George & Susanna Chandler, born Sept'r 13, baptized Oct. 9.

1757. Joseph son of James & Tabitha Christian, born Sept'r 4.

1758. Henry son of Antho. & Ann Cole, born Feb'ry 11.

1758. Lucy Daughter of James & Ann Clarkson, born Apr. 9.

1758. John son of Benja. & Sarah Collier, born Aug'st 7.

1758. Lyddall Son of Richard & Susanna Crump, born Aug'st 28.

1758. John Pinchback son of Charles & Sarah Crump, born Aug'st 28.

1758. David Son of Wm. & Elizabeth Cook, born Apr. 10, baptized Dec'r 10.

1767. Nathaniel Son of Nath. & Sarah Crump, born April 5.

1767. Archelaus Son of Rich'd & Susanna Crump, born Jan'ry 13.

1767. Kesandra Dau' of Robt. & Alice Crump, born Mar. 17.

1767. John son of Wm. & Mary Chancey, born Mar. 3, baptized April 26.

1767. Nath'l son of ——— ———, born May 4.

1758. Thomas son of John & Elizabeth Cox, born Nov'r 26.

1758. Clara Daughter of Nath'l & Sarah Crump, born Nov'r 23, baptized Dec'r 31.

1759. Sarah son of (?) John & Patty Crump, born Jan'ry 16, baptized Feb'ry 18.

1759. Robert Wentworth son of Wm. & Eliza. Clopton, born Sept'r 24.

1759. Alley Daughter of Joel & Sarah Christian, born Aug'st 26, baptized Octo. 28.

1760. John & Nancy Daughters of Robt. & Frances Clopton, born Nov'r 4, baptized Jan'ry 27.

1760. Mary Daughter of John & Eliza. Cox, born Feb'y 8.

1760. Elizabeth Daughter of Charles & Sarah Crump, born Feb'ry 25.

1760. Elizabeth Daughter of Richard & Susanna Crump born March 10.

1760. Leonard son of Nathan & Sarah Crump born Apr. 25, baptized June 8.

1765. Sarah Ravencroft Daughter of Chas. H. Cox & Ann his wife born June 24.

1767. Susannah Daughter of Chas. H. Cox & Ann his wife born Jan'ry 28.

1768. Edward Pye of Richard & Mary Chamberlayne born Jan'ry 16.

1768. Hannah Negro girl belonging to Eliz^a Crump born April 5, baptized June 5.

1768. Sharard son of John & Patty Crump born June 25, baptized July 31.

1768. Eliz^a Daughter of James & Ann Clark born June 11, baptized July 31.

1768. William Son of Wm. & Rebeckah Sherman born Aug'st 1. This is in its wrong place.

1768. Sarah Hewlet of Robt. & Fras. Clopton born July 22, baptized Sep'r 18.

1768. George Woodward Son of Chas. Henry & Ann Cox born Sept'r 10.

1769. Cathrine Daughter of Robt. & Alice Crump born Mar. 31.

1764. John son of William & Sarah Crittenden born Nov'r 3.

1767. William son of Do. born April 22.

1769. William son of Wm. and Mary Chancey born Aug'st 5, baptized Sep'r 3.

1769. John son of Henry & Martha Christian born May 25.

1769. Haviliah son of Benedict & Eliz^a Crump born April 8.

1761. Rich'd Hazelwood son of Jno. & Mary Crittenden born March 6.

1763. Salley of Do. born Jan'ry 14.

1763. John of Do. born Mar. 29.

1767.   Mary of Do. born Ap'l 13.

1769.   Eliza Smith of Do. born Oct'r 22.

1771.   David Son of John Condon & Ann Ritter his wife born Jan'ry 2.

1771.   Nancey Daughter of Chas. H. Cox & Ann his wife born June 18, baptized July 28.

1772.   Martha of John & Mary Crump born Nov'r 5, baptized Jan'ry 10:75.

1772.   Anna Dudley Coleman of Thos. & Anna Coleman born Sep'r 26.

1772.   Chas. son of Jno. and Mary Crittenden born Dec'r 15.

1774.   John Hunt son of John & Mildred Christian born Sep'r 1st.

1775.   Thos. the Son of Chas. H. & Ann Cox born April 3, baptized May 30.

1775.   Cathrine of John & Patty Crump born April 22, baptized May 28.

1774.   Nancy Daughter of John & Ann Ritter Condon his wife was born June 7.

1783.   Boller Cock Castle Son of Mary Castle Born 25th May.

1794.   Jno. P. Crump Son of Bene[t] & Susanna Crump dyed April 5.

D.

1758.   Mary Daughter of James and Martha Danforth born Decr. 8.

1753.   Eliz[a] Ann Daughter of Millington and Sarah Dixon born May 30.

1753.   Mary Daughter of William & Agnes Drake born Nov'r 13, baptized Dec'r 18.

1753.   William Son of Ambrose & Hannah Dudley born Dec'r 18.

1754.   Susanna Daughter of Griffith & Ann Dickinson born March 14, baptized Apr. 7.

1754.   Lucy Daughter of John and Susanna Dollard born Apr. 5.

1754.   Bartholomew Son of William and Mary Dungee born Aug'st 3, baptized Sept'r 7.

1755.   Mary Daughter of Millington & Sarah Dixon born Oct. 15, baptized Nov'r 16.

1755. Joel Son of William & Agnes Drake born Dec'r 9.

1756. Sarah Daughter of Walter and Mary Daniel, born Sept. 28, baptized Nov. 7.

1744. Will Negro Boy belonging to Edwin Daingerfield, born Feb'ry 13.

1757. Sarah Daughter of Millington & Sarah Dixon, born July 2.

1757. Susann Daughter of John & Susanna Dollard, born Aug'st 12, baptized Oct'r 23.

1758. James Son of Ambrose & Hannah Dudley, born Feb'ry 27.

1758. Mary Daughter of Walter & Mary Daniel, born Sept'r 17, baptized Oct'r 29.

1767. Wm. Daniel son of Walter & Mary Daniel, born Octo. 4.

1768. Epaphroditus son of Wm Gilliam (This is in the wrong place), born Jan'y 20.

1767. John of Wm. & Martha Davis was born Dec'r 13.

1769. Sarah of Robt. & Rachel Drake, born Jan'ry 9.

1769. Molley of Wm. Cook Dennett & Calron his wife, born Do. 23.

1770. William Drake, aged about 63 years, Departed Octo. 24.

1770. John Amons of Wm. C. Dennett & Calron his wife, born Dec'r 6, baptized Jan'ry 20.

1771. William son of Robert & Rachel Drake, born May 30.

1773. Thos. Darnold was born (Sig'd by Nich's Darnold) May 14.

1775. John son of William & Fra^s Dudley, born Jan'ry 19.

1775. Eliz^a of Geo: & Lucy Heath, born April 10, baptized May 28.

1782. Mary Daughter of James Davis & Mary his wife, born Sept'r 10.

1784. John son of James & Mary Davis his wife, born Octo'r 8.

1786. Elizabeth Daughter of James & Mary Davis, born Oct'r 26.

1784. Sally Daughter of Anto. Davis & Ann his wife, born Octo'r 11.

1786. William of Do & Do, born Sept'r 10.

1792. Mary Ann Daughter of Anthony Davis & Ann, born Aug'st 22.

1795. Kitty Daughter of Anthony Davis & Ann his wife, born May 22.

1797. Thomas Evans Son of Anthony Davis & Ann his wife, born Dec'r 18.

1801. Fanny dau. of Anthony Davis & Ann, born April 8.

E.

1752. George Negro Boy belonging to Joseph & Mary Ellison, born July 18.

1754. David Negro Boy belonging to Joseph & Mary Ellison, born June 23.

F.

1760. Sam negro Boy belonging to John Finch, born Aug'st 24, baptized Sept. 24.

1753. Jonathan son of John & Elizabeth Flewellin, born May 17, baptized June 24.

1753. Susanna Daughter of Ed^{wd} and Eliza. Finch, born May 7, baptized July 1.

1753. Aggee Daughter of John & Rebecca Finch, born July 31, baptized Nov'r 4.

1755. Moss son of Ed^{wd} & Eliz^a Finch, born Feb'ry 5

1755. William son of Robert & Mary Forbes, born August 1.

1756. John Bassett Son of Henry & Ann Frances, born April 19, baptized May 23.

1756. Nathan'l Bassett son of Henry & Ann Frances, born May 18.

1757. Henry Son of Edward & Elizabeth Finch, born Dec'r 29.

1760. Mary Daughter of Henry & Sarah Finch, born Dec'r 28.

1757. Mary Cocke & Eliz^a Twins Daughters of Brothers & Sarah Finch, born August 31.

1758. Thomas Son of Edmund & Mary Forbes, born Jan'ry 28, baptized Feb'ry 26.

1758. Caleb son of Henry & Ann Frances, born March 6.

1758. John Son of John & Mary Ferris, born August 10, baptized May 7.

1758. Alley Daughter of Robert & Mary Forbes, born Nov'r 15, baptized Dec'r 17.

1759. Elizabeth Daughter of Frances & Elizabeth Foster born May 10.

1759. Sarah Daughter of Brother & Sarah Finch born July 25, baptized Aug'st 26.

1760. John son of Edmund & Mary Forbes born Jan'ry 25, baptized Feb'ry 24.

1760. Thomas Son of Nath'l Bassett & Ann Francis born May 24.

1767. Martha Daughter of Fra^s Forster & Eliz^a his wife born Dec'r 26.

1768. William son of Samuel Trower & Lucy Trower born Jan'ry 9.

1767. Lucy Daughter of Edwd & Eliz^a Finch born Dec'r 19.

1768. Ben a Negro belonging to John Finch born May 7, baptized August 21.

1768. Sarah Waddy of Henry & Sarah Finch born July 8.

1768. Samuel Firth of Samuel & Susanna Firth born Nov'r 10.

1769. Peter Negro Boy belonging to John Finch born Dec'r 24, baptized April 1st, '70.

1770. Molley of Henry Sarah Finch born July 20.

1771. Fra^s of Francis & Eliz^a Forster born March 14.

1771. Rebekah of Robt. & Agness Furbush born April 10.

1771. Edward son of Henry & Sarah Finch born Dec'r 4.

1773. Adam son of Edward & Eliz^a Finch born May 30.

1774. Rich^d son of Henry & Sarah Finch born Nov'r 7.

1783. Pleasant son of James Finch & Judith his wife born March 8.

1785. Betsy Daughter of Do. born March 1.

G.

1758. Ralph the son of Richard & Dyonysia Graves born March 8.

1758. Fanney Negro Girl belonging to John Green born May 28.

1757. James Negro Boy belonging to Richard Graves born Dec'r 16.

1757. Ned Negro Boy belonging to Richard Graves born April 25.

1759. Sarah Cobb Daughter of Richard & Dyonysia Graves born Dec. 30.

1753. Charles Henry son of Rich^d & Dyonysia Graves born June 1, baptized July 1.

1754. Ann Daughter of Hanstey & Susanna Grubbs born Oct. 6, baptized Nov'r 10.

1755. Mary Daughter of Richard & Dyonysia Graves born Feb'ry 6.

1755. Thomas Son of William & Martha Gregory born Aug'st 22.

1756. William Son of Richard & Dionysia Graves born August 2, baptized September 5.

1760. Judith Negro Girl belonging to John Green born Dec'r 10.

1757. Isaac son of William & Martha Gregory born Nov'r 6, baptized September.

1758. Thomas son of Thomas & Theodosia Goodwin born Sept'r 10.

1758. Susanna Daughter of Hensley & Susanna Grubbs born May 15, baptized June 18.

1759. William son of John & Elizabeth Glen born Feb'ry 24, baptized in March.

1760. Edmund son of William & Martha Gregory born Jan'ry 25, baptized October.

1760. John son of Nicholas & Temperance Goldwell born Jan'ry 12, baptized June.

1768. Epaphroditus son of William Gilliam born Jan'ry 20.

1768. Eliz^a Goocher of Domini & Ann Goocher baptized June 2.

1763. Sarah Green Departed this Life Nov'r 23rd.

1768. Phillis a negro belonging to John Green born July 28.

1768. Thos. Son of John and Eliz^a Glenn born Nov'r 28, baptized Jan'ry 22.

1769. Sarah Daughter of Jacob & Eliz^a Gaulding born Aug'st 5, baptized Sept. 7.

1769. Catharine Daughter of John & Mildret Gording born Dec. 12.

1770. Mathew son of Jno. & Eliz^a Glenn born Dec'r 20, baptized Feb'ry 3d.

1771. Bob negro belonging to Ithamar Green born Decemb. 12.

1772. —— child of Jacob & Eliz^a Gaulding born Feb'ry 4.

1773. Thos. Son of Hezekiah & Molly Hardin born April 19, wrong place.

1773. Pleasant son of Jno. & Eliz^a Glenn born May 11.

1781. Pleasant Glenn departed this life July 8.

1767. John Son of Lyddall & Ann [Bacon?].

1785. Elizabeth Winfree Daughter of Jno. & Frances Glenn born Jan'ry 12.

1768. Epaphroditus Son of William Gilliam born Jan'ry 20.

1755. Thos. Son of William & Martha Gregory born Aug. 22.

1788. Kitty Daughter of Mary Glenn born Mar. 3.

1786. Mary Moody Daughter of John Glenn & Frances his wife born Ap'l 26th.

1788. Nancy Daughter of Jno. Glenn & Frances his wife born Aug. 18.

H.

1756. Daniel a Negro Boy belonging to William Hilliard born Decem'r 23.

1758. William Son of Frances & Joyce Harris born Feb'ry 26.

1757. Jane Negroe child belonging to Martin Hewlett born Decem'r 10.

1758. Cate Negro girl belonging to Thomas Hilliard died Nov'r 3.

1756. Susanna Negro girl belonging to Thomas Hilliard born Octob'r 11.

1757. Jane Negro girl belonging to James Morris born Feb'ry 25.

1757. Daniel Negro Boy belonging to William Hilliard died Dec'r 10.

1758. Judy Negro girl belonging to John Hilliard born March 21.

1758. Jeremiah Negro Boy belonging to John Hutcheson born June 22.

1757. Sue Negro Girl belonging to Thomas Hilliard baptized June 26.

1757. Anthony Negro Boy belonging to John Hutchinson born July 30, baptized October 2.

1755. Frances wife of William Hopkins dyed Dec'r 10.

1755. William Hopkins died Dec'r 16.

1756. Calesby Negro Boy belonging to Thomas Hilliard born June 25.

1759. Judy Negro Boy belonging to Thomas Hilliard born Jan'ry 3.

1758. Joseph Negro Boy belonging to Jeremiah Hilliard born Dec'r 22.

1759. Frederick Sackville son of Ralph & Agnes Hankey born Feb'ry 20.

1759. Isham Negro Boy belonging to Thomas Hilliard born April 5.

1759. Thomas Hilliard Junior died Jan'ry 1.

1760. Elizabeth Chamberlayne Daughter of David & Mary Harfield born July 4, baptized Aug'st 12.

1759. Joseph Negro Boy belonging to Jeremiah Hilliard baptized May 6.

1759. Peter Negro Boy belonging to Jeremiah Hilliard baptized May 6.

1759. George son of Thomas & Elizabeth Hatten born Feb'ry 8, baptized March 10.

1759. Susanna Johnson Negro Girl belonging to Thomas Hilliard born Jan'ry 16.

1759. Sterling son of William & Sarah Hopkins born Dec'r 5.

1759. Unity Wife of William Hilliard died Dec'r 3.

1753. Thomas Son of Epaphroditus & Mary Howle born Sept. 1.

1753. Judith Daughter of John & Ann Howle born Sept'r 26, baptized Nov'r 11.

1754. Susanna Daughter of John & Elizabeth Howle, born March 9, baptized May 12.

1754. Jno. & Milly son & Daughter of Anthony & Mary Waddy, born Apr. 9.

1754. Jenny Daughter of John & Agnes Hamlet, born March 25, baptized May 24.

1754. John Son of William & Ann Hewlett, born July 17, baptized Aug't 18.

1754. Tamar Daughter of John Hilliard, born Aug't 22.

1754. William son of William & Margaret Hatten, born Sept'r 2, baptized Octo'r 27.

1755. William son of William & Unity Hilliard, born Jan'y 20, baptized March 2.

1755. Rebeca Daughter of John & Lucy Hamlet, born Jan'y 28.

1755. Absalom son of John & Annis Hughes, born June 16, baptized July 13.

1755. Fanny Daughter of Robert & Eliz^a Hollings, born July 4, baptized Aug't 3.

1755. Walter son of Francis & Joyce Harris, born Oct'r 24, baptized Dec'r 21.

1756. Epaphroditus Son of Epaphroditus & Mary Howle, born Feb'ry 13.

1756. Mary Daughter of William & Frances Hatten, born Feb'ry 19, baptized April 18.

1756. Gideon Son of Absalom & Hannah Howle, born April 10.

1756. Edmund Son of William & Mary Hewlett, born June 2.

1757. Keziah Daughter of John & Keziah Hilliard, born Jan'y 20.

1757. Stephen Son of John & Annis Hughes, born March 22.

1761. Lewellin son of Christopher & Elizabeth Hudson, born Nov'r 9, baptized Dec'r 14.

1757. Wm. Tragu Son of John & Sarah Hopkins, born March 25.

1757. Elizabeth Daughter of John & Ann Howle, born March 12, baptized May 1.

1767. Geo. son of Geo: Heath & Lucy his wife, born Sept'r 29.

1767. Rich'd son of Martin Hewlet & Sarah his wife, born May 18.

1767. John son of Wm. Hewlet & Fra^s his wife, born March 11, died Sept. 5, 1784.

1767. Wm. son of William Hazelgrove & Lucy his wife, born Jan'ry 7.

1768. Mary of Do., born Oct. 21, baptized Dec. 11.

1769. Eliz^a of Wm. & Fra^s Hewlet, born Aug. 13.

177–. Pleasant son of —— Hylliard, born Dec'r 27.

1773. Benskin Herman son of William & Molly Hylliard, born May 24.

1773. Benjamin Hilliard was born Novem'r 25.

1775. Susannah Daughter of Martin & Sarah Hewlet, born Mar. 18, baptized May 28.

1775. Goldwell son of Hezekiah & Molly Harden, born July 8, baptized Aug't 6.

1757. Sally Daughter of John & Eliz^a Howle, born April 10, baptized June 12.

1757. Joseph son of John & Mary Howle, born May 7, baptized July 31.

1757. Mary Daughter of William & Unity Hilliard, born Octo. 19, baptized Dec'r 11.

1758. Jane Daughter of Ralph & Agnes Hankey, born Oct. 12.

1758. Mary Daughter of Lewis & Naomi Hancock, born Dec'r 14, baptized January 15.

1758. Elizabeth Williamson Daughter of Thomas & Mary Hilliard, born Jan'y 10, baptized Feb'ry 19.

1758. Fanny Daughter of Absalom & Hannah Howle, born Feb'y 6.

1758. Benjamin son of William & Frances Hatton, born Feb'ry 9, baptized Apr. 9.

1758. Henrietta Daughter of William & Lucy Hazlegrove, born May 20.

1758. Jeremiah son of Jerem^{ah} Kerenhappuck Hilliard, born May 21, baptized June 25.

1758. Ann Daughter of William & Mary Harris, born Aug't 23, baptized October 1.

1759. Susanna Daughter of George & Agnes Hamlet, born Feb'ry 4, baptized Mar. 4.

1759. James son of Epaphroditus & Mary Howle, born Feb'ry 26.

1759. Frederick Sackville son of Ralph & Agnes Hankey, born Feb'ry 20, baptized April 1.

1759. Joyce Daughter of John & Lucy Hamlyn, born Apr. 18, baptized May 20.

1759. John son of John & Keziah Hilliard, born Apr. 27, baptized May 27.

1759. Reuben son of William & Frances Hatton, born May 11.

1759. Betty Daughter of John & Eliz^a Howle, born July 12, baptized October 14.

1760. John son of John & Sarah Hopkins, born Feb'ry 25, baptized March 23.

1760. John son of Robert & Eliz* Hollinge, born March 1.

1760. Charles son of Absalom & Hanna Howle, born March 2, baptized May 4.

1760. Thomas son of Jeremiah & Kerenhappuck Hilliard, born April 11, baptized May 18.

1760. Lewis son of William & Lucy Hazlegrove, born May 2, baptized June 29.

1760. James son of John & Ann Howle, born June 13.

1760. Thomas son of Thomas & Eliz* Hatton, born June 30, baptized Aug't 10.

1766. Wm. son of Thomas Hatton & Eliz* his wife, born Nov'r 21.

1767. Thomas Hilliard, died Jan'ry 17.

1767. Roger a negro boy belonging to Frances Hilliard, born March 22.

1762. John son of Thos. Hatton & Eliz* his wife, born April 13.

1764. Eliz* Daughter of Thomas & Eliz* Hatton, born October 17.

1767. Thos. Cleyborne of Wm. & Molly Hilliard, born Jan'ry 29.

1768. Armistead son of Micajah & Mary Hilliard, born May 28, baptized June 26th.

1768. Sarah Negro girl belonging to Micajah Hilliard, born May 13.

1768. Thos. son of George & Agness Hamblett, born Apr. 30, baptized July 30th.

1768. Geo: Fleet Hoomes son of Stephen F. Hoomes, born Apr. 9, baptized May 24.

1768. Jeremiah Hilliard departed this Life April 8th.

1768. Abram belonging to Keren Hilliard, born June 25.

1768. John Godfrey ——— of Robert Trowel & Mary his wife, born July 12, baptized Aug't 21st.

1768. John of Rich'd & Ann Howle, born Oct'r 8, baptized Dec'r 11.

1768. Francis of James & Susannah Howle, born Oct'r 28, baptized Feb'ry 12.

1768. Nancy of Epaphroditus & Mary Howle, born July 6.

11

176-. Lewis of Do, born Feb'ry 5.

1768. Tabitha of Do, born June 28.

1769. Daniel of Do, born Apr. 20th.

1769. John of Jesse & Mildris Hall, born Octo'r 8.

1770. Bartlett of Micajah & Mary Hilliard, born Feb'y 28, baptized Ap'l 8th.

1769. James Negro Boy belonging to Eliz^a Hollings, born Dec'r 7, baptized April.

1770. Mary Oakley of George Heath, born March 11, baptized April 24.

1769. Rich'd son of Wm. & Moley Hilliard, born Decem'br 16, baptized April 29.

1770.· Rich'd son of Rich'd & Ann Howle, born Jan'y 25, baptized April 29.

1770. Eve negro belonging to Keren H. Hilliard, born Aug'st 15.

1771. Susannah first Daughter of Gideon & Mary Hill of Hanover born Feb'ry 6.

1771. Robert Carter third son of Wm. & Frances Hewlet born March 31.

1771. Sarah & Betsey twin Daughters of Robt. & Mary Howel born March 22, baptized April 28.   Free Molatto.

1772. Thos. of Rich^d & Ann Howle born March 29.

1772. Becke Daughter of Martin & Sarah Hewlet born May 30.

1773. William son of Martin & Susannah Hewlet born Jan'ry 16, baptized Feb'y 28.

1773. Lucy Hunt of George & Lucy Heath born Jan'ry 16.

1773. Thos. of Hezekiah & Molley Haiden born Apl. 19.

1782. Mary Ann of Lucy Howel born May 27.

1740. Austin Hewlet son of Martin & Susanna Hewlett born Apl. 1st.

1764. Anna Daughter Austin & Rebecca Hewlett born Nov'r 9.

1766. Sally Born of Ditto July 11.

1768. James Born of Ditto Apl. 16.

1770. Martha Born of Ditto Feb'ry 28.

1772. Elizabeth Born of Ditto Oct. 11, died July 30, 1775.

1775. Henry Born of Ditto May 6th, died Augt. 1, 1775.

1777. Elizabeth Ballard Born of Ditto Sept'r 6.

1785. Robert son to Thomas & Lucy Howel born Feb'ry 20.

1755. Elizª of George & Lucy Heath born April 10th, baptized May 28th.

1773. Thos. son of Hezekiah & Molley Hardin born April 19.

1786. John Hopkins Departed this life, aged about 54 years, July 16th.

1765. Richᵈ Heath son of Geo. & Lucy Heath born Jan'y 20.

1793. Lucy Hunt & Epaphroditus twin Daughter & Son of Lewis & Elizabeth Howle born Sept. 30.

1787. Susanna Daughter of Thos. & Lucy Howel born April 17.

1790. Rebecca Daughter of Do. Do. born do. 27.

1794. Elizabeth Daughter of Do. Do. born Mar. 12.

1795. Richᵈ Heath son of Geo. & Lucy Heath Departed March 20.

I.

1757. William son of Thomas and Anna Ivy born March 29, baptized May 3.

1760. Cloe Negro girl belonging to Thomas Ivy born Aug'st 14.

1759. Mary Daughter of Thomas & Anna Ivy born Decem'r 9.

1753. Milley Daughter of Matthew & Judith Johnson born May 7.

1753. Benjamin son of Thomas & Elizª Johnson born Aug'st 12, baptized Sept'r 30.

1754. John Hardy Son of James & Sarah Ingram born May 27, baptized June 30.

1755. Rebecca Daughter of Daniel & Mary Jameson born April 5, baptized May 4.

1756. Susanna Daughter of Matthew & Judith Johnson born Nov'r 6, baptized Jan'ry 11.

1756. Patty Daughter of Thomas & Elizabeth Johnson born Jan'ry 24.

1756. Mary Daughter of James & Sarah Ingram born Feb'ry 6, baptized March 21.

1757. Jacob son of Tobias & Eliza. Johnson born Jan'ry 23, baptized May 29.

1757. Susanna Daughter of Daniel & Mary Jameson born Sept'r 4.

1758. Cicely Daughter of Thomas & Eliz^a Johnson born Jan'ry 2, baptized April 2.

1758. Mary Daughter of Tobias & Elizabeth Johnson born Feb'ry 3, baptized Apr. 16.

1758. Elizabeth Daughter of James & Sarah Ingram born Aug'st 21, baptized Sep'r 24.

1759. Joseph son of Francis & Ann Joseph born June 6.

1759. Isaac son of Thos. & Eliz^a Johnson born May 29, baptized July 8.

1760. Elizabeth Daughter of Daniel & Mary Jameson born June 10, baptized July 13.

1763. Freman son of William & Mildred Jameson born Feb'ry 10.

1765. Frances Daughter of Do. Do. born Sep'r 15.

1767. Ralph son of Do. Do. born Oct'r 15.

1769. Sally Daughter of Do. Do. born Oct'r 1st.

1771. Eliza. Daughter of Do. Do. born Jan'ry 30.

K.

1756. Ann Daughter of James & Sarah Kempton born Feb'ry 3.

1769. Benjamin of Wm. & Ann Keiningham born 22 Jan'y, baptized Mar. 18.

L.

1748. William Turner son of Charles Lemay born Aug'st 24.

1752. Mary Daughter of Charles Lemay born Novem'r 19.

1754. Jane Daughter of Charles Lemay born October 22.

1748. Judith a Negroe Girl belonging to John Lewis Sen'r born Febr'y 10.

1756. Robin a Negro Boy belonging to John Lewis Sen'r born October 4.

1753. Ann a Negro Girl belonging to John Lewis Sen'r born Decem'r 1.

1757. Charles the Son of Charles & Susannah Lemay born Feb'ry 8.

1758. John the Son of Edward & Ann Langford born Sept'r 16.

1750. Lucy Daughter of William & Sarah Lacy born February 3, baptized March 5.

1750. Jesse son of Sandy & Elizabeth Linzey born January 15.

1760. Kiddy Daughter of Wm. & Sarah Lacy born March 26, baptized May 4.

1753. William Son of Edward & Ann Langford born Jan'ry 24, baptized March 17.

1754. Richard Littlepage Son of John & Frances Lacy born March 22.

1754. Thomas Son of William & Martha Leonard born Sept'r 13.

1755. Elizabeth George & Frances Lewis's Daughter born Jan'ry 6, baptized March 2.

1755. William son of William & Sarah Lacy born Feb'ry 7.

1755. David son of John & Elizabeth Lewellin born Aug'st 15.

1756. Ann Daughter of John & Frances Lacey born Dec'r 25, baptized Jan'ry 25.

1756. Jesse son of Sandy & Eliza Linsey born Jan'ry 15.

1756. Edmund Son of Edward & Ann Langford born March 21.

1760. Moses Negro Boy belonging to John Lacy born Aug'st 22.

1757. Edmund son of Henry & Sarah Lacy born May 9.

1757. James Son of William & Martha Leonard born May 24.

1758. Edward son of John & Frances Lacey born Nov'r 23.

1758. Sarah Daughter of George & Frances Lewis born Nov'r 19.

1758. John son of Edward & Ann Langford born Sept'r 16.

1759. Ann Daughter of Henry & Sarah Lacy born Aug'st 24.

1762. Thos. Bates of Henry & Sarah Lacy born April 5.

1764. Mary of Henry & Sarah Lacy born June 1.

1768. Susanna of Daniel & Frances Lyon born May 4, baptized June 12.

1768. Bartholomew son of John & Frances Lacy born Nov'r 23d, baptized Jan'ry 22, '69.

1769. Archer son of Wm Lacy & Sarah his wife, born Feb'ry 4.

1768. Thomas negro belonging to Do, born 23 October.

1768. Dufery negro of do, born Dec'r 9.

1770. Eliza Daughter of Daniel & Fra^s Lyon, born Jan'ry 2.

1771. Thos. of Dan'l Lucas & Sarah his wife free mulatto, born May 7, baptized June 10.

1773. Joseph son of Dan'l & Lucy Lucas mollattos, born Feb'ry 7, baptized Mar. 14.

1775. Dan¹ of Dan¹ & Sarah Lucas, born Mar. 19.

1775. John & Wm. Twins of Dan¹ & Fra⁸ Lyon, born Nov'r 19, baptized Jan'ry 21.

1786. William Sone of Joseph & Lucy Lucas, born Jan'ry 28.

1788. Nancy Daughter to Do. & Do., born Feb'ry 23.

1792. Josiah Lucas son of Joseph & Lucy Lucas, born Dec'r 8.

1794. Abraham son of Joseph and Lucy Lucas, born Oct. 5.

M.

1756. Leadenhall Negro Boy belonging to James Moss, born Septem'br 27.

1756. Benjamin Negro Boy belonging to William Moore, born October 22, baptized Nov'r 28.

1758. Sam Negro Boy belonging to William Marston, born June 15, baptized August 19.

1756. Will Negro Boy belonging to Samuel Moss, born October 8.

1751. Henry son of James & Mary Moriss, born June 16, baptized June 28.

1760. Susanna Negro girl belonging to Jas. Morris, Jr., born Oct'r 4.

1760. David Negro Boy belonging to Sam'l Moss, born Jan'ry 4.

1759. James son of Joshua and Susanna Martin, born Sept'r 18.

1760. Peter Negro Boy belonging to Susanna Moss, born March 4.

1760. Betsy Daughter of Edward & Ann Morgan, born May 26, baptized July 20.

1759. Cloe Negro girl belonging to William Moore, born Octob'r 26, baptized Feb'ry 23, 1760.

1753. Ann Daughter of Thomas and Ann Martin, born May 1, baptized July 8.

1753. Nathaniel son of Cornelius & Eliz'a Matthews, born Feb'ry 1, baptized May 3.

1754. William son of William & Elizabeth Moore, born March 10, baptized May 5.

1754. Thomas son of Edward & Ann Morgan, born May 22.

1754. Elizabeth Daughter Archeleus & Ann Meanly, born Sept'r 13, baptized October 12.

1755. Nathaniel son of Charles & Catharine Manning, born Feb'ry 26.

1755. Isham Son of Paul & Ann Menitree, born Aug'st 20, baptized Sept'r 28.

1755. James son of Thomas & Ann Martin, born Aug'st 18, baptized Nov'r 2.

1756. Susanna Daughter of Absalom & Susanna Meanly, born March 14.

1756. James & William son of James & Ann McGehee, born March 31.

1756. Edward son of Edward & Ann Morgan, born May 2.

1756. Elizabeth Daughter of Thomas & Judith Mitchel, born Oct'r 14, baptized Nov'r 14.

1756. Thomas son of Cornelius & Elizᵃ Matthews, born Nov'r 10, baptized Dec'r 12.

1756. Kiddy Daughter of Archelaus & Ann Meanly, born Nov'r 18, baptized Dec'r 25.

1760. James Morris dyed Nov'r 30.

1760. Mary wife of s'd James Morris dyed Dec'r 2.

1758. Elizabeth Daughter of Thomas & Ann Martin, born Dec'r 25.

1758. Nathaniel son of David & Sarah Mitchel, born April 18.

1758. Frances Daughter of Ed^{wd} & Ann Morgan, born Apr. 6, baptized May 28.

1757. John son of Jacob & Sarah Meanly, born Aug'st 23.

1758. Elizabeth Daughter of Nathan' & Elizᵃ Massie, born Dec'r 15.

1758. Nancy Daughter of Archelaus & Ann Meanly, born Nov'r 26.

1758. Robert Jarret son of Absalom & Susanna Meanly, born Dec'r 27.

1758. Thomas son of Sylvanus & Hannah Massie, born Dec'r 26, baptized Febry 4.

1759. Ann Daughter of Paul & Ann Minetree, born June 18, baptized July 22.

1759. Thomas son of William & Ann Moss, born Aug'st 1, baptized Sept'r 23.

1760. Molly Daughter of Thomas & Ann Martin, born Jan'ry 28.

1760. Mary Daughter of Jacob & Sarah Meanley, born May 24, babtized July 27.

1766. John Cowles son of John & Susanna Morris, born December 4, baptized Decem'r 17.

1766. James son of Jas. Moriss & Alice his wife, born Decem'br 27.

1767. James Morris in the line above, died June 7th.

1762. Susanna Daughter of James & Alice Moriss, born May 29.

1764. Julius son of Jas. & Alice Moriss, born Octob'r 21.

1767. Ellyson son of Tho* & Eliz* Martin, born Aug'st 23.

1768. Lucy of Ed^wd Morgan & Ann his wife, born April 1, baptized May 15.

1768. W^m of W^m & Rebekah Pearman (This Posted in its place), born Ap'l 6, baptized May 15.

1766. Bartee son of John & Mary Miller, born April 9, baptized May 15.

1768. Dabney son of John & Mary Miller, born April —, baptized April 15.

1768. Alice Daughter of Jas. & Alice Moriss, born May 4, baptized June 5.

1768. Nancy of Wm. & Ann Moss, born Sept'r 23, baptized Jan'ry 21, 1769.

1768. Joannah Girl belonging to Jas. Morris, born Sept'r —, baptized July 22.

1768. Dabney son of John & Mary Miller, born June 30.

1766. John Moriss Departed Dec'r.

1764. William Marston & Euphan Netherland was married May 29th.

1766. Robert son of William & Euphan Marston, born April 8th.

1766. Wm. Taylor son of Do., born November 10.

1768. Thomas son of Do., born May 13.

1771. Bartho. son of Do., born August 20.

1772. Rich'd Hubbard son of William & Lucy Hubbard Muncy, born May 14.

1772. Patsey Daughter of Ed^{wd} & Ann Morgan, born July 25.

1772. Watt negro child born Belonging to Bathia Moss, born Sept'r 12.

1773. Betsey Daughter of Wm. & Anne Moss, born May 1st.

1773. Betsey of J^{no} & Catharine Mallary, born June 19.

1773. Iveson son of Benj. & Ann Mederass, born May 29.

1773. Sarah Moon dau. Jno. & Rebekah, B.

1775. William of W^{m} & Ann Moss Born October 3d & Baptized 17th December.

1776. Archelaus son of Archelaus & Mary Mitchel, born 23d Jan'ry, Bapt'd 5th April.

1782. Julius Moss of Sarah Moss a free negro Born March 25th.

1783. Wm. son to Do., Born Sept'r 27.

1785. John son to Do., Do., Born April 1.

1768. Nancy Dau^r of John & Temperance Morris born Dec'r 24, baptized Feb'ry 5th, '69.

1769. Jane Daughter of Dav^d & Eliz^a Merry born Jan'ry 30.

1766. Mary of Gedion & Kisandry Mitchel born Sept. 30.

1768. Wilson of Don son born Apr. 12.

1769. Gideon son of Dav^d & Sarah Mitchel born July 11, baptized Aug't 20.

1769. Archals son of Archelas & Ann Meanly born Sep'r 27.

1770. John son of Ansell & Mary Martin born June 1.

1770. Charles of Samuel & Mary Mannin born May 26.

1770. Salley Daug^r of Julious & Usley Martin born Augt. 17, baptized Sep'r 16.

1770. Susannah Dau^r of William & Ann Moss born Sep'r 16, baptized Nov'r 11.

1771. James Vaiden Son of James & Alice Moriss born Jan'ry 12, baptized Feb. 24.

1771. James a Negro belonging to Sam'l Moss born April 4, baptized June 2nd.

1771. Alice the wife of Jas. Moriss Departed Sunday 10 Novem'r.

1771. John son of Jno. & Temperance Moriss born Dec'r 12.

1772. Ann the wife of William Morris departed Thursday 28 May.

1772. A Negro child belong'g to Sam'l Mannin Nam'd Oct'r 10.

1772. Lucy belonging to James Moriss born Dec'r 6, baptized Jan'ry 10, '73.

1773. Catey belonging to Do. born Feb'ry 7.

1774. Sarah & Martha (Twins) of Jas. & Eliz^a Moriss born June 18, baptized July 24.

1772. Lucy a Negro girl belonging to Jas. Morriss born June 2nd.

1775. Agness a Negro girl belonging to Jas. Morris born May 20, baptized Saturday.

1775. Phatha a Negro belonging to Do. born June 25.

1776. James Moriss son of James & Mary Moriss departed this Life 16th Nov'r.

1768. Nancy of Wm. & Ann Moss born Sept'r 23, baptized Jan. 1.

1778. Tabitha of Wm. & Ann Moss born Feb'y 8.

1765. William son of Willie & Dorotha McKenzie born Aug't 26.

The office and Prison Burnt the night of the 15th July, 1787. August the 7th Sawney a Negro boy belonging to Mr. Wm. Chamberlayne was condemned to Be Hanged By Our Court for Being a Partie in the Said Firing, the Same Day Mr. Thos. Green Confess'd He was an Assistant likewise and the whole Executed By a Mr. John Price Posey who came with Mr. John P. Custis into this country His Steward.   the same Day the Said Posey was comited to the care of a strong Guard who carefully Kept Til Wednesday the 15th When a call'd Court is Ordered By Wm. H. Macon Gent. a Justice for the County to Inquire and Have a full Hearing of said Posey's Burning Said Prison & office Aug'st 15th, 1787, Being the Day appointed For the above Examination.   Present Eight Members and the Examination began about 12 o'clock and continued till near Sun Set.   When the Question was put and the Court was of Opinion He the said Posey should have a further Hearing accordingly was sent to the great Gail the Next Day being the 16th, the first of Octo'r His tryal came on in the Gen'l Court and Found Gilty when he appeal'd to the High Courts of Chancery & being Found Gilty appealed to the Court of Appeals When there was Nine out of Ten Found Him Gilty After which Judge Lyon after a most Learned Speech Which Drew tears from near all present Ask'd the Dreadful Question (To Wit) if he could shew cause why the Sentence of Death Should not pass against him Which so shok'd the prisoner that for some time the organs of speech had left him til at Length He spoke to this Effect that he was Gilty of the charge and pray'd Mercy. Jan'y 18th, 1788, was then appointed for the Execution the time arriving, He prayed a week which was granted and on Jan'y the 25 He was Executed at the gallows in Richmond, Bro't Down & Buried in this county. Tis to be noted the above Posey serv'd in this county as a Magistrate some time and once Represented it in general Assembly.

P.

1756. Moses a Negro Boy belonging to Wm. Poindexter Born June 28.

1758. Phillis a negro girl belonging to John Poindexter baptized May 29.

1758. Mary Daughter of Susanna Patterson born Feb'ry 12, baptized Sep. 4.

1757. Tom Negro Boy belonging to William Purcell born April 18.

1757. Frank Negro Boy belonging to William Purcell born April 18.

1759. Ben Negro Boy belonging to John Pearson born May 27.

1759. Francis Poindexter Daughter of Robert & Mary Pollard born August.

1759. Millsy Negro girl belonging to Wm. Poindexter born Sept'r 8.

1759. Jack Negro Boy belonging to Wm. Poindexter born Apr. 8.

1759. Ann Daughter of Wm. & Ann Poindexter born Nov. 22.

1759. Aaron Negro Boy belonging to Wm. Poindexter born Oct. 15.

1760. Henry Son of Jacob & Hannah Poindexter born Apr. 14.

1759. Milley Negro girl belonging to Jacob Poindexter born Nov'r 3.

1760. Elizabeth Daughter of Jno. & Frances Ann Pinchback born Jan. 11, baptized April 13.

1759. Lucy Negro girl belonging to Henry Pearson born Apr. 25, died July 8.

1760. Robert Mingo Negro boy belonging to Jno. Poindexter born Feb'ry 29.

1753. Charles son of Henry & Rebecca Pearson born Sept'r 16.

1753. Jane Daughter of James & Jane Pollard born Nov'r 1.

1753. Frances Daughter of Thomas & Marg^t Peasley, born Jan'y 16.

1753. George son of Charles & Eliz^a Pearson, born Feb'ry 15.

1754. Ann Daughter of David & Mary Patterson, born June 18.

1754. Sarah Daughter of Jonathan & Eliz^a Patterson, born June 17, baptized July 21.

1754. Jonathan Bourchier son of J^{no} & Sarah Pearson, born Aug'st 7, baptized Sept'r 8.

1755. Mary Ann Daughter of Mary Perkins widow, born March 18, baptized April 20.

1755. Jonathan Son of William & Ann Poindexter, born March 25, baptized Apr. 27.

1755. Lucy Daughter of Solomon & Susanna Peasley, born Aug'st 24, baptized Sept'r 21.

1755. Elizabeth Daughter of John & Catharine Parker, born Sept'r 21, baptized Nov'r 9.

1756. Ann Daughter of Rob't & Mary Pollard, born Jan'ry 18, baptized Feb'ry 15.

1756. Ann Daughter of Thos. & Margaret Paisley, born Feb'ry 15.

1756. William son of Henry & Rebecca Pearson, born March 28, baptized May 9.

1756. Thomas Son of John & Eliz^a Pearson, born Aug'st 13, baptized Sept'r 13.

1756. James son of James & Jane Pollard, born August 9.

1757. Ann Daughter of Jonathan & Elizᵃ Patterson, born Dec'r 30.

1757. John son of George & Charity Porter, born May 23, baptized June 19.

1757. Jacob son of William & Ann Poindexter, born October 6.

1757. William son of Thomas & Mary Paisley, born Jan'ry 12, baptized March 12.

1758. Ann Daughter of Joseph & Agnes Pond, born Dec'r 12, baptized March 19.

1758. Sarah Daughter of Jacob & Hannah Poindexter, born May 28, baptized July 2.

1758. Mourning son of Henry & Rebecca Pearson, born Nov'r 11, baptized Jan'ry 14, 1759.

1758. Susanna Daughter of Thomas & Mary Pointer, born Dec'r 6, baptized Feb'ry 11.

1760. Absalom son of James & Susanna Pollard, born Jan'y 1.

1760. William son of George & Charity Porter, born Dec'r 2, baptized Feb'ry 3.

1760. Benjamin son of Joseph & Agnes Pond, born Jan'ry 10.

1760. Lucy Daughter of Thomas & Margaret Paisley, born Feb'ry 21, baptized April 13.

1760. Henry son of Jacob & Hannah Poindexter, born Apr. 14, baptized May 11.

1769. Archelaus son of John & Lucy Perkins, born July 6, baptized Aug't 4.

1767. Geo. son of Geo. & Frances Poindexter, born Mar. 29.

1767. John Bailey son of John & Sarah Pearson, born Mar. 19.

1767. Wm. son of Callum & Mary Parrish, born Oct'r 21.

1768. Joseph Ferguson, baptized Jan'ry 5, died 6th.

1768. Wᵐ of Wᵐ & Rebekah Pearman, born Ap'l 6, baptized Jan'y 15.

1768. Frances of Jⁿᵒ & Sarah Pearson, born Oct'r 29. Elizᵃ Parke born ———.

1768. Ann Christian of Jacob & Elizᵃ Parkinson, born May 24, baptized June 26.

1768. Christiany of John & Fraˢ Ann Pinchback, born May 29, baptized July 10.

1769. Geo: son to Robᵗ & Mary Pollard, born Jan'ry 10, baptized Mar. 5.

1769. William Pearse departed this Life who came from N. England 19th July.

1769. William Passons of Dav^d & Mary Pearson, born July 29, baptized Oct'r 1.

—— —— Callum of Mary Parrish, born Aug'st 23, baptized Oct'r 22.

—— —— son of Jno & Fra^s Ann Pinchback, born Feb'ry 19.

—— —— of Jacob & Eliz^a Parkinson, born Nov'r 11, baptized Dec'r 23.

—— —— of Martha Patteson, born Do. 3, baptized Jan'ry 6th.

—— —— Robt. & Mary Pollard, born May 18, baptized June 30.

—— —— Daughter of J^{no} & Fr^{as} Ann Pinchbeck, born Novem'r 6.

—— —— Edwd Love & Molley Pecock, born April 2.

—— —— son of Jacob & Eliz^a Parkinson, born Sept'r 3.

—— Mary Ann of Nimrod Poindexter & Ann his wife, born Feb'y 11.

—— Sherod Negro boy Belonging to Joseph Parkinson, born Dec'r 19.

1776. Wm. Sone to Joseph Parkinson & Elisabeth his wife, born Aug'st 14.

1777. John sone to Do. & Do., born Jan'y 22.

1773. Joseph Henry son to Jos. & Elisabeth Parkinson, born Oct'r 2, died Jan'ry 20, 1776.

1775. Mary Daughter to Jos. & Elisabeth Parkinson, born May 3d, who departed Oct. 4th, 1773.

1781. Elizabeth Winfree D. to J. & E. Parkeson, born March 17.

1783. James Moody son to Do., born Sept'r 10.

1785. Sarah Parkeson Departed this Life Jan'y 6th.

1776. Betsey Daughter of Mary Patterson, born Dec'r 31.

1777. Polley Daughter of Jane Pollard, born Dec'r 30.

1785. John Parkison Departed this Life Sept'r 9.

1785. Josiah Parkison of Jos. & Eliz^a Parkison, born Sept'r 7.

1772. Lewis Poindexter of Wm. & Ann Poindexter, born Sept'r 3rd.

1775. Rob't son of Isaac & Ann Perkins, born Ap'l 16.

R.

1759. Elizabeth Daughter of Wm. & Ann Roper, born Feb'ry 27.

1758. Beck Negro Girl belonging to Wm. Ragland, born Octr 12.

George Negro Boy belonging to Wm. Ragland born May 21.

1759. Martha Daughter of John & Eliz^a Roper, born March 14.

1753. William son of Nath'l & Blandina Ragland, born May 29.

1753. Henry son of John & Sarah Roach born July 29.

1753. William son of John & Eliza. Roan born Feb'ry 23.

1754. John son of Thomas & Mary Richardson born Jan'ry 26.

1754. James son of Edmund & Ann Richardson born June 11, baptized July 7.

1754. Sarah Daughter of Ware & Mary Rocket born July 26, baptized Aug'st 25.

1754. Sarah Daughter of John & Eliz^a Roper Aug'st 25, baptized Sept'r 29.

1755. Oray Daughter of John & Sarah Roach born Feb'ry 26.

1755. Gideon son of William & Sarah Ragland.

1755. Mary Ann Daughter of Mary Perkins born March 8, baptized April 20.

1755. Rebecca Daughter of John & Judith Ragland born Aug'st 26, baptized Sept'r 24.

1756. Elizabeth Daughter of John & Eliz^a Roan born April 27. baptized May 30.

1756. William son of John & Elizabeth Roper born October 25.

1757. Francis Ware son of Ware & Mary Rocket born Dec'r 30, baptized January 30.

1757. Littlebury son of John & Sarah Roach born Feb'ry 9, baptized March 13.

1757. Nathaniel son of William & Sarah Ragland born March 2.

1757. Mary Dove Daughter of Thomas & Mary Richardson born Oct. 8, baptized Nov'r 6.

1758. Edmund son of Nathaniel & Blandina Ragland born Dec'r 6, baptized Jan'ry 8.

1758. Milly Daughter of John & Sarah Roach born Nov'r 23.

1759. William son of William & Sarah Ragland born Apr. 24.

1759. Elizabeth Daughter of William & Ann Roper born Sept'r 27.

1767. Richard Richardson son of John Richardson & Sarah his wife born Dec'r 23d.

1768. John son of Lucy Redcross born Sept'r 26th.

1769. Judith Negro girl belonging to Wm. Ragland born Janu'y 25.

1769. Rachel Negro belong'ng to Do. born March 12.

1769. Nancey Daughter of Geo. & Arrana Richardson born May 17, baptized June 18.

1770. Milley Negro girl belonging to Edwd Richardson born Decem'r 23.

1770. Alley Negro child of Wm Ropers born Aug't 14.

1770. Eliz^a of Thos. & Mary Roper born Dec'r 9th, baptized Ja'ry 6.

1771. John son of Jno. & Sarah Richardson born Mar. 31.

1772. A Negro child belong'ng to Jacob Ragland.

1779. Holt sone to Jessey Richardson and Susanna his wife born Sep'r 19th, baptized Oct'r 31st.

1787. Charles Royster Hanged himself March 14.

S.

1776. John son Henry & Elizabeth Slaughter born March 20th.

1757. Betty Negroe girl belonging to Jno. Smith in Middlesex born May 5th.

1758. Jenny Negro girl belonging to Thos. Sherman born March 18, baptized May 21.

1756. Michael Negroe Boy belonging to John Smith born February 4.

1758. Jude Negro Girl belonging to John Slaughter born August 5.

1758. Milley Negro Girl belonging to John Smith born May 15, baptized July 16.

1748. Richard Son of John & Anne Smith born Septem'r 20.

1760. Thomas Smithers died March 4.

1760. Henry Scruggs died March 18.

1759. Will Negro Boy belonging to Jno. Slaughter born October 10.

1753. John son of Richard & Frances Sherlock born May 17.

1754. Tabitha Kumi Daughter of William & Susanna Sharp, born Oct'r 25, baptized Dec'r 8.

1755. Sally Daughter of Thomas & Frances Sherman, born Dec'r 29, baptized Feb'ry 19.

1755. Susanna Daughter of William & Rebecca Sherman, born Dec'r 21, baptized Feb'ry 2.

1756. Mary Daughter Samuel & Eliz^a Scruggs, born January 1, baptized March 14.

1756. Elizabeth Daughter of Alexander & Sarah Strange, born Feb'ry 14, baptized March 28.

1756. Sally Duke Daughter of John & Hannah Sherman, born May 2, baptized Jan'ry 13.

1757. John son of Lewis & Judith Smith, born Octo'r 15.

1758. Nathaniel son of John & Fanny Slaughter, born Jan'ry 2, baptized Feb'ry 12.

1758. Nancy, John & Hannah Sherman, born July 9.

1758. Ann Daughter Samuel & Elizabeth Scruggs, born Aug'st 14, baptized Sept'r 10.

1758. Harry Duke son of Thomas & Frances Sherman, born Aug'st 20.

1758. Joyce Daughter of Marston Duke & Judith Sherman, born Sept'r 4.

1759. John Brothers son of Thomas & Mary Smithers, born Feb'ry 10, baptized Ap'l 8.

1759. Lewis son of Lewis & Judith Smith, born April 14.

1759. Mary Daughter of John & Fanny Slaughter, born Aug'st 30, baptized October 31.

1760. James son of Julius & Sabry Scruggs, born Dec'r 25.

1767. Myme Negro child belonging to Mr. John Smith, born July 26.

1767. Alce Negro child belonging to Do., born Aug'st 24.

1768. Nancey Daughter of Thomas Smithers & Sarah, born Jan'ry 21.

1767. John son of Joseph & Eliz^a Swinney, born Nov'r 24.

1768. Eliz^a of Thos. & Mary Steward, born June 25, baptized July 31.

1768. Sarah More of Jos. & Sarah Sherman, born July 13, baptized August 28.

1768. William son of W^m & Rebekah Sherman, born Aug'st 1st, baptized Sept'r 18.

1768. James son of the Rev'd Mr. James Semple & Rebekah his wife, born Sept'r 7, baptized Octo'r 9th.

1768. Sam'l son of Robt. & Susan Sharp, born Sept'r 24.

1768. Robt. Furnew or Furlong of J^{no} & Eliz^a Smith, born Octo'r 16.

1768. Frances of Michael & Eliz^a Sherman, born Nov'r 16, baptized Jan'ry 1.

1770. Dickey & Molly Son & Dau. of Thos. & Mary Steward, born April 19, baptized May 27.

1770. Milley Negro Belonging to Edwd S. [no date].

1770. Jonathan son of Jos. & Eliz^a Swinney, born June 11, baptized July 22.

1770. Lucy of Marshal & Rebekah Sherman, born June 23, baptized July 20.

1770. Fra^s Daug^r of Robt. & Susannah Sharp, born Dec'r 5, baptized Jan'ry 6.

1770. Robt. son of Michael & Eliz^a Sherman, born Dec'r 23d, baptized Jan'ry 27.

1771. Mary Ann Frances of Th^{os} & Susannah Sanders, born March 25, baptized Ap'l 28.

1771. John of John & Eliz^a Smith, born July 24.

1771. Nathl son of Tho. & Sarah Smithers, born May 18.

1772. Betsey of Saml & Fra^s Standley, born Aug'st 17.

1774. Wm. of Thos & Susannah Sanders, born Feb'ry 6.

1774. Wm. of John & Eliz^a Smith, born Feb'ry 10.

1774. William son of Th^{os} & Sarah Smythers, born Feb'ry 11, baptized Ap'l 9.

1775. Sarah Scott daug^r of Robt. & Susannah Sharp, born Aug'st 9.

1776. Eliz^a Daughter of John & Judith Stephenson, born Feb'ry 16.

1784. John Smith Departed this Life Jan'y 31.

1768. Wm. son of Wm. & Rebecca Sherman, born Aug' 1.

1784. John sone of Lewis & Ann Smith born July 28.

1786. Dionysia Daughter to Do. & Do. born Feb'ry 15.

T.

1756. Martha Daughter of William & Mary Terrell born Sept'r 12.

1757. Lucy Negro girl belonging to Richard Tyrie Jun'r born October 31, baptized May 1st, 1758.

1758. William son of William & Mary Terrell born October 8, baptized Novem'r 12.

1757. Sam Negro Boy belonging to William Terrell born April 20.

1757. Elimeleck Negro Boy belonging to William Terrell born June 25.

1757. Leonard son of Richard & Mary Taylor born Decem'r 22.

1757. David Negro Boy belonging to Richard Taylor born July 30.

David Negro Boy belonging to Richard Taylor baptized May 28.

1759. Solomon Negro Boy belonging to Richard Taylor born May 27.

1759. Milly Negro belonging to Richard Taylor born Feb'ry 2.

1744. Richard Negro Boy belonging to Elizabeth Scruggs born May 8, baptized May 8, 1757.

1748. Lucy Negro girl belonging to Elizabeth Scruggs born May 8, baptized Sept. 8, 1757.

1747. Betty Negro girl belonging to Elizabeth Scruggs born May 8, baptized May 8, 1757.

1751. Roger Negro Boy belonging to Elizabeth Scruggs born Sept'r 8, baptized May 8, 1757.

1754. Magarett Negro girl belonging to Eliz^a Scruggs born June 8, baptized May 8, 1757.

1756. Milley Negro girl belonging to Elizabeth Scruggs born May 8, baptized May 8, 1757.

1754. Susanna Daughter of Samson & Mary Tucker born July 31, baptized Sept. 22.

1754. George son of James & Elizabeth Taylor born Aug'st 12.

1755. George son of James & Hannah Turner born March 5.

1755. Elizabeth Daughter of James & Mary Taylor born Nov'r 7, baptized Dec'r 14.

1756. John son of William & Eliz^a Talman born Feb'ry 27, baptized Apr. 11.

1756. Milley Daughter of Christopher & Mary Toler born March 17, baptized May 21.

1757. Sarah Daughter of John & Mary Thomson born October 27, baptized March 6.

1760. Ann Daughter of Charles & Jane Turner born May 21.

1757. Wm. & Martha Son & Daughter of Jas. & Hannah Turner born Oct'r 20.

1758. Leonard son of Richard & Mary Taylor born Dec'r 22, baptized Feb'ry 5.

1758. William son of Wm. & Mary Terril born Octo'r 8.

1758. Elizabeth Daughter of William & Eliz^a Talman born Jan'ry 15, baptized Nov'r 19.

1759. Martin Son of Valentine & Elizabeth Tucker born Nov'r 4, baptized Feb'ry 25.

1759. John son of Charles & Jane Turner born Feb'ry 19.

1759. Clarke son of Richard & Mary Taylor born Apr. 1.

1760. William son of John & Eliz^a Taylor born Feb'ry 3, baptized March 2.

1760. James son of John & Mary Thomson born Dec'r 12, baptized Apl. 20.

1760. Anna Daughter of William & Eliz^a Talman born Apr. 6, baptized May 11.

1760. Ann Daughter of Charles & Jane Turner born May 21, baptized June 22.

1760. Mary Daughter of James & Hannah Turner born June 12.

1767. James son of Wm. & Eliz^a Talman born June 17.

1767. Eliz^a Daughter of Calib & Mary Ann Turner born October 10.

1767. Martha Daughter of Rich'd & Mary Tyree born October 30.

1769. Waddey son of Nath'l & Mary Turner, born April 2, baptized May 7th.

1770. Sally Daug'r of Rich'd & Mary Tyree, born Aug'st 3, baptized Sept'r 16th.

1771. Eve Daughter of Tho⁸ & Susannah Tyree, born March 11, baptized Ap'l 28.

1760. Nancy Daughter of Rich'd & Mary Tyree, born Sep'r 27.

1763. Mary Dau' of Do., born June 6.

1765. Tabitha Daughter of Do., born May 8.

1771. John son of Nath. Turner & Mary his wife, born June 18.

1773. Salley Lacy of Tho⁸ & Susannah Tyree, born May 6.

1775. Amigillicai of Tho⁸ Tyree dec'd & Susannah his wife, born March 1, baptized April 9th.

1768. Wm. son of Sam'l & Lucy trower, born Jan'y 9th, baptized June 28.

V.

1756. Lewis son of William & Eliz⁸ Vaughan, born June 19.

1758. Lucy Negro girl belonging to Elizabeth Vaiden, born May 15.

1757. Agnis negro girl belonging to Willm Vaiden, born Aug'st 1st.

1758. Judy Negro Woman belonging to Wm Vaughan, born May 28.

1757. John Vaiden died Nov'r 13.

1757. Cate negro girl belonging to John Vaiden, born Jan'y 13.

1758. Dick Negro Boy belonging to William Vaiden, born March 11th.

1758. Lucy Negro girl belonging to Eliz⁸ Vaiden, born June 25.

1756. Tod Negro Boy belonging to William Vaughan, born Sept'r 4, baptized October 10.

1760. William Vaiden Jun', died Feb'ry 20.

1760. George Negro Boy belonging to Susanna Vaiden, born Feb'ry 12.

1760. Susanna Negro Girl belonging to Isaac Vaiden, born Sept'r 12.

1760. James Negro Boy belonging to Isaac Vaiden, born Sept'r 24.

1754. Mary Daughter of William & Elizabeth Vaughan, born May 4.

1754. Mary Daughter of John & Elizabeth Vaiden, born Sept'r 17, baptized Oct'r 6.

1754. Zachariah son of Edward & Ann Valentine, born October 8.

1761. Nancey Negro Woman belonging to Sarah Vaughan, died Feb'ry 18.

1761. Jenny Negro Girl belonging to Sarah Vaughan, born Feb'ry 22.

1760. Timothy Vaughan died Nov'r 18.

1757. Susanna Daughter of John & Elizabeth Vaughan, born July 6.

1757. Jemima Daughter of Thomas & Rebecca Vannerson, born July 14.

1759. Elizabeth of William & Elizabeth Vaughan, born March 27, baptized May 6.

1759. Jeremiah son of Isaac & Elizabeth Vaiden, born Octob'r 31.

1766. Micajah son of Joseph & Judith Vaiden, born Sep'r 12.

1768. Gilbyrd Negro Boy belonging to Joseph Vaiden, born Jan'y 17.

1768. Phannee Negro Girl belonging to Sarah Vaughan, born May 9th.

1768. John Negro Boy of Henry Vaiden, born Dec'r 2nd.

1769. Nancey Daughter of Jos. & Judith Vaiden, born Ap'l 13.

1769. Sarah Negro Girl of Do., born Aug'st 3rd.

1770. Sarah Vaughn Dau'r of Tim'y & Sarah Vaughan, departed Feb'ry 16.

1771. Squire a Negro Boy belonging to Sarah Vaughan, born Feb'y 14.

1771. William son of William & Nancey Vaughan, born May 30, baptized July 21.

1772. Nanny Negro child belong. to Sarah Vaughan, born May 4.

1772. Sarah Vaughan departed Thursday the 21 May.

A negro child belonging to Tim'y Vaughan died 7 June.

1769. Henry son of Isaac & Eliza Vaiden Born May 13.

1773. Joseph Negro Child Belonging to Tim Vaughan born June 30.

1774. Elizabeth Wife of Wm. Vaughan died 14 April.

1774. Wm. Vaughan died Sept'r 7.

1774. Sarah Daughter of Henry & Eliz' Vaughan born Nov'r 29, baptized Jan'y 1st, '75.

1774. Joseph Son of Stanhope & Anne Vaughan born Nov'r 21.

1773. Nancey Daug' of Wm. & Nancey Vaughan born Mar. 24.

1774. Polly of Wm. & Nancey Vaughan born Aug'st 4th.

1776. Edmund Son of Henry & Eliz' Rebeca Vaughan born July 5, baptized Aug't 11.

W.

1758. Martha Daughter of Charles & Mary Waddill born October 6.

1758. John Burnett son of George & Elizabeth Walton born August 7.

1758. Violett Negro girl belonging to George Wilkinson baptized June 18.

1755. Augustine son of Richard & Mary Winfree born April 3.

1757. Lydia Negro girl belong'ng to George Webb born June 4.

1757. Temperance Negro girl belonging to George Webb born June 11th.

1758. Silas belonging to Charles Waddill born July 26.

1756. Bess Negro girl belonging to John Wilkinson born Novem'r 10.

1756. Judith Daughter of John & Judith Wilkinson born Decem'r 29.

1757. Phill Negro Boy belonging to John Wilkinson born May 5.

1757. Sarah Negro girl belonging to Noel Waddill baptized Oct. 1.

1757. May Negro girl belonging to Noel Waddill baptized Oct. 9.

1756. Benjamin son of Charles Waddill born August 13.

1759. Lucy Negro girl belonging to John Wilkinson baptized July 15.

1759. Dorcas Negro girl belonging to John Wilkinson baptized July 15.

1759.   Cloe Negro belong'ng to John Wilkinson baptized July 15.

1759.   Harwood son of John & Judith Wilkinson born August 25.

1758.   Patt Negro girl belonging to John Wilkinson born Dec'r 3.

1760.   Lucy Negro girl belonging to Robert Clemons Warden born June 1st, baptized July 27.

1753.   Noel son of George & Susannah Waddill born Sep'r 29.

1753.   Mary Daughter of Izard & Mary Wilkinson born Dec'r 1st.

1753.   William son of Joseph & Mary Walton born Feb'ry 11.

1753.   John son of Peter & Elizabeth Winfree born Feb'ry 1.

1754.   Noel son of John & Hannah Waddil born August 6.

1754.   Walter son of William & Sarah Wade born August 31.

1754.   Frances daughter of John & Judith Wilkinson born August 19.

1755.   Frances Izard Daughter of Geo. & Susan Wilkinson born Dec'r 23, baptized Jan'y 23.

1755.   Judith Daughter of David & Tabitha Wilkinson born Feb'y 10.

1755.   Susanna Daughter of Matthew & Fanny Whitlock born March 11, baptized April 6.

1755.   Turner Thomas & Judith Waddil born March 1.

1755.   Austin Son of Richard & Mary Winfree born April 3.

1755.   George son of Geo. & Eliz\a Walton born Sept'r 27, baptized Oct. 26.

1756.   Wm. & Mary son & daughter of John & Agnes Walker, born Dec'r 14, baptized Jan'y 18.

1756.   Lyddal son of Izard & Mary Wilkinson, born Dec'r 10.

1756.   Reuben son of Richard & Frances Whitlock, born March 3.

1756.   Frances Daughter of Joseph & Mary Walton, born July 4, baptized July 28.

1756.   Benjamin son of Charles & Mary Waddill, born Aug'st 13, baptized Sept'r 19.

1760.   George Walton died Dec'r 12.

1767.   William son of William & Sarah Wade, born May 18.

1757. George son of George & Susanna Wilkinson, born Apr. 27, baptized June 26.

1757. Elizabeth Daughter of Robert & Ann Wilkins, born July 10.

1757. Frances Daughter of David & Tabitha Wilkinson, born July 3.

1757. Jacob son of George & Susanna Waddill, born Aug'st 4, baptized Sept'r 18.

1757. Jesse son of Joseph & Mary Walton, born Nov'r 7.

1757. Robert son of Jeremiah & Joanna Wilkins, born Oct'r 18.

1758. John Burnett son George & Eliz^a Walton, born Aug'st 7.

1758. Harry Duke son of Samuel & Mary Woodward, born Sept'r 3.

1766. Edwd son of Robt. C. Warren & Jane his wife, born Nov'r 9.

1767. John Stanup son of John & Mary Wright, born Aug. 27.

1764. Geo: Woodward died First Ap'l.

1758. Philemon son of George & Susanna Woodward, born Aug'st 24.

1758. Martha Daughter of Charles & Mary Waddil, born Octob'r 2, baptized Novem'r 12.

1758. George son of James & Mary Waddil, born Decem'r 2.

1759. William son of William & Sarah Wilkinson, born Jan'ry 31.

1759. Mary son of William & Sarah Wade, born May 6, baptized June 24.

1759. William son of David & Tabitha Wilkinson, born May 26, baptized July 1.

1759. Samuel son of Joseph & Rachel Weaver, born July 1, baptized July 29.

1760. Ann Daughter of Robert & Ann Wilkins, born Dec'r 12.

1760. Elizabeth Daughter of John & Agnes Walker, born Jan'ry 18, baptized Apr. 4.

1760. Susanna Daughter of George & Susanna Wilkinson, born May 11.

1767. Susanna Daughter of Edwin & Eliz^a Waddill, born October 4.

1763. Peyton son of Joseph & Dorothy Wyatt, born Nov'r 15.

1767. Joseph son of Do., born August 24.

1768. Parkes of Wm. & Sarah Wilkinson, born Nov'r 4, baptized Jan'y 1.

1768. Nancey of Wm. & Ann Moss, born Sept'r 23, baptized Jan'y (wrong place).

1768. Tho⁸ of James & Sarah Wilson, born Oct'r 22, baptized Jan'y 1.

1769. James son of Robt. & Ann Wilkins, born April 25.

1771. Stephen a Negro Boy belonging to Ro. C. Warren, born March 5.

1771. William Dennis son of Charles & Mary Waddell, born June 9.

1772. Silvy a negro girl belong. to Jos. Wyatt, born July 2.

1773. John son of Robt. & Ann Wilkins was born April 22.

1781. Robt. C. Warren Departed, aged about 56 years, Octob'r 3.

1781. Rich'd Henry son to Austin & Jane Winfree, born March 19.

1754. John & Milly son & Daughter of Antho: & Mary Waddy, born April 9.

1784. James Wilson son to Austin & Jane Winfree, born Jan'ry 28.

Y.

1763. Sally Hewlett born J. 28.

1768. Mary Dau'r of Rich'd & Sarah Yates born Dec'r 21.

1768. James Negro Boy belonging to R'd Yates born Jan'y 1.

1769. Mary Daughter of Rich'd & Sarah Yates died Sepr.

1772. Sarah Moriss of Rich'd & Sarah his wife born Jan'y 4.

1772. Sarah ye wife of Rich'd Yates departed Jan'y 8.

1776. Betsey the Daughter of Mary Paterson born Decemb'r 31 (in its right place).

1778. Tabitha Daughter of William & Ann Moss was born February 8th (in its right place).

INDEX.

54, 55, 77, 78, 101, 111, 119, 124, 133, 157; Lyddall 76, 146, 147, 157; Sara 147; Sarah 8, 54, 55; Susanna 8, 77, 78, 101, 119.

Bailey, Ann 77, 140, 146; Anne 78, 142 ; Anselm 7, 140, 147 ; Charles 79; Deary 77; Edward 1, 56, 77, 79, 148; Elizabeth 113, 148, Elsy 55, Francis 79, James 77, 146, 148, Jeremiah 132, John 1, 7, 9, 46, 55, 56, 76, 77, 78, 140, Judith 142, 146, 147, Lucy 9, 77, 146, Mary, 9, 78, 113, 132, 142, 148, Martha 78, Mathew 55, Parke 77, Parkes 148, Robert 78, 113, 132, 142, Sarah 78, Samuel 146, 147, Tabith 9, Thomas 9, 76, 148, William 76, 146.

Bairey, Amea 54.

Baisey, George 55.

Baker, Ann 137, Mary 51, Susanna 137, William 137.

Ballard, Elizabeth 138, Mary 138, William 138.

Banks, Andrew 117, Henry 117, Lacy 117, Mary 50.

Bardrick, Constantine 8, Elizabeth 8, 54, Henry 3, 8, 54.

Barker, Charles 1, 54, Elizabeth 112, Fridkin 100, Fidkin 112, John 1, Osilla 100, Rebeck. 1, Rebecca 54.

Barkwell, Elizabeth 133; Eliza 148; Eve 148; John 133, 148; Sally 148; Thomas 148.

Barley, Sam 54.

Barns, John 77; Thomas 77.

Barnes, Elinor 147; Elizabeth 141; Francis 55, 146, 147; Henry 143; Jack 55; Littlebury 147; Margery 78; Margret 143; Martha 147; Mary 130; Peter 147; Sarah 78; Tabitha 146, 147; Thos. 78, 79, 129, 147.

Barnett, Absalom 148; Gregory 54; John 2; Lucy 147; Martha 146, 147, 148; Mary 147; Nathan 2, 147; Peter 146, 147, 148; Rebecca 147; William 146.

Barry, Sarah 142.

Bartwell, John 121; Sarah 121; William 121.

Bassett, Ann 155, Anne 2, 77, Ellenor 54, 100, Elizabeth, 55, 100; Francis 48, Jane 8, John 2, 55, 77, 100, Mary 76, Nathaniel

155, Thomas 2, 3, 8, 9, 47, 54, 55, 76, 78, 155, Ursula 9, William 9, 55, 76, 77, 78, 101.

Battin, Mary 132, Sarah 132, William 132.

Baughan, Ann 111, Anne 1, Elizabeth 2, Elkahah 111, James 100, John 1, 2, 100, Joseph 1, 3, 111, Rebecca 52.

Bayley, Ann 131.

Baizey, Jane 8.

Bayzy, William 3.

Beek, William 3.

Beer, David 77, Richard 77.

Beetty, Joseph 54.

Bell, Bethea 7, David 2, 3, 7, Edward 1, Mary 1, Rebecca 48.

Bereel, Benjamin 47.

Bettes, Edward 8, 40, 54, Gideon 8, Hester 8, 54, Rachel 8, Uriah 8.

Bettus, Edward 55, Rachel 55.

Benns, David 114, Elizabeth 114, Peter 114.

Biby, John 3.

Bigger, Wm. 1.

Bingham, Jane 1, Wm. 1.

Binn, Abraham 1, Joe 1.

Binns, Amadiah 2, Ann 147, Anne 77, Charity 142, Christopher 2, 3, 78, David 77, 78, 128, 142, Daniel 147, Edm'd 147, Elizabeth 78, 142, Fras. 147, John 147, Joseph 128, Martha 147, Mary 147, Sarah 118, Thomas 118, 147, William 118, 121, 147.

Birkett, Ed. 55.

Black, John 54.

Blackburne, Rowland 47, 54.

Blackstone, Ann 117, James 117, 129, 139, Rachel 117.

Blackwell, James 1, 2, 46, 54, John 1, Lydia 1, Mary 2, 54.

Boastman, Lucy 146, Sherwood 146.

Bolton, Charles 100, Elizabeth 78, Henry 146, Judith 100, Mary 146, Sarah 146, Thomas 100, William 78.

Bomps, Robert 1.

Bon, Henry 2, Jane 2.

Bone, Henry 2.

Borer, Robert 46.

Borne, Henry 2, John 2.

Bostick, Charles 54, Mary 54, Venicia 47.

Boswell, Anne 148, Fras. 148, Martha 148, Parrobo 148.

Doe, Alice 7, Rachel 7.
Dollard, Edward 140, Francis 7,
James 8, 127, John 127, 140, 152,
153, Lucy 152, Margaret 7, Sa-
rah 121, Susann 153, Susanna
127, 140, 152, Thomas 121, Wil-
liam 7, 59, 121.
Doller, Eliz. 7, James 7.
Dorrill, Edward 58.
Douglas, Geo. 7, Robt. 7.
Dowe, Nitt'e 7, Wm. 7.
Drake, Agnes 152, 153, Ann 136,
Joel 153, Mary 152, Raehel 153,
Robt. 153, Sara 153, Sarah 114,
124, 136, Thos. 124, William
114, 124, 136, 152, 153.
Drummond, Wm. 59.
Dudley, Ambrose 120, 152, 153,
Eliza. 120, Fras. 153, Hannah
152, 153, James 120, 153, John
153, Wm. 152, 153.
Dumas, Jeremiah 7, Mathew 7.
Dungee, Bart. 152, Mary 152, Wm.
152.
Dynd, Margaret 15.

Elliott, Mary 9, Thos. 9.
Ellis, Alexander 59, 81, Ann 59,
Francis 59, 81, Sarah 52.
Elmore, Ellmore, Bathiah 10, Eliz-
abeth 10, 82, Harris 10, John
81, 82, Lucy 82, Mary 10, 59,
Peter 9, 10, 59, 81, 82, Rebecca
9, Sarah 82, Will 9, Wm. 82.
Ellison, General 82, John 9, Joseph
154, Mary 154, Sivilla 9.
England, Eliz. 10, John 10, Mourn-
ing 81, Wm. 10.
Englebrite, John 62.
Eperson, Epperson, John 9, 10, Pall
9, Wm. 10.
Esrot, Hugh 9, Jane 9.
Evans, Anne 82, John 9, Mary 9,
10, Rich. 10, Thos. 82.

Farell, Farrell, Daniel 84, 120, Eliz-
abeth 84, 133, Jos. 84, Rich 84.
Fennell, Eliz. 12, John 12, Sarah 12.
Fergison, Ferguson, Fergusson,
Ann 84, George 84, Hannah
11, James 11, Jane 114, 122,
John 85, 114, 122, Jos. 173, Ju-
dith 12, Peninnah 85, Sarah 85,
Wm. 11, 114.
Ferris, Agnes 130, John 130, 154,
Mary 154, Sarah 130.
Fewterel, Wm. 60,

Fidkin, Thos. 59.
Field, Madam 12, 59, 60, 84, Alice
84, Peter 11. 59.
Fielding, Mary 84, Wm. 84.
Finall, Jas. 11, John 11.
Finch, Adam 155, Aggee 154, Bet-
sey 155, Brother 155, Chas. 85,
Dorothy 129. Edward 11, 12, 60,
84, 154, 155, Eliz. 154. 155,
Francis 129, Henry 11, 84, 85,
129, 139. 154, 155, John 12, 85,
129, 138, 154, 155, Lucy, 155,
Martha 60, 84, Margaret 129,
Mary 11, 154, Molly 155, Moss 154,
Pleasant 155. Richard, 155 Re-
becca 154, Sabra 85, 129, 138,
Sarah 154, 155. Susanna 84, 154,
William 84.
Firth, Elizabeth 85, Sam 32, 61,
Sam'l 155, Susan 155, Thomas
85, Wm. 85.
Fleming, Charles 11, 84, Eliz. 11,
Hannah 84, John 59, Sarah 12,
Susannah 11, Tarleton 84.
Fluellen, Eliz. 154, John 154, Lucy
84.
Flower, Alex. 84, Jesse 84.
Forbes, Forbess, Allen 154, Edm'd
111, 154, Elizabeth 111, 118,
127, 137, George 118, John 127,
155, Mary 60, 154, 155, Robert
154, Sara 84, Thomas 137, 154,
William 84, 111, 118, 127, 137,
154.
Forgos, Wm. 59.
Forsbush, Wm. 84.
Foster, Agnes 99, Elizabeth 11, 154,
Fras. 154, Jane 12, 60, John 12,
59, 60, 84, 99, Joseph 11, 83, 84,
131, 132, 140, Luce 11, Lucy
84, Martha 155, Mary 60, 84,
Thomas 59, Wm. 59.
Fox, Fras. 84, John 84.
Frances, Ann 154, Bassett 154, Ca-
leb 154, Henry 154, John 154,
Nathan'l 154.
Freeman, Barbary 11, James 59,
Wm. 11.
Furbush, Agnes 155, Rebecca 155,
Robt. 155.
Fusell, Fussell, Fras. 84, Sarah 60,
84, Thos. 84.
Fuzell, Fuzzell, Eliz. 11, Martha 12,
Sarah 11, Thomas 12.

Galing, Galling, Anne 13. John 13,
Math. 13.

Gannaway, Hannah 123, 138, John 85, 131, Marmaduke 123, 138, Sarah 138, Wm. 85.
Gardner, Martha 60, Wm. 60.
Garland, Edward 13.
Garrard, James 2, Jos. 2, Judith 13.
Garratt, Thos. 14, Tyler 14.
Garrett, James 13
Garwood, Fras. 61, 85, Sarah 85, Thos. 85.
Gauling, Ann 120, Honour 14, John 14, 120, Martha 60.
Gaulding, Eliz. 156, 157, Jacob 156, 157, Sarah 156.
Gawling, Alex. 85, John 85.
Gentry, Eliz. 12, Mabel 13, Nich 12, 13, Peter 12, Samuel 12.
Gibbon, Mary 129.
Gilbert, Susanna 85.
Gill, Stephen 60.
Gillam, Gilliam, Eliz. 13, Epaph. 153, James, 134, John 12, Martha 134, Marg't 13, Rebecca 136, Rich. 12, 13, 136, Ruth 134, Wm. 153.
Glass, Robt. 13, Thos. 13.
Glenn, Ann 47, Eliz. 156, 157, Fras. 157, James 146, John 156, 157, Kitty 157, Mathew, 156, Mary 46, 157, Nancy 157, Pleas. 157, Thos. 156, Wm. 156.
Goderds, Vincent 67,
Goldwell, John 156, Nich. 156, Temperance 156.
Goocher, Ann 156, Domini 156, Eliz. 156.
Goodall Elizabeth 85, Jas. 85, Mary 85, Thos. 85.
Goodin, Alex. 14, Thos. 14.
Goodman, Benj. 13, Samuel 13.
Goodwin, Eliz. 13, Fras. 13, Jacob 13, John 13, Peter 13, Theodosia 86, 156, Thos. 86, 156, Wm. 86.
Gording, Catherine 156, John 156, Mildret 156.
Goodin, Alex'r. 13, Chas. 13.
Gore, Chas. 61.
Gowan, Aaron 134, George 134, Sarah 134.
Granger. Elizabeth 13. Thos. 13,
Grant, Frances 85, Mildrett 85, Thos. 85.
Graves, Charles 156. Dyonysia 155, 156. Eliz. 13, Math. 13, Mary 156, Ralph 155, Rich. 155, 156, Sara 155, Susanna 13, Wm. 156.

Gray, Sam. 60, Eliz. 138, Martha 138, Wm. 142.
Green, Edw. 13, 60, 85, Edmund 61, Eliz. 113, 121, 139, Forest 60, 85, 86, Ithamar 139, 156, Jane 13, 14,50, 60, Jas. 13, 14, 113, John 14, 86, 113, 121, 139, 155, 156, Martha 85, Mary 13, 60, 86, Thos. 85, 170, Wm. 14, 60, 85, 121, Zacharis 86.
Greenhill, Paschal 61.
Greenkills, Dr. 67, 70, 85.
Gregory, Edm'd 156, Isaac 156, John 60, Martha 156, Thos. 156, Wm. 156.
Grindley, Ellinor 85, Fras. 85, Hugh 60, 61, 85, Mary 85, Sarah 60.
Grose, Ann 50.
Grubbs, Hensley 156, Susan 156.
Guillam, Guilliam, Agnes 14. Eliz. 61, James 14, John 14, 85. Marg't 61, Martha 85, Richard 60, 85, 118, Rebecca 118, Sarah 85. Wm. 61, 85, 118.
Gunnell, Anne 13, Judith 13, William 13.
Hacher, Martha 47.
Haiden, Hezekiah 162, Molley 162, Thos. 162,
Hall, Jesse 162, John 86, 127, 162, Mildris 162. Sam 86. Sarah 127.
Hamblet, Agnes 161, George 161, Thos. 161.
Hamlet, Agnes 158, George 160, Jenny 158, John 158, 159, Lucy 159, Rebecca 159, Susan 160.
Hamlyn, John 160, Joyce 160, Lucy 160.
Hancock, John 62, Mary 62.
Hankey, Agnes 158, 160, Fred 158, 160, Jane 160, Lewis 160, Mary 160, Naomi 160, Ralph 158, 160.
Hanna, Mary 15, Peter 15.
Hanson, Angelica 138, Eliz. 138, James 138.
Hardcastle, Hannah 16, John 15, Wm. 15, 16.
Hardon, Hardden, Anne 16, Goldwell 160, Hezekiah 157, 160, 163, Judith 86, Math. 16, 86, Molley 157, 160, 163, Thos. 163.
Hardyman, Judith 87.
Harfield, David 113, 158, Eliz. 158, Grace 113, Mary 138, 158, Matthew 138, Miriam 138, Michael 48, 113.

Labamore, John 90, Judith 90, Mary 90.

Lacy, Angelica 64, 91, 106, 124, Ann 165, Archer 165, Bartholomew 165, Edmund 165, Edward 165, Elizabeth 91, Frances 165, Henry 64, 91, 106, 124 165, John 165, Kiddy 165. Lucy 165, Mary 165, Richard 165, Sarah 165, Thomas 165, Ursula 64, 91, William 165.

Lake, Mary 19, Peter 19. Wm. 19

Lamb, Jane 19, Rich'd 19, 63.

Lang. John, 64.

Langford, Ann 164. 165. Edw. 92, 164, 165; Eliz. 91, 165, Henry 90, John 90, 91, 92, 164, 165, Rebecca 92, Wm. 165.

Lancaster, John 92, Joyce 92, Mary 92.

Lanceston, Richard 19, Robt. 19.

Lane. Hannah 48.

Laneford, John 19, Martha 19.

Laurence, Geo. 63.

Lawson, Elenor 19. John 19, Judith 19.

Leake, Jane 19, Josias 137, Rich. 20, Sarah 137, Wm. 19, 20, 137.

Leigh, Margaret 91, Mary 92, Walter 91, 92.

Lemay, Chas. 164, Jane 164, Mary 164, Susannah 164, Wm. 164,

Leonard, James 165, Martha 165, Thos. 165, Wm. 165.

Le Strange, Leman 122, Julius 122, Sarah 122.

Lewis, Abraham 19, Angelico 21, Chas. 89, 90, 104, David 19, Edward 20, Eliz. 32, 90, 165, Francis 104, 111, 165, Geo. 165, Gwin 22, Jane 91, John 19, 20, 32, 63, 89, 90, 164, Mary 20, Nath. 104, Nicholas 20, 21, 32, 89, 111, Owen 32, 63. 90, Robt. 91, 104, Sara 104, Sarah 165, Susan 104, Wm. 32, 64, 111.

Lewellen, Elizabeth 165, Daniel 165.

Lewes, John 19.

Lightfoot, Alice 19, Anne 19, Elizabeth 89, 107, Frances 21, 126, 141, Goodrich 21, 22, 63, 64, John 19, 21, 63, 112, 115, 126, 129, 131, 141, 142, Mary 20, 21, 91, 115, 126, 141, Sherwood 21, 32, 63, 64, 89, 90, 91, 92, 115,

132, Thomas 22, 63, 64, 89, 90, 91.

Lillingston, Mary 64.

Lines, Mary 91.

Linzey, Elizabeth 165, Jesse 165, Sandy 165.

Littlepage, Alice 20, Edmond 21, Eliz. 20, 32, 89, Frances 20, 62, 63, 90, 91, 92, James 32, John 32, Judith 32, Madam 107, Oreano 125, Richard 19. 20, 21, 22, 32, 63, 90, 125, 130, 139, Susan 90.

Levermore, Barbara 32.

Longworthy, John 63.

Louch, Philip 90, Wm. 90.

Lowell, Chas. 19, Geo. 19, Jno. 19.

Lowill, Geo. 20, Sarah 20.

Lucas, Charles 90, Daniel 166, Forrester 90, Joseph 166, Josiah 166, John 64, 90, Lucy 166, Nancy 166, Sarah 166, Wm. 63, 166.

Luck, John 19, 20, Mary 20, Richard 19, Sam 20, Wm. 19.

Ludwell, Col. 49.

Lyddall, Geo. 64.

Lyon, Daniel 165, 166, Elizabeth 165, Frances, 165, 166, John 166, Susannah 165, Wm. 166.

Macdlin, Richard 24.

Maccomick, Grezel 94, Martha 94.

Macheke, Thos. 22, Wm. 22.

Machen, David 23, Edward 23, Thos. 23.

Mackdaniel, Dansel 64.

Mackgert, Daniel 24, Sarah 24,.

Mackgill, David, 96.

Mackhany, Daniel 27, Wm. 27.

Mackquery, John 92, Mary 92.

Maclagehe, Catherine 47.

Macon, Ann 94, 124, Anne 22, 66, Elizabeth 116, Gideon 22, 23, 24, Henry 95, James 24, John 23. 24, 66, Judith 130, Lucy 94, Martha 22, 24, 93, Mary 95, 116, 130, Sarah 116, Thomas 94, William 23, 24, 60, 92, 93, 94, 95, 116, 124, 130.

Macoy, John 23, Mark 23.

Madox, Maddox, John 24, 25, 27, 93, Mary 25, Michael 27, Sarah 24, Susanna 25, Robt. 25, Wm. 93.

Major, Frances 23, John 24, Robert

Merry, David 169, Eliz. 169, Jane 169.

Meux, Eliz. 65, 66, 126, 136, Francis, 115, Jno. 27, 28, 65, 66, 92, 93, Richard 27, 28, 96, 115, 126, 136, 139, Thomas 136.

Middlebrook, Thos. 97.

Millington, Margaret 23, Wm. 23, 26, 65.

Miller, Bartee 168, Dabney 168, Jno. 168, Mary 168.

Mills, Henry 22, Nicholas 22.

Mims, Anne 27, Benj. 27, Lionel 27, Lineal 48, Sarah 28, 50, Thos. 23, 25, 27, 28, 48, 65.

Minetree, Ann 168, Paul 168.

Michell, Anne 25, Archelaus 26, John 23, Martha 23, 26, Mary 23, 26, Stephen 23, 24, 25, 26, Thos. 23, 24.

Mitchell, Alice 66, Ann 113, 123, 136, Anne 96, Archelaus 94, 97, 113, 123, 136, 169, David 125, 167, 169, Eliz. 95, 96, 97, 122, 127, 138, 167, Evan 27, George 122, 137, Gideon 169, Hannah 50, Jane 137, Judith 167, Kisandry 169, Lucy 123, Leazan 94, Mary 66, 125, 136, 169, Nath. 167, Rebecca 127, Robert 125, Sarah 167, 169, Stephen 27, 28, 64, 65, 66, 92, 94, Susannah 113, 122, Susan 137, Thos. 34, 92, 94, 95, 96, 97, 125, 127, 138, 167, Val. 28, William 97.

Mochi, John 22, Mary 22, Robert 22.

Moon, Eliz. 28, 66, Jacob 92, John 127, 169, Judith 94, Mary 65, 92. Peter 27, 28, 48, 66, 92, Phillis 25, 92, Rebecca 169, Ruth 92, Sarah 169, Stephen 25, 26, 27, 65, 66, 92, 94.

Moore, Agnes 97, 118, Anne 24, Cassandra 23, Cath. 67, 94, Daniel 98, Edward 28, 66, 92, Eliz. 24, 26, 27, 28, 93, 114, 115, 167, Francis 66, Geo. 23, 25, Hannah 95, 115, Jas. 23, 24, 26, 28, 93, Johanna 50, John 23, 24, 26, 28, 66, 92, 95, 97, 113, Jude 24, Lucy 28, Margaret 97, Marmaduke 23, 95, 97, 113, 115, Martha 26, Mary 23, 67, 95, 97, 137, Nicholas 23, Pelham 23, 24, 65, 66, 67, 93, 94, 95, 97, Peter 22, Rebecca 24, 95, Robt. 28,

66, 97, 137, Sarah 28, 95, 97, 129, Stephen 22, 66, Susan 111, Susanna 95, 98, 117, Thos. 24, 27, 28, 111, 137, Valentine 118, Wm. 24, 98, 111, 117, 166, 167.

Moorman, Andrew 22, Eliz. 23, Mary 22, Thos. 22.

Morfield, Jno. 64.

Morgan, Amy, 23, 94, Ann 166, 167, 168, 169, Betsy 166, Edward 23, 65, 92, 93, 94, 95, 96, 97, 98, 120, 166, 167, 168, Eliz. 97, 117, Frances 167, Hannah 96, 120, Jno. 93, Lucy 120, Patsy 169, Robt. 23, 97, 117, Susanna 92, Thos. 167.

Morris, Alice 168, 169, Ann 97, 126, 141, 170, Benj. 66, Chas. 23, 28, 95, Edward 22, 26, 27, Eliz. 22, 97, 130, 170, Frances 126, Henry 166, Jas. 26, 130, 138, 142, 157, 166, 167, 168, 169, 170, Jane 66, Jno. 28, 138, 141, 168, 169, Judith 95, Julius 166, Mary 22, 130, 138, 166, 167, 170, Nancy 169, Rebecca 22, Rich. 186, Robt. 22, 23, 65, 66, Sarah 186, Susan 168, Susanna 27, 94, Tabitha 65, 92, 95, Temperance 169, Wm. 22, 65, 92, 94, 95, 97, 126, 141, 170.

Moss, Mosse, Alex. 94, 112, Ann 119, 168, 169, 170, 186, Anne, 26, 65, 94, 138, Bathia 97, 169, Bethia 138, Betsey 169, Chas. 97, Eliz. 49, 66, 97, James 26, 28, 56, 65, 93, 97, 166, John 94, 169, Joyce 28, 97, Judith 26, 122, Julius 169, Lucy 96, Mary 93, Nancy 186, Rebecca 140, Sam'l 26, 97, 122, 138, 166, 169, Sarah 169, Susan 169, Susanna, 97, 119, 166, Tabithia 170, 186, Thos. 22, 26, 28, 66, 96, 97, 119, 143, 168, Wm. 22, 28, 66, 93, 94, 97, 168, 169, 170, 186.

Mossom, David, 112, 121, 122, 124, 126, 127, 129, 131, 132, 133, 137, 138, 141, 144.

Mulattoes 6, 16, 53, 55, 91.

Munk, Johanna 50

Murfield, Daniel 48.

Murran, Jno. 23.

Murrant, Susanna 65.

Mutton, Wm. 64.

Mux, Jno. 94.

Penick, Edw'd 30, Wm. 30.
Penstone, Francis 67.
Pepper, Eliz. 100, Jane 100, Stephen 100.
Perday, Hannah 31, Nicholas 31.
Perkins, Ann 30, 174, Archelaus 173, Christian 114, Eliz. 30, Isaac 174, Isabel 114, Isabella 118, 125, John 133, 173, Judith 31, Lucy 173, Mary 118, 133, 172, Robt. 174, Sarah 198, Wm. 30, 31, 67, 98, 114, 118, 125, 133.
Pere, Richd. 67.
Perry, James 30, 31, Francis 30, Robt. 31.
Person, Chas. 29, 30, 31, George 29, John 30.
Pettery, John 72.
Phillips, Eliz. 98, Geo. 67, John 98.
Pickring, Eliz. 30, Gabriel 30.
Pierson, Frances 31, Rowland 67, Wm. 31.
Pillomore, Elizabeth 22.
Pinchback, Ann 127, Christiany 173, Eliz. 22, 98, 100, 127, 172, Frances 172, 173, 174, John 100, 172, 173, 174, Mary 98, Sarah 100, Thos. 98, 99, 100.
Pines, Rich. 29, Susanna 29, Mrs. 60.
Pinick, Edwd. 28, Eliz. 28.
Piram, Jas. 29, Susannah 29.
Pirant, Jas. 30, Wm. 30.
Plant, Anne 29 Eliz. 28, 29, 50, Mary 28, Wm. 28, 29.
Plantine, Peter 30, Wm. 30.
Plumley, Eliz. 131, 140, George 131, Jno. 140, Samuel 131, 140.
Poindexter, Ann 119, 131, 143, 171, 172, 173, 174, Anne 47, Armistead 50, Carter 52, Edwin 50, 51, Eliz. 30, 48, 120, 133, Frances 50, 51, 173, Geo. 28, 30, 31, 32, 50, 51, 67, 68, 98, 99, 100, 112, 133, 134, 141, 173, Hannah 172, 173, Henry 99, 172, 173, Jacob 98, 99, 100, 172, 173, Jas. 50, 51, John 100, 119, 131, 140, 143, 171, 172, Jonathan 172, Judith 30, Julius Cesar 98, Lewis 174, Lyghtfoot 50, 51, Mary 31, 32, 120, 174, Nimrod 143, 174, Parke 50, 51, Phillip 31, 120, 133, 142, Rebecca 100, Robert 50, 51, Sarah 30, 50, 51, 98, 99, 173, Susannah 30, 50, 51, 141,

Susan 29, Thos. 30, Wm. 98 171, 173, 174.
Poiner, John 67.
Pointer, Mary 173, Susanna 173, Thos. 173.
Pollard, Absalom 173, Ann 172, Francis 171, Geo. 173, James 172, 173, Jane 172, 174, Mary 171, 172, 173, 174, Polly 174, Robt. 171, 172, 174, Susanna 173.
Pond, Agnes 173, Ann 173, Benj. 173, Eliz. 98, Joseph 173, Lydia 115, Martha 98, Mary 126, Matt. 115, 126, Phyllis 115, 126.
Pontin, Thos. 29, 30, Wm. 30.
Porter, Anne 31, Charity 173, Henry 31, Judeth 50, Wm. 173.
Posey, John Price 170.
Powel, Susanna 67.
Pratt, Peter 67.
Prerdd, Eliz. 30, Mary 30, Mio 30.
Preoy, Robt. 98, Sussanna 98.
Price, Ann 113, James 113, Jane 67, John 67.
Pritchard, Jno. 116, Thomas Davis 116.
Prior, Anne 31.
Proctor, William 63.
Pruet, Jane 138, John 138, Sarah 138.
Pryer, Eliz. 32, Wm. 32.
Pryor, Nich. 99, Wm. 99.
Pullam, Anne 30, Benj. 30, James 30, Wm. 29, 30.
Pully, John 68.
Purcell, Wm. 171.
Purdie, Jane 31, Susanna 31,
Pyrant, James 30.

Ragland, Ann 125, 131, Blandina 175, Edward 175, Eliz. 101, 124, 132, 136, Gideon 101, 175, Hannah 139, Jacob 176, Joll 142, John 124, 125, 132, 139, 175, Judith 125, 139, 175, Nath. 124, 132, 136, 175, Rebecca 175, Sarah 131, 142 175, 176, Thomas 101, Wm. 101, 131, 136, 142, 175, 176.
Raglin, Jacob 34, Thos. 34.
Ragling, Evan 33, 34, 68, Isaac 34, Jno. 34. Thos. 34, 68, Wm. 33.
Randall, Eliz. 32, Jno. 32.
Ray, Launcelot 68.
Raxford, Jno. 33, Wm. 33.

177, Sarah 105, Thomas 104, Wm. 37.

Semple, Jas. 178, Rebekah 178.

Serwoll, Mary 35, Tim. 35.

Sheperson, Geo. 35, Mary 35.

Shepherdson, Geo. 36, Jno, 36.

Shailer, Johannah 69.

Sharp, Sharpe, Cath. 70, Frances 178, Madam 103, Robert 178, Samuel 178, Sarah 178, Scott 178, Susanna 68, 177, 178, Tabitha Kumi 177, Thos. 41, 68, 69, Wm. 177.

Sheller, Jno. 50.

Sherlock, Frances 177, Jno. 177, Rich'd 177.

Sherman, Duke 177, Eliz. 178, Frances, 177, 178, Hannah 177, Harry 177, Jas. 178, Jno. 177, Joseph 135, Joyce 177, Judith 177, Lucy 178, Marston 177, Marshal 178, Michael 104, 130, 135, 178, Nancy 177, Rebecca 151, 177, 178, Robt 178, Sally 177, Sarah 104, 178, Susanna 151, 177, Thos. 176, 177, Wm. 151, 175, 178.

Showers, Eliz. 126, Jno. 126, Mellicent 126.

Skropbe, Anne 37, Tho. 37.

Simes, Anne 40, Hannah 40, Mathews 40. 50.

Simons, Jno. 72, Salomon 36, Thos. 36, 50.

Simson, Jno. 51.

Simpson, Jno. 69.

Simes, Wm. 70.

Skiner, Marg't 35, Mary 35, Rich'd 35.

Slaughter, Eliz. 176, Fanny 177, Henry 176, Jno. 176, 177, Mary 177. Nath. 177.

Slayden, Arthur 70, 105, 116, 125, 136, John 105, Martha 136, Rachel 105, 116, 135, 136, Sarah 125. Wm. 70, 116.

Sledd, Eliz. 104, Milly 104, Wm. 104.

Smith, Absalom 36, Ann 115, 119, 178, Anne 36, 176, Chas. 36, David 34, 35, 68, Dinah 69, Dionysia 178, Dorothy 70, Eliz. 34 35, 36, 48, 59, 103, 178 Francis 68, Geo. 35, 41, 69, Jas. 37, 41, 69, 103, Jane 140, Jno. 34, 36, 51, 119, 140, 176, 177, 178, Judith 177, Lewis 177, 178,

Marg't 69, Mary 35, 36, 41, 42, Nath. 36, 68, 115, 132, Richard 176, Robt. 178, Sam'l 41, 42, 69, 70, 103, Susanna 35, 115, 132, Thos. 33, 36, 70, Wm. 36, 37, 178.

Smithers, Jno. 178, Nancy 177, Nath. 178, Sarah 177, 178, Thos. 176, 177, 178, Wm. 178.

Snead, Henry 35, Jno. 35, Rebecca 35, Thos. 35, Wm. 35.

Snorve (probably Snowe), Mary 34, Rebec. 34, Richard 34.

Snowe, Richard 50.

Soane, Henry 104.

Spain, Ann 35, Mary 35.

Speare, Spearr or Speere, Ann 36, 68, Alice 41, 69, Austin 103, Charley 69 Edward 36, 69, Eliz. 37, Geo. 35, 36, Henry 103, 116, Hezekiah 134, James 36, Jane 69, John 36, 41, 50, 68, 103, 116, 134, Joyce 134, Judith 103, Margaret 41, 116, Mary 69, Robert 35, 36, 37, 41, 68, 69, 70, 103, Ruth 37, 41, 68, 69, Wm. 41, 68.

Spencer, Ann 34. Benj. 134, Mary 134, Susannah 34, 68, Thos. 34, 35, 68.

Sporell, Ann 34, Mary 34, Robt. 34, Spradlin, Andrew 35, 36, Anne 36, Martha 36.

Sprague, Amey 41, Susanna 41, Wm. 41.

Sprosen, Eliz. 41.

Sproson, Sarah 70.

Spurlock, Anne 41, Drury 41, Eliz. 35, Frances 35, Juda 36, Rebecca 35, 36, Rich. 37, Robert 35, 36, 37, Sarah 51, Susan 52, Wm. 41, 50

Squires, Madam 40, Rich. 68.

Stanly, Standly. Betsy 178, Frances 178. James 35, John 35, Samuel 35, 178, Thos. 35.

Stegall, Jane 35, Moses 69, Samuel 35, Wm. 69.

Stephens, Thos. 68.

Stephenson, Eliz. 178, John 178, Judith 178.

Stevens, Wm. 36.

Stewart, Dickey 178, Eliz. 177, Mary 177, Molly 178, Thos. 177, 178.

Stiles, John 35.

Stils, John 69, Martha 69.